Child-to-Child: A Resource Book

Edited by
Grazyna Bonati and Hugh Hawes

The Child-to-Child Trust

First published in London, in 1992.

British Library Cataloguing in Publication Data
Child-to-Child: A Resource Book
     I. Bonati, Grazyna II. Hawes, Hugh
     613.07

ISBN 0-946182-01-9

This resource book is available from TALC (Teaching-aids At Low Cost),
P.O. Box 49, St. Albans, Herts AL1 4AX, UK. Fax: (0727) - 46852

The **Child-to-Child Trust** would like to thank **British Gas** and Save the **Children Fund** for their help in the publication of this resource book.

Child-to-Child: A Resource Book

Preface

This Child-to-Child Resource Book contains several sections (also available as separate booklets) which have been collected in one volume for easy reference. It contains many of the most important Child-to-Child publications from recent years and we hope that it contains most of the information needed to use the Child-to-Child approach effectively.

This book begins with an introduction to Child-to-Child and gives some examples of the many ways in which it has been used round the world. Section 1 contains all the Child-to-Child Activity Sheets with a special box on each giving more examples of how these have been used and finally an extra sheet on "Making Our Own Activity Sheets" in response to particular local problems has been created. Section 2, "Approaches to Learning and Teaching", gives a detailed description of the Child-to-Child methodology with many examples.

Section 3 offers practical advice on how to plan and organise an evaluation. It shows that evaluation is not as mysterious as it may appear and that even children can and should be involved in evaluating their activities. There is also a section on how to run a workshop. The final section is a list of Child-to-Child publications indicating the languages in which they are available and where they can be obtained. The list is far from complete and we would be grateful for information about any publications not included.

It is impossible to credit everyone who has contributed to this publication. Many people from around the world have worked on the various sections and contributed the results of their experiences over many years of using Child-to-Child approaches. We would like to take this opportunity of thanking everyone who has helped.

We should also be grateful for your comments and suggestions and be happy to help you solve any difficulties you may be encountering. Please contact The Child-to-Child Trust, Institute of Education, 20 Bedford Way, London, WC1H 0AL, UK.

Table of Contents

SECTION 2 - APPROACHES TO LEARNING AND TEACHING

SECTION 3 - DOING IT BETTER - A SIMPLE GUIDE TO EVALUATION

INTRODUCTION

PART I - EVALUATION AND THE CHILD-TO-CHILD APPROACH

PART II - EVALUATING CHILD-TO-CHILD ACTIVITIES

SECTION 4 - HOW TO RUN A WORKSHOP AND SIMILAR OCCASIONS

SECTION 5 - CHILD-TO-CHILD PUBLICATIONS

CHILD-TO-CHILD

The Child-to-Child approach

The Child-to-Child approach to health education was introduced in 1978, following the Alma Alta Declaration on Primary Health Care and prior to the International Year of the Child. It helps us to realise the potential of **children** to spread health ideas and practices to other children, families and communities.

The first Child-to-Child programme started at the University of London. Here teachers and doctors from the Institutes of Child Health and Education, working with colleagues from all over the world, developed many of the ideas and activities included in this book.

The Child-to-Child approach has now spread all over the world and wherever it is found we will also find the same partnership of health and education workers developing the same central ideas.

These are the ideas:

- Health is a very important part of every child's education. Unless we learn to be healthy we cannot live happily or study well.

- Health is everyone's concern - not just that of doctors and other health workers. Children have just as much responsibility as adults to keep themselves healthy and to help others become healthy and stay healthy.

- The most important way of remaining healthy is to prevent illness from taking place. But even when children and adults are ill there are simple things which all of us can do to help them get better.

  There are also important **signs** of illness which we can learn to recognise. In this way we may be able to get help quickly so that it is easier to treat sickness.

- **Health** does not only mean being well in body. It also means having a bright and active mind and a happy, healthy life. Children can also help themselves and others towards this kind of health.

- Good health is based upon sound knowledge about health. Unless we **know** and **understand** the really important facts, ideas and skills necessary for good health we cannot spread our ideas properly.

How can children spread health ideas and practices?

There are many different ways in which children can spread health ideas and teach others good health practices:

Older children can help younger ones

They can: care for them;
             teach them;
             show them a good example.

Children can help others of the same age

* Children learn from each other by doing things together.
* Children who have been to school can help others who have not had the chance to do so.

Children can pass on health messages and take health action in their families and communities

* Sometimes they can spread knowledge they have learned in school. (e.g. Mary learns about the importance of immunisation. Mother takes baby to be immunised.)
* Sometimes they teach by example. (e.g. John makes a new toy for baby. Grandmother helps baby play with it.)
* Sometimes they can work together to spread ideas and take action in the community. (e.g. The health scouts make a fence round the well ... and hold a party afterwards.)

What's old about Child-to-Child and what's new?

Some people say that Child-to-Child is part of the traditional way in which families helped each other. This is true and very important. But Child-to-Child activities go beyond the traditions of the past:

- They give children **new knowledge and skills** and a better understanding of what they are doing. They also make learning more interesting and more fun.

- They give a **new look** to health education in school. Instead of teaching children health **facts** about their **own health,** they encourage them to take **health action** for **themselves and others.** This links school learning with home and community needs and helps children learn to grow up into responsible adults.

- Because they encourage children to **work together** for the good of others, they develop their self-respect and sense of worth. This also encourages adults to value and trust children more.

Child-to-Child as an approach to learning and teaching in school

Once we accept the Child-to-Child approach to health education in schools we find that it has important effects on the way we teach and learn because:

- Child-to-Child approaches link what **we learn now** with **what we do now.**

- Child-to-Child approaches link what we do **in class** with what we do **out of class** and **at home.**

- Child-to-Child approaches cannot be learnt in one lesson and forgotten ... they are learnt and developed over a longer time and we continue to apply them for the rest of our lives.

Things learnt at school ...

... are immediately put into practice

For this reason most Child-to-Child activities in health need to be introduced in a series of steps:

> **STEP 1**
> Choosing the right health idea
> Understanding it well

So we must choose activities which are:

- important
- do-able by children
- fun to do

Once we select the topic we must understand it properly. In each sheet there is an **IDEA** which is very clearly stated. Make sure this idea is understood.

THE IDEA

Every living thing needs water to live, but dirty water can make us ill. We must be careful to keep water clean and safe: where it is found; when we carry it home; and when we store it and use it.

Ways of developing better understanding include:

- Practical activities to reinforce the ideas, e.g.:
  - measuring arm circumference;
  - using the 'Road to Health' chart;
  - mixing a rehydration drink.

- Role-play, drama and games to understand how people feel and react, e.g.:
  - plays to illustrate people's attitudes to immunisation;
  - games to understand what it is like to be blind;
  - role-play to explore how to say **'No'** to people who offer cigarettes or drugs.

- Making up and telling stories to relate health problems to real life, e.g.:
  - imaginative stories: 'my life as a fly';
  - problem-posing stories: 'preventing accidents';
  - 'what happened next?' stories.

- Making and using pictures to develop understanding, e.g.:
  - discussion based on a picture of malnutrition;
  - creating a comic strip on washing hands;
  - role-play based on a picture of bottle-feeding.

STEP 2
Finding out more

In every case a health problem and the activities linked with it have to be seen **in the light of local needs.**
- There will be **local** examples of the problem.
- There will be **local** variations, **local** names, **local** practices.
- There will be **local** beliefs.
We need to find out about them.

Finding-out activities can include:

- Finding-out among ourselves, e.g.:
  - how many babies and young children in our families had accidents in the last three months?
  - what kinds?

- Finding-out at home, e.g.:
  - in what ways do we prevent accidents?
  - what dangers are still present to young children?

- Finding-out in the community, e.g.:
  - where do flies breed?
  - how many people recognise the **danger signs** of pneumonia?

Is this situation the same as ...

... this one?

STEP 3
Discussing what we have found out

This involves deepening our knowledge as a result of the new information we have obtained. The same **understanding activities** listed above can be used.

STEP 4
Planning action

Children need to discuss and plan what action they can take either **individually,** when they go out of the classroom and back into their homes, or **together,** when they are able to support each other and so, possibly, achieve even more. Often children will need to be helped in what they do. Planning activities thus include:

- Discussing (in groups) possible action (role-play can help);
- Choosing the best course of action;
- Drawing up an action plan:

> WHAT can we do?
> WHEN can we do it?
> WHO can do what?
> HOW can we start?
> WHO can help us?

(Children's action is most useful if others can be asked to help, e.g. families, teachers, health workers.)

STEP 5
Taking action

This may be **in school** (particularly in matters of hygiene and safety) or, more frequently, **at home** or **in the community.**

These **doing** activities include:

- Practical activities at home, e.g. covering food; new games to play with the baby.

- Sharing new ideas and messages with the family, e.g. what I learnt about immunisation.
- Activities in the community, including **helping activities**, e.g. protecting water supplies, spreading messages through campaigns, drama, health songs, etc.
- Myself, my home, my school as a **good example** for others.

STEP 6
Discussing results

After action has been taken, children must come back and discuss what has happened.

- How were their ideas and activities received?
- Who listened .. and who didn't?
- Who took action?
- What were the results?
- Should we try again?
- How can we do better next time?
- How can we make the new practice an everyday habit?

Activities in class and outside class

Sometimes Child-to-Child activities are based on classroom teaching either in Health or Science lessons or during other subject periods. (Often health topics such as child growth and nutrition prove a very effective basis for developing learning skills like making graphs in mathematics or effective comprehension in language.)

Activities are usually developed over a period of time rather than in a single lesson. Class teaching alternates with activities at home and in the community.

1. Health objectives which everyone agrees

Sometimes a whole school or, better still, a whole community can agree on a list of **the most important, local health objectives,** including the health messages (facts, skills and attitudes) that ... 'every child should know and has a responsibility to pass on'.

The UNICEF/Unesco/WHO book, **Facts for Life,** lists such messages. Many are contained in the activity sheets in this book. If everyone knows these priorities, then there will be complete agreement that they should form part of children's learning, and children will receive encouragement and support to pass them on.

2. School health plans

Sometimes a school can agree an action plan to help everyone receive and understand such messages. Staff, parents and even children can list those that they think are most vital for children to know and do.

OUR SCHOOL HEALTH PRIORITIES	
PROBLEMS	WHAT WE CAN DO
Much malaria in wet season	Fill in water puddles, find and kill mosquito larvae.
Stomach upsets in children. Deaths in babies from dehydration	Keep Latrines clean. Learn to make special drinks

They can then plan how they will help to achieve them:
- through health teaching;
- through reinforcing the ideas in other subjects;
- through action to make the school a good example;
- through community activities organised by the school.

They can then decide how to check to what extent these plans are being followed and what results are being achieved.

3. A Child-to-Child school

Sometimes whole schools can be a living example of Child-to-Child in action. Staff and children agree a set of rules to live by:

- "In a Child-to-Child school, we should all know ..."
- "In a Child-to-Child school, we practise ..."

- "In a Child-to-Child school, we spread these ideas ..."

Child-to-Child schools nearly always set up a Health Committee (of children, teachers and community members) to plan and organise activities. Children are usually **paired,** with an older child responsible for a younger one.

Finally there is nearly always one or more action groups such as health clubs or health scout groups who take action in the community. In the best Child-to-Child schools both children and teachers are extremely proud of what they are and what they are achieving.

Back to the classroom

But all the activities described above must be based on sound knowledge and on active methods of learning and teaching, leading to real understanding. That is why this approach to science teaching is so important.

Child-to-Child Outside School

Not all Child-to-Child activities are school-based. Whenever children meet, activities can be organised. Sometimes schools are not the kind of places which encourage children to meet and do things for others. Sometimes they are cut off (or cut themselves off) from communities.

For this reason, Child-to-Child activities in many countries are based on:
- youth groups;
- health centres;
- refugee camps;
- programmes for disadvantaged children.

Sometimes activities are quite informal, spread by radio programmes, books or from one child (or group of children) to another.

But wherever Child-to-Child activities occur, the following conditions are necessary for their success.

The right knowledge and skills

Correct knowledge and practice is at the centre of effective health care. Incorrect knowledge or skills (however enthusiastically spread) may do more harm than good.

...... to meet the right needs

Not all needs are present in all contexts. Not all can be best met by children. The power of children is best used when it is focussed on what children do best.

...... introduced in the right way

The six steps outlined earlier are appropriate both in and out of school, but different messages have to be spread by children in different ways. Depending on the message, the needs and the culture of a society.

• One child

• A group of children

}

- spreading knowledge to
- teaching skills to
- demonstrating by example to
- working together with

}

- a younger child
- younger children
- a same-age child
- same age children
- a family
- families
- the community

What is difficult, but yet so very important, is to decide in each separate case which of these activities and channels is most effective and most acceptable.

CHILD-TO-CHILD IN ACTION

Child-to-Child is an **approach** to health and education and not a rigid set of content and principles. For this reason, there is no one 'right' way of introducing it - many different approaches can be introduced at the same time and complement each other. This section gives examples of different approaches used from all over the world - and suggests possible action that could be taken by those working to introduce and extend Child-to-Child.

Since Child-to-Child was launched in 1978, its ideas and activities have spread very widely and have been taken up in varying degrees in at least 70 countries. Though originally used mostly in developing countries, there is increasing interest and activity in industrialised countries such as Britain. The principles of children helping each other and of children taking an active part in health promotion are equally relevant in any community.

CHILD-TO-CHILD MATERIALS AND IDEAS AS A RESOURCE FOR HEALTH EDUCATORS

Child-to-Child publications from London and Paris as a resource

Child-to-Child publications, especially activity sheets and story books, are widely used in their original forms as resource materials in international and national programmes. Lists of materials and sources from which they can be obtained are included in Section 5 of this resource book.

Translation, Adaptation and Origination of Local Materials

Many countries have translated Child-to-Child materials into local languages usually with adaptations to suit local priorities.

In many other cases as in India, Ecuador and Zambia, new materials have been originated based on the Child-to-Child approach.

Action possible

Assess the use and applicability of published Child-to-Child material. Where it appears useful make it available, either directly to project workers and health educators or through libraries and resource centres. Aid agencies such as UNESCO, UNICEF and British Council as well as NGO's such as CARITAS, Bread for the World, CARE and Save the Children are often sympathetic to the funding and distribution of such materials. Since Activity Sheets and this publication are copyright free they may be reproduced locally.

Action possible

- Find out availability of translated and adapted Child-to-Child materials and make them available where they are needed.

- Organise workshops and writing teams where possible and desirable. Be sure that there is competent medical advice available to each writing group. Funding is often possible for such activities from the agencies mentioned above as well as from local industries.

Child-to-Child approaches as components of resource books for health educators

Many influential books such as Young and Durston's *Primary Health Education*; Werner and Bower's *Helping Health Workers Learn* and Gibbs and Mutunga's *Health into Mathematics* incorporate Child-to-Child activities, as do many books printed round the world.

Action possible

- Identify and use such resource books in preference to others which do not incorporate active and child-centred approaches.

- Incorporate copyright-free Child-to-Child materials into locally produced resource books in Health Education.

Child-to-Child approaches as a component of national curricula and education material

In the widest sense it is possible to emphasise the Child-to-Child approach as desirable throughout the primary school curriculum and to state it as part of the general aims of education at this level. This is a policy favoured both by UNESCO and UNICEF and a number of national governments (eg. Zambia and Chile). Thus children are actively encouraged to help younger and weaker ones within a school situation and to adopt an attitude to development which seeks to spread good practice from school back to the community, e.g. in health, environmental protection and active citizenship.

In a narrower sense many countries (e.g. Guinea, Nepal, Myanmar, Nicaragua) have announced Child-to-Child as a recommended approach within their health education syllabus. In some cases where the approach is recommended the Child-to-Child logo is inserted in the syllabus or recommended texts.

Action possible

- Include a public statement of the importance of children as communicators in the aims of the curriculum. Discuss this approach with different syllabus panels within Curriculum Development Centres to see how they would incorporate it within their methodology.

- Incorporate Child-to-Child approaches and activities into the health education curriculum and materials (In Sierra Leone a special working party was convened to examine the Child-to-Child activity sheets alongside the health syllabus and integrate them).

- Discuss how Teacher Education can incorporate and introduce these new curricular approaches (see next section).

Child-to-Child approaches introduced into pre-service and in-service training of teachers

In a number of countries (e.g. Uganda, Sierra Leone, Zambia) Child-to-Child approaches have been introduced in teachers' colleges. They form part of the health education curriculum and, through links with pilot schools also involved in Child-to-Child approaches, teachers in training can join theory with practice. Colleges set lists of minimum health competencies (including the ten priority areas contained in UNICEF's *Facts for Life*) which every student leaving college should master and have a duty to pass on to children.

Action possible

- Review existing curricula for health education in teachers' colleges alongside a list of Child-to-Child activities. Incorporate these activities where possible.

- Generate a list of minimum health competencies which every student should possess and pass on to others. Design a college health plan which should incorporate these competencies either through direct teaching, through the medium of other subjects in the curriculum, or through the interaction of students in the college and in the community.

- Identify, motivate, and monitor a small number of Child-to-Child schools close to the college.

- Organise short in-service courses to introduce and discuss the Child-to-Child approach and/or arrange 'add-on' days or sessions within existing in-service programmes.

- Make Child-to-Child activities part of teaching practice.

CHILD-to-child

Look at your list of things found at home which can cause cuts and wounds. Find safe places at home for knives and other dangerous things. Make sure young children cannot reach them.

Keep children from playing in the road.

Child-to-Child methodology has been introduced into many school textbooks around the world. This example concerning safety is from a Ugandan primary science textbook.

Child-to-Child and school-based curricula

Although syllabuses and, sometimes, textbooks are prescribed nationally, schools have very great power to interpret and vary them to suit their own needs. Moreover schools retain complete control of what happens outside the classroom and between school and community. In many countries, e.g. Kenya, Mali, India (New Delhi) and Uganda, individual schools are developing their own health action plans - linking teachers, children, parents and community members. These school plans are made side-by-side with new national-level health syllabuses.

Plans often include the following:

- An agreement by children, teachers, local health workers that 'this is a Child-to-Child school'. Hence, one which is an example to other schools and to the community.

- A school health action plan - where certain health priorities are agreed - probably on a term-by-term basis. These priorities (examples: clean safe water; malaria, etc.) form part of direct teaching, reinforcement across the curriculum, and action by children in school and community.

- A school health committee (including children and parents) who organise and monitor the activities.

- Some form of 'pairing' where older children are responsible for younger ones in school, at home or both.

- Links with the community and the local health workers and with national campaigns such Anti-AIDS campaigns as in Uganda and Zambia.

However, in many countries e.g. Sudan, Indonesia, Kenya and Mexico, children have been very successfully organised into school health clubs, health scouts, or, in Indonesia, a special movement called 'Little Doctors' co-ordinated and advised by health workers.

The advantage of these voluntary groups are that they are very easy to establish alongside the formal system and because the children who form them are highly motivated they are often successful and effective. The main disadvantage is that many children do not have the opportunity to join them. Often it is these very children who need to have their confidence and motivation built up through participation in such programmes, and whose parents may also need particular help, who are unable to participate in them.

Action possible

- Help organise and stimulate individual schools to become Child-to-Child schools and to make their own plans. (Parents often encourage this once they have seen how good the Child-to-Child schools are.)

- Organise some way for different schools to share ideas and experience and to show their achievements to other schools and communities. (In India, for instance, Health Fairs are organised based on Child-to-Child schools.)

Action possible

- Survey groups that have already been established - e.g. Red Cross or Red Crescent clubs, 'Anti-Aids' clubs and find out which Child-to-Child ideas have already been introduced.

- Consider starting a programme of health clubs or health scouts where these do not exist.

Remember

- *It is better to start small and build upon success.*

- *It is essential that such health clubs/scout programmes have support and help from local health workers.*

- *Remember that activities planned for clubs must be interesting, active and rewarding for children. They must have fun doing them.*

Programmes based on schools - but carried out entirely through out-of-class activities

Sometimes it is not possible to integrate Child-to-Child activities with the regular school teaching programme. Health education may not be a school subject or the existing programme is too overloaded, inflexible or examination-oriented.

Schools linked with health centres and/or used as part of national health campaigns

Sometimes (as in India (Bombay) or Gambia) community health programmes or individual health centres make special links with groups of schools within the community served by the health centre. Health workers come into the schools and give school children special training on how to carry out their work as health promoters. In Bombay, for instance, special health problems in a particular slum were targeted (e.g. scabies and anaemia) and school children participated in very successful campaigns to help eliminate these.

Sometimes national programmes, often with UNICEF assistance, have involved school children as agents for health campaigns as in the highly successful immunisation campaign in Togo.

Action possible

• When health programmes and centres identify schools as partners they need fully to involve heads, teachers and local inspectors. These in turn need to guarantee time and support. Discussion could also take place on how other subjects could help emphasise the priority themes, e.g. graphs in mathematics, maps and surveys in social studies, posters in art and craft are all areas where many important health themes can be discussed.

• When national campaigns are launched, a similar partnership is necessary. Demands on schools should be kept reasonable. (Say, perhaps one theme each year; Immunisation; AIDS; Safety; Breast feeding, etc.).

Schools linked with other schools and communities

• In many countries there are areas (often in cities) where some schools are more fortunate than others, or where some children have an opportunity to go to school while others are denied it. In India (Delhi and Madras) some children in higher-cost schools 'adopt' schools and communities (with children who do not go to school) in slum areas. They are involved in:

  • Passing on information and ideas (often through plays and songs) to these communities.
  • Making toys, games and story books for younger children in poorer schools and families.
  • Making playgrounds.
  • Helping in literacy classes.

• Schools in some industrialised countries, e.g. the United Kingdom, have developed links with schools and communities in Africa. They learn about, and learn to admire the health action taken by African children to help their families and communities and in return contribute to buy health texts and story books for these schools.

Action possible

• Establish school links either within countries or between them. Set them up in such a way that children from more financially fortunate schools can relate to others in a sense of equality rather than with any feeling of patronage. Both should gain from the relationship.

• Make sure that links are maintained over a long period of time.

Below you can see an example taken from a leaflet called, "Fun with Health", produced for UK schools. The leaflet contains a health game with many important health messages.

Try the Fun with Health Game

In the middle pages of this leaflet is a simple game. It will help you to understand more about the kind of health activities which children are doing all over the world.

 Work with a partner or in small groups

 Match the pictures with the sentences

 Ask yourselves these questions
○ Which of these health activities could you do with your friends?

○ What other Child-to-Child activities could you do here? For example activities to improve the environment or to prevent accidents.

○ Children in Britain do not die from many of the diseases that affect children in developing countries but we have our own special problems. If children from those countries were to come to Britain, what kinds of things would you warn them about?

 Make up a story or a play about one of the picture sentences.

 Plan a 'healthy lifestyles' campaign.

Schools linked with pre-schools and pre-school children

One of the most effective ways in which older children can help in the health and development of babies and pre-school children is by playing with them in an interesting and stimulating way. Research has shown that little children who have good mental stimulation are healthier and do better at school later. Many Child-to-Child activities worldwide help child development in different ways.

In Kenya, district centres for early childhood education identify schools, pre-schools and their communities within an area. Children in school make toys and play areas for younger ones. Toy-making workshops and activities have taken place in many countries, for instance India (Orissa); Nepal, Zanzibar, often using ideas provided in the Child-to-Child book, **Toys for Fun.**

In Botswana, school children named *little teachers* have each been given responsibility for a child about to enter school. They teach them simple health facts, assist them in keeping themselves clean and even help with early pre-reading and number games. Research indicates that the *little teachers* do better in their studies than other children without their responsibilities. One reason may be that their sense of responsibility and initiative has been increased.

Action possible

- Attempt to establish local links between schools, pre-schools and communities. Children in school thus become responsible for playing games, making toys, and 'teaching' skills to others - from the time they are born.
- Have toy-making workshops and competitions by children and between schools.
- Teach **all** children (boys as well as girls) in upper primary and secondary schools the kind of play and stimulation little children need at different ages and why this is important.

Schools in and for Children in Refugee Camps

Children in refugee camps benefit in two ways from using Child-to-Child approaches. It helps improve their health and, by giving children recognised responsibilities, increases their self-esteem.

Child-to-Child activities are used in schools in refugee camps in Ethiopia, Pakistan, Thailand, Lebanon and many other countries.

Action possible

- If schools have been built in refugee camps, encourage the children in them to take up some Child-to-Child activities. In particular, they will benefit if they set up teams of health scouts to spread health messages and improve health practices in the camp.
- Badges, membership certificates, caps or other items of clothing can help to give members of these groups a sense of identity and pride in their achievements.
- Schools and school children can also take particular responsibility for growth monitoring, and with helping and playing with babies and young children.

Taken from "Child-to-Child: A Manual for Teachers."

CHILD-TO-CHILD ACTION ORGANISED OUTSIDE FORMAL EDUCATION

Child-to-Child approaches can be spread through youth groups composed of either younger or older children.

In many countries e.g. India (Orissa), Nigeria, Sudan, children enrolled in scout or health scout groups learn how to pass on priority health messages as part of their training. The badge system based on competency used in youth groups is a very suitable way of promoting and measuring Child-to-Child activities. Traditionally given for skills in subjects like first aid and cookery, it is already being extended in many programmes to include topics such as water safety, child care, management of diarrhoea, prevention of malaria. Members of these health scout groups need not be school children. Children who cannot read are well able to spread health messages.

Adolescent children and youth are increasingly seen as very suitable agents for spreading health messages, sometimes directly to the community (as in Chile), sometimes through Youth-to-Child programmes where young people work to mobilise children of school age. This has been tried out on a very large scale in India (through the Intensive School Health Education Project in 10 states).

Action possible

- Plan and organise Health Scout programmes incorporating both school and non-school children.

- Review health activities undertaken by existing groups such as scouts, guides or youth brigades. How can they be improved? Can more Child-to-Child content be usefully incorporated?

- Review how national youth movements can help to empower other children to take positive health action.

Health Scouts trained in First Aid.

Child-to-Child activities as part of the training of doctors and health workers

Contact with the Child-to-Child approach, particularly if they can see it in action at community level, should help doctors to realise the importance of primary health care and of working with the community, including its children, to promote it.

Doctors working with community health programmes can often profitably make use of children, both in and out of school, to spread health messages. Often Child-to-Child materials are very useful too in helping health workers to communicate with young people. Thus Child-to-Child ideas and activities are very widely used e.g. in community health programmes for doctors, e.g. Semarang, Indonesia) in nurse training programmes (e.g. Zanzibar) and in training of para-medical staff and community health workers (e.g. Lagos, Nigeria).

Action possible

- Make Child-to-Child materials available to staff of medical and health worker training.

- Organise discussions of the value of this approach and how these materials can be profitably incorporated.

- Encourage local doctors to participate in community and school Child-to-Child activities.

Child-to-Child activities through the mass media

Many countries have become aware of the great potential of children as communicators over the radio and television. Children are particularly effective because they bring a sense of freshness and vitality to the messages they convey. In a sense they thus act as the conscience of the community. Effective and popular radio and television health programmes organised round children's activities exist, e.g. in Nepal, Bolivia, Ecuador, Uganda and India. Child-to-Child issues a resource pack (pamphlet and tape) to help those who wish to use radio in this way.

Action possible

- Review possibilities of using children to project health messages through mass media if they have not already done so.

- One way of initiating this would be to hold a one-day workshop for those who might be interested to discuss possible action and priorities. Funds for such a workshop might easily be obtained through Aid agencies or non-government organisations.

- Later organise training for teachers and pupils in techniques of using the media. (A radio pack including a written guide and cassettes is available through Child-to-Child).

Child-to-Child and children in specially difficult circumstances

This is an area of great complexity - but one in which children may often offer help to others of a kind and quality which no adult can give. There are different categories of such children.

Refugee children - mentioned above.

Disabled children may be helped through the establishment of a self-help group or centre such as Project Projimo (Mexico); through special emphasis placed on their needs in ongoing Child-to-Child programmes as in Kenya (Nairobi), or through special campaigns, targeting one particular area of disability e.g. eye disease in India (Andhra Pradesh).

Street and working children Many programmes for assisting street and working children use some elements of Child-to-Child material (Brazil, Liberia, Philippines, Benin). These children are particularly vulnerable to health risks so provision for health education is especially important. However, materials and approaches need to be very carefully adapted to meet their particular local needs.

Action possible

- Provide Werner's 'Disabled Village Children' as a resource wherever possible. (Apart from providing a great fund of practical ideas, the book has an excellent section on Child-to-Child.).

- Consider a national campaign (in school and out) sensitizing all children to the needs of disabled ones and the attitudes of understanding and co-operation necessary for them to be effectively integrated with other children.

Action possible

- Make Child-to-Child materials and activities available to programme organisers for street and working children.

- Discuss how far messages can be used and adapted and if so by whom? Involve children themselves in suggesting ways of adopting existing messages and in selecting and preparing new ones.

- In cases where residential or day centres have been set up, adapt material and involve children in helping others - particularly in situations where mixed ages are common (as in the successful 'Mobile Creches' programme in Bombay, India, with children of mobile construction workers.)

Some suggestions for a playground where many children, including disabled children, can play together (from "Disabled Village Children", by David Werner).

Children victims of war and disaster
(To an increasing extent this also involves a new group, the orphans of AIDS epidemics.)

Action possible

Identify such groups - discuss appropriate health action which they need and can take. The action of helping to provide for others is an important element for these children since it raises their own self esteem and sense of belonging. However such groups need close and careful support.

Child-to-Child and children in clinics and hospitals
Many small scale activities are possible and have been attempted where children are resident in hospitals (as in Northern Kenya). Older children can be mobilised to play with, read to and teach health skills to younger ones. This raises children's morale as well as passing on useful ideas.

Action possible

Where children of mixed ages regularly attend clinics and hospitals, introduce Child-to-Child either through older children helping younger ones or by getting groups of older children to prepare activities such as drama and songs for other patients.

CO-ORDINATING CHILD-TO-CHILD

As can be seen from the many examples given, Child-to-Child activities can (and should) take place at different levels and in different ways.

However they should always complement each other and never compete with one another for funds or for influence.

It is also vital that different activities within a country and within a region should share information, materials and plans.

For this reason various means have been used to co-ordinate and inform. These include:

National Child-to-Child associations. Usually with a committee representative of many Child-to-Child interests and with one or more paid workers (sometimes seconded from government but usually paid by a non-government organisation). There are associations in, for instance, Burkina Faso, Uganda and Botswana.

National programmes - set up within Ministries of Health and/or Education and often with the active involvement of UNICEF. These are usually coordinated by government staff whose duties are not exclusively confined to Child-to-Child.

Such a pattern may be found in India, Zambia, Nepal, Lesotho and many other countries.

Individual institutions recognised as a resource or information base for Child-to-Child. (Again these may be partly supported by Aid cooperation or non-government organisations.) In Africa, Asia and Latin America, a number of such institutions have emerged, often as a result of the particular interest of a member or group of persons. These include, for instance:

Voluntary Health Education Association, New Delhi,
Centre for Health Education and Nutrition Awareness (CHETNA), Ahmedabad, India.
College of Health, University of Lagos, Nigeria.
The University of Gezira, Sudan.
The University of Cuenca, Ecuador.
Institute for Teacher Education, Kyambogo, Uganda.
The Child Development Centre of China, Beijing.
The Health Network based on AMREF, Nairobi, Kenya.

Within Britain, France and Belgium a number of university centres of interest are also developing. The Universities of London, Paris, Liège, Leeds and Bristol all have active units.

Regional Centres. As yet co-ordination at regional level has to be achieved, though in one area, the Eastern Mediterranean, WHO, UNICEF and UNESCO cooperation in a prototype action-orientated curriculum incorporating much Child-to-Child material is well advanced. It is very likely that the future will see regional resource bases and information centres emerging as they have been identified as a prime need in the development of the Child-to-Child network.

Action possible

Discuss, activate and support co-ordination and resource centres especially at national level. Modest funding, prudently employed can help enormously in the co-ordination and dissemination of ideas and in the generation and spread of new approaches and materials.

CHILD-TO-CHILD

ACTIVITY SHEETS

CHILD-TO-CHILD

ACTIVITY
SHEETS

CHILD-TO-CHILD

HOW TO USE THE CHILD-TO-CHILD ACTIVITY SHEETS

THE IDEA

Child-to-Child is a way of teaching about health which encourages children to participate actively in the process of learning and to put into practice what they learn.

The activity sheets in this package are designed to help you teach health education in a more exciting way using the Child-to-Child approach.

In the Child-to-Child approach we select topics:

- which are really **important** for the health of children and communities;
- which can be **well understood** and are of **interest** to children;
- which children can **act** on.

Children enjoy being involved and it helps them to learn better. This makes teaching more fun and more effective.

What Topics Are Most Important?

Government health services and organisations such as WHO and UNICEF now know the main causes of most avoidable deaths and diseases. We now know how to prevent these, and how to care for people when they are sick so that they can be cured. Child-to-Child materials help to pass on this knowledge.

However, preventing people being sick is not enough. They must also live safe and happy lives. Child-to-Child ideas and activities also help children to **grow up happily and to develop their minds and bodies.**

We are all teachers: school teachers (1); parents (2); older children (3); religious leaders (4); health workers (5); craftsmen (6).

What Action Can Children Take?

Child-to-Child activities all over the world have proved that children can improve their own health and that of others through:

- caring for younger brothers and sisters and other young children in the community (**Child-to-Child**);
- influencing other children in their community, especially those with less opportunities and education than themselves (**Children-to-Children**);
- spreading health ideas and messages within their own communities (**Children-and-Community**);
- sharing information with their families (**Child-with-Family**).

BY SPREADING AND SHARING IDEAS CHILDREN ALSO IMPROVE THEIR OWN HEALTH

Experience has proved that Child-to-Child activities fall into distinct categories which are best introduced in the following sequence:

UNDERSTANDING activities, e.g.:

- the main causes of diarrhoea and dehydration;
- why dehydration kills;
- how to recognise it.

FINDING-OUT activities, e.g.:

- the number of children who have had diarrhoea;
- how do people treat it?

PLANNING ACTION activities, e.g.:

- what can 'I' do to prevent diarrhoea?
- what can 'we' do if another child is affected?

DOING activities, e.g.:

- making and mixing the special drink (oral rehydration solution);
- giving the special drink to others;
- persuading others to use it.

DISCUSSING RESULTS activities, e.g.:

- how many of 'us' can make the special drink?
- how many have passed on the ideas to others in our family and community?

What Are Activity Sheets?

Topics for the activity sheets have been grouped under separate headings:

- Child Growth and Development
- Nutrition
- Personal and Community Hygiene
- Safety
- Recognising and Helping the Disabled
- Prevention and Cure of Disease

Every year new sheets are added to these groups.

Each sheet is divided into several sections:

- A clear statement of the main idea.

- More information about the subject, as a resource for those using the sheet.

- A wide selection of suggested activities to choose from, e.g.:

  - **finding-out** activities;
  - **discussion** and other classroom activities;
  - **doing** activities.

- A separate section of **follow-up** activities (evaluation). This section contains ideas and suggestions to find out:

  - if children have understood the new ideas properly;
  - what action they have taken;
  - whether people in the community now know more, understand better and have changed their actions.

Using The Sheets

- Sheets are resource material and can be used in a variety of ways.

- Each sheet can be used separately though some are closely related.

- There is no special order to the way in which sheets are grouped. Different countries and localities have different needs and schemes for health education. Sheets can be selected to fit these needs.

- Although the sheets can help teachers and others prepare for their teaching, they are not lesson plans:

  - Each contains far too much information and activity for a single lesson.

  - Many of the activities suggested are designed to be used outside a classroom setting, at home and in the community.

The following guidelines may be useful in helping you to use a sheet as a basis for introducing and spreading a health idea.

1. Understanding the idea

Make sure you fully understand the **idea** at the beginning of the sheet, e.g.:

THE IDEA

Diarrhoea is dangerous because it can both kill and cause malnutrition. It can be prevented by keeping clean, using clean water and by eating properly. Children who get diarrhoea may die because they become dehydrated, that is, their bodies lose too much water. The liquid they lose must be put back in their bodies. A Special Drink can be made by children to help replace the lost water when a child has diarrhoea and prevent dehydration.

THE IDEA

Everything living needs water to live, but dirty water can make us ill. We must be careful to keep water clean and safe - where it is found, when we carry it home, and when we store and use it.

The next part of the sheet is also very important because it gives more detailed information related to this idea.

It is essential that the health message you teach and children spread is correct.

A WRONG MESSAGE WELL TAUGHT
CAN DO MORE HARM THAN GOOD.

---

2. Selecting the right material for your learners and their communities

Make sure that the content you select is helpful for those who will use it and that examples given are familiar and fit in with the life and experience of the learners.

3. Selecting and using activities

Communicating Information

Effective learning depends on the ability of teachers to:

- pass on their own knowledge and enthusiasm;
- communicate through words and pictures.

```
BUT ACTIVE PARTICIPATION OF THE CHILDREN
IS EQUALLY VITAL
AT ALL STAGES IN THE LEARNING PROCESS
```

Understanding Activities

Ways of developing better understanding include:

- Practical activities to reinforce the ideas, e.g.:

  - measuring arm circumference (Sheet No. 2.2);
  - using the 'Road to Health' chart (Sheet No. 1.7);
  - mixing a rehydration drink (Sheet No. 6.1).

- Role play, drama and games to understand how people feel and react, e.g.:

  - plays to illustrate people's attitudes to immunisation;
  - games to understand what it is like to be blind;
  - role playing to explore how to say 'No' to people who offer cigarettes or drugs.

- Making up and telling stories to relate health problems to real life, e.g.:

  - imaginative stories: 'my life as a fly';
  - problem-posing stories: 'preventing accidents';
  - 'what happened next?' stories.

- Making and using pictures to develop understanding, e.g.:

  - discussion based on a picture of malnutrition;
  - creating a comic strip on washing hands;
  - role play based on a picture of bottle-feeding.

Finding-out Activities

- Finding-out among ourselves, e.g.:

  - how many babies and young children in our families had accidents in the last three months?
  - what kinds?

- Finding-out at home, e.g.:

  - what do we do to prevent accidents?
  - what dangers are still present to young children?

- Finding-out in the community, e.g.:

  - where do flies breed?
  - how many people recognise the 'danger signs' of pneumonia?

Planning Activities

- In groups, discussing possible action. (Role-play can help.)

- Who can help us? Children's action is most useful if others can be asked to help, e.g. families, teachers, health workers.

- Making a plan of action:

  WHAT can we do?
  WHEN can we do it?
  WHO can do what?
  HOW can we start?

Doing Activities

- **Practical activities at home,** e.g. covering food; new games to play with the baby.

- **Sharing new ideas and messages with the family,** e.g. what I learnt about immunisation.

- Activities in the community including 'helping activities' such as protecting water supplies and spreading messages through campaigns, drama, health songs, etc.

- Myself, my home, my school as a **good example** for others.

But often it means **changing** the content and approaches in the sheets and sometimes it involves writing new ones. Nearly always the sheets that are changed or newly written are more useful than the original sheets because they are closer to the needs of local teachers, children and communities.

> CHILD-TO-CHILD WELCOMES YOU TO TRANSLATE AND ADAPT THESE SHEETS. THERE IS NO COPYRIGHT ON CHILD-TO-CHILD MATERIALS.

Discussing Results Activities

- **Testing knowledge and skills,** e.g. how many of us ... how many at home ... know why the 'Road to Health' chart is important and how to fill it in?

- **Observing attitudes and practices,** e.g. are we more careful about home safety? Have we changed our approach to feeding babies at home?

- **Doing it better next time.** As a result of what we have found out, how can we find out more, take new action, change our habits?

Adapting The Sheets For Local Conditions and Writing New Ones

The sheets are written for use all over the world, but people and places are different. Often groups of teachers and health workers have met to **adapt** sheets to local needs. This usually takes place in a workshop.

Often sheets need to be **translated** into other languages. (Before translating you should check with Child-to-Child London to see whether this has already been done.) After translation be sure that the sheets are read through by qualified health professionals.

Some Suggestions for Adapting The Sheets

When adapting the sheets remember to:

- **relate the content to local conditions and resources.** Urban and rural areas differ; richer and poorer communities differ. Sometimes a sheet will need to cover more than one set of needs.

- **be sensitive to local culture, beliefs and customs.** In particular the sheets should avoid any statements and pictures which could offend people.

- **take into account real-life difficulties,** e.g. shortage of fuel may make it impossible to boil water, shortage of money or food may make some nutrition messages impossible to carry out.

- **develop an understanding and sympathetic attitude to local beliefs about health and diseases** and to encourage beneficial practices.

PLAYING WITH YOUNGER CHILDREN

THE IDEA

All babies and young children like to play. They can be helped to play better. Better play makes children grow and learn well. Better play helps children and parents to understand one another. Different ages need different kinds of games, and older children can help younger children to play better.

Children everywhere spend some time looking after younger brothers and sisters. They are often told what **not** to do when looking after the baby: "**Don't** let her near the fire!" "**Don't** let her hurt herself!" They are seldom told what they **can** do with the baby.

This sheet talks about **why** children need to play, **what kinds of play** are suitable for children at different ages, and **how children can help each other to play.**

Children Like to Play

All babies and young children like to play from an early age. Babies like to watch things moving, like the shadow of a tree against the sun. Later, they like to reach out to grab hair, or some pretty beads or a dish. When they can walk and run, they also like to hide, to jump, to skip and to twist around. As soon as they can understand and begin to talk, they like to play games using words: "Where's my nose?" or "Find the ball". We can encourage them to do all these things and even more. We can help them to play better and do many different kinds of things.

Where and how these activities have been used

This sheet has been used widely and is useful everywhere since children develop through play. Specially vital in big cities and refugee camps where family support is no longer strong or the child's surroundings may not be very stimulating. Through play the child explores his body, then his environment, and learns to establish relations with the outside world.

In Bombay, the children of mobile construction workers are brought together in special day centres, "Mobile Creches". They work in mixed age groups. Older children play games and invent games for younger ones but this is only part of an integrated programme of child health and development which focusses on basic literacy and numeracy skills, good health and hygiene practices and developing self-reliance. The older children learn about the milestones of motor development and the play activities which can be used to promote these.

In Botswana, children at school "adopt" younger pre-school children and help them develop through playing games and teaching activities to give them a sound start when they enter school. These activities involve songs, dances, games and drawing while preparing children for reading, writing and other skills.

In Kenya, pre-schools and schools are linked so that they work together as one "team" with families for the benefit of pre-school children in the home and in the family.

Why Better Play?

Older children may ask, "Don't all children play? Why do we need to learn about **better** play, about **different kinds** of play?"

- Better play makes the baby or young child more lively, using all parts of its mind and body together.
- Better play uses voice, eyes and hands. This helps the child and older people to understand one another and communicate better, which will help at school.
- Better play helps young ones to:
  - look at things around them;
  - try out new actions and activities;
  - make their own small experiments with their hands, their eyes, their voices.

In this way, they are always learning new skills and finding out for themselves about new things, and thus to:
  - use their bodies well;
  - talk and use language better;
  - think and later solve problems;
  - use their imaginations.

As they get older, better play helps children to learn to share and cooperate with others.

ACTIVITIES

Older children can help to organise better play for young children by understanding that children enjoy different kinds of play at different ages, as the following activities suggest.

Activities for Young Babies

Older children can begin by looking at babies in their own homes. How do they play? What can they do at different ages? What makes them laugh? What makes them move their hands, their heads, their eyes, their legs? What do they do when someone comes into the room? when someone takes their hand? when someone talks to them?

How can we help babies to learn to do more things? Here are some ways; children themselves may suggest others.

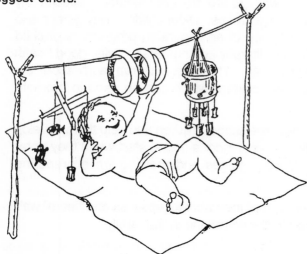

When they are very small, babies learn mainly through being **touched**. They need to be gently handled as much as possible by those who love them.

Little ones also like to **look** at things like a hand moving slowly in front of them, or a mobile hung above their bed. They enjoy people hiding their faces suddenly behind a corner or behind a piece of cloth.

They also like to **listen**. They like to hear the sound made by stones rattling in a tin can or of seeds in a dry pod. They will turn to discover where hands are being clapped. **Most important**, they like to hear someone **talking** to them. We should always talk with babies and encourage them to talk back. The sounds they make are their own language. Language is perhaps the most important thing for babies to learn. Babies like to listen to music. Sing to them.

Activities for Babies Learning to Crawl

Babies like to use their bodies. Put them on their stomachs so that they can push themselves up. Help babies to sit. Put things just out of reach so that they have to find them. Give babies spoons, sticks and noisy things like pans and tins to hit. Give them things to pick up and play with.

Don't forget to keep talking to babies and encourage them to imitate words. Make baby laugh. Make baby look at you. Tell baby what you are doing: "I'm going to cook your food now". Baby will start to copy you.

Activities for Babies Learning to Walk

Help babies to stand up. Be ready to catch them when they try to walk. Babies like to be thrown carefully up and down. Take them for small walks, show them things, and talk to them about what they see around them. Give them things to push and pull.

Toddlers like to **do** things. Let them help when they are being dressed. They can learn to talk about their clothes and what they are doing. Give them matchboxes or tins with seeds and stones they can remove. (Be careful they don't put them in their mouth or nose!) They like to climb into cardboard cartons and hide behind chairs.

Activities for Pre-school Children

Long before they go to school, young children want to learn. They need to be given challenges through many different kinds of play and activities. Older children can help with this. It is very important to remember that even when young children have a smaller baby in the home who needs mother's attention they still need plenty of talk and play.

Older children can observe and discuss what things younger children like to do by themselves or with other children; what games they like to play; what new games we can teach them. Can these games be played with boys or girls or both? Are they played alone or with two people or more? Do they need special materials or a special place?

Water, Sand and Mud
Children will play for hours with water and sand. Give them a few materials like different sized tins, gourds and calabashes. What can children use them for? Try putting holes in some of them. Thin bamboo, paw-paw or banana stems, or hollow reeds make good pipes and gutters. They can be used with soap and water for blowing bubbles. Tins, seed pods and pieces of wood make boats.

Building Games
Maize cobs, matchboxes, scraps of wood and cardboard can be used by children for building. Soft pith from palm fronds, grass stalks, banana leaves and thorns can be used for making or building things. Sisal, bark and other materials can be used for weaving. What other materials can be found for building and weaving?

Riddles, Songs and Stories
The stories, songs and riddles which young children learn can teach them to use language well, and help them to understand their culture and its values.

Taking Things to Pieces
Children can also learn how things work by taking things apart. Anything safe and no longer in use will do (pieces of old cars, broken clocks, locally made animal traps).

Sense Games
Children's senses of **feeling, smelling and hearing** can be used in play. Scraps of cloth, shells or stones can be put into bags for children to identify by feel.

Scraps of soap, onion, flowers or anything else with a strong smell can be wrapped in paper with tiny holes in it. The children can smell them and guess what they are. Other things can be put into tins to identify by sound only when the tin is shaken.

Pretend Games
Children love to pretend they are mother or father or teacher. Supply them with materials they can use to make these games more interesting, like things for making a house, preparing food, making dolls, playing at shopping or market, or dressing up.

Adventure Games
Young children need to be very active. They like to run and play tag games. Fallen trees and steep banks are good places to climb and slide down. Simple swings can be made with rope and old tyres, which are also good to roll and to climb through. Stilts can be made with big tins and string. Large stones can be placed so that children have difficulty stepping from one to the other.

Learning What Adults Do
Small children will enjoy a visit to a workshop, a bakery, or any other place where they can see work being done by adults in their community. Encourage children to talk about what they have seen when they get home.

Playing with the Sun
Children can play tag with their shadows. They can draw round their shadows in the dust, or make the shadow of their finger point at stones. They can make their shadows carry, kick or stand on other children's shadows. Children can play games with mirrors or shiny pieces of tin.

Music
Music can be used in many ways in games. Children can be active while music is playing, or drums are being beaten, and stop when the music stops. This teaches them to listen carefully. Music can be used for dancing. This helps them to listen and to move at the same time.

Musical instruments can be made out of reeds and gourds. Children can clap their hands, sing, beat on

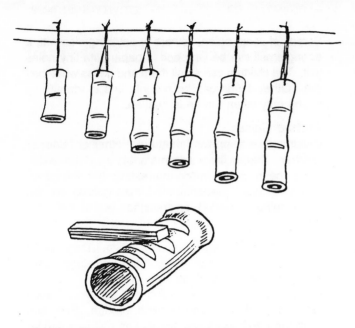

tins for drums, or shake gourds with seeds in them. Even blowing on the edge of a piece of paper or over the mouth of a bottle can make music.

Other Games

Children can learn from other games like flying kites, playing with tops and hoops, clapping, counting and singing games, hop scotch, and other skipping and running games. If cheap paper and pencils can be found, children can draw.

Organising Play

Older children can help younger ones to play better in a variety of ways:

*   **at home,** older children can help by talking about play activities with their mothers and fathers, by making a special place for children's play, by setting aside and looking after a special box for baby's and children's play materials;
*   **in creches and nursery groups,** older children not only can learn from the nursery teacher, but can help to make materials for play and to look after them;
*   **at school,** older children can set up play areas, and organise and help care for materials for the younger classes;
*   **at clinics** and other meeting places, older children can organise play materials for younger children attending with their parents.

If children want to help organise better play for younger children, they can:

*   talk things over among themselves, with mother and father, and plan how to bring play materials into their own homes, how to organise them, how to care for them;
*   discuss with the nursery school teacher, the childminder, the community worker or the nursing sister how best to help;
*   persuade head teachers and community members that the school or meeting place can be used to set up a play activity.

FOLLOW-UP

This is discussed at the end of **Toys and Games for Young Children** (Sheet 1.2).

USING THIS SHEET

Mothers and fathers will be especially interested in new ways of playing with younger children, and older children can tell them about these. Many other people can also help:

*   **school teachers** can introduce ideas in the curriculum, carry out projects at school, and help to raise money;
*   **school headmasters** can make time and space available at school for better play activities for younger pupils and preschool groups;
*   **health workers** at home and in clinics can explain the advantages of better play, and spread the idea of talking more to the baby;
*   **preschool leaders** can use and demonstrate better play ideas in their own programmes;
*   **press and radio, women's groups, religious groups, political and cultural organisations** can demonstrate and talk about the idea of better play, and of talking to babies and little children;
*   **youth leaders and community workers** can help older children to organise play for younger children.

Most important of all, older children can help by making toys, learning new games, playing and talking with the younger children.

This sheet should be used together with **Toys and Games for Younger Children** (Sheet 1.2) which concentrates on play materials (where to get them, how to make them, and how to use them), and **Playing with Babies** (Sheet 1.6).

TOYS AND GAMES FOR YOUNG CHILDREN

THE IDEA

It is important that children learn to use play materials of many different kinds. This helps them to experiment, to use their imagination and to use the muscles in every part of their bodies (eyes, arms, hands and feet). Excellent playthings can be made with materials which cost nothing.

All communities are rich in materials for play activities. Children themselves are very good at finding playthings, and are always trying out new ones and thinking of ways of playing with them. But they never think of **all** the materials they can use, and **all** the best ways of using them. They need help to add to the ideas they already have.

Children can **collect together** all the different ideas and materials which could be used for making toys and playthings, and **talk about** and **share** the different things they can make for their younger brothers and sisters.

This sheet discusses **how** older children can play with their younger brothers and sisters, **where** they can find materials, **what** to make and **how** to make it.

This child has as many good toys ...

... as this one

Where and how these activities have been used

Many countries encourage older children to make toys for younger ones. Sometimes there are national competitions as in **China** (Child Development Centre, Beijing).

In **Uganda**, older classes in schools make toys for younger ones - and this helps to develop a bond between these "school brothers" and "school sisters".

The book, *Toys for Fun,* published by Child-to-Child gives ideas of simple toys which can be made from locally available, low-cost and waste materials. Many of these have been made and used, e.g. in **Nepal** and **Zanzibar**. Children and teachers were able after a little help to follow the diagrams and make the toys suggested. But children also proved very creative and came up with many new ideas themselves. However, toy-making is not usually seen as an end in itself but an integral part of encouraging older children to stimulate the development of younger children.

The book, *Health into Mathematics,* has a whole section on making toys and games which involve many mathematical skills such as accuracy and measurement.

Remember making and creating toys and games for others helps the child who makes them as much as it does the child who plays with them.

Older children should always remember to make sure that play materials for young children are safe. They must avoid:

- things with sharp edges;
- small pieces which young children could swallow or put in their noses or ears;
- plastic bags which can suffocate little children.

ACTIVITIES

Collecting Play Materials

Older children will be able to find play materials in many different places in the community:

- **at home:** sand, gourds, tins, boxes, etc.
- **from shops:** scraps of cloth, packing material, bottle tops, cartons, paper, etc.
- **in the community:** cornstalks, stones, clay, grasses, seed pods, dye from local plants, etc.
- **from local craftsmen:** scraps of cloth, wood, metal, leather, etc.
- **from local musicians:** materials (and advice) for making simple musical instruments.
- **from local industries:** waste paper and packaging, broken or used parts, wood, etc.

Making Play Materials

School time can be made available for older children to make play materials for young ones. Here are some examples:

The art and craft lesson: toys like cars, dolls and models; games equipment like balls, hoops and ropes; paints and brushes for making pictures; puppets; building blocks.

The language lesson: books with stories and pictures; reading cards with pictures and words; posters and charts.

The music lesson: instruments like drums, rattles and flutes; collections of songs and singing games.

The maths or science lesson: puzzles, shapes and dominoes; games like Snakes and Ladders, Ludo.

Organising Play Materials

Don't forget that play materials which have been collected will need to be stored and cared for. Can a special place for children's play materials, even a special box, be set aside at home? at school? at the clinic? How can older children help to care for children's play areas in these places?

Using Play Materials

Older children can decide to collect materials for younger children which are as interesting as possible. They can think about all the different things that children can learn from the games they play with these materials.

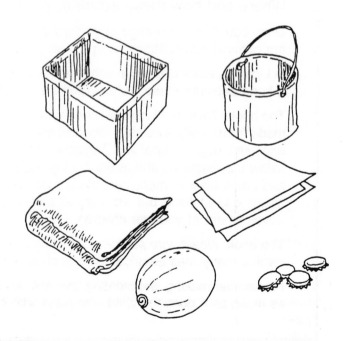

Playing with Hands

When babies grow older they learn by doing difficult things with their hands. What materials can be used by young children for building? for weaving? for cutting, drawing and pasting? What games, like cat's cradle, can encourage young children to be clever with their hands?

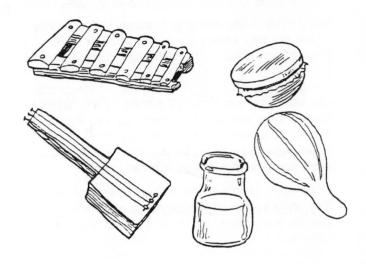

Clay or mud can be given to children. They can make many things from it. Encourage them to use materials like sticks and leaves with clay, to make model houses, animals and many other things, real or imaginary.

Matchboxes and small tins can be filled with things like small seeds. Children can learn to put things in them and take things out of them under supervision.

Sorting Things

Young children like to sort things. They can be given many different kinds of things to play with and sort: like flowers with different colours and different smells, scraps of cloth which look and feel different, dull things and shiny things, big things and small things.

Dressing Up

Older children can provide materials to help younger ones dress up and pretend. Children only need a little help to dress up. Paper, leaves, sticks and bits of cloth can easily be used to make hats, dresses, and other 'pretend clothes'.

Active Play

Preschool children learn by being very active and using their bodies. Older children can design games of throwing and catching, jumping and skipping, climbing and sliding, etc., that help the younger children use the muscles in their bodies. What kinds of equipment do children need? What can this equipment be made from?

Making Music

Young children love to make music. Older children can make simple drums and rattles, and teach younger ones to dance and sing and play their instruments in time with songs.

Other Kinds of Play

Young children love playing with water. Older children can provide materials that float and sink in water, or make water flow long distances. They can make reed pipes of different sizes that water flows out of at different rates, or that can be used for blowing bubbles.

What different shapes and sizes of containers can be collected for younger ones to use when playing with water and mud?

All children love to draw and paint. Scrap paper, cardboard, newspapers, etc., can be used for young children to paint and draw on. Paints can be made from inks, dyes or local plants. Brushes can be made from chewed sticks. Glue can be made from a local food like flour, mixed with a little water.

Talking and Listening

All children love to learn through talking and listening. Older children can collect stories, songs and riddles for younger children. Make sure to find opportunities to encourage the younger children themselves to talk. Make playing introduce ideas like 'bigger than, smaller than, the same as, smoother, rougher and heavier' and other phrases.

Teach younger children traditional games, make other games like these or make up new games.

AS-11

Helping the "Childminder"

Many children who do not go to school look after very young children while parents are away or working. Older school children, or youth group members, can be divided into smaller groups. Each group can be in charge of a certain number of houses. These groups can take play activities to the children who stay at home. They can also help them learn to read and count. At school, older children can make picture books, toys and simple games which can be used by other children who care for younger ones.

Often these children have their own ideas to share: they know traditional games, songs and stories, and can be encouraged to teach these to the school children.

Helping at the Clinic

Often little children who come to clinics need toys and games to play with while they are waiting. Sometimes mothers who come to clinics with their babies bring along other children who need to play. Older children can help by making toys for these clinics and even help to play with the children there.

FOLLOW-UP

(This section refers to Sheets 1.1 and 1.2 on play.)

Find out how many of the children have younger brothers and sisters, or older brothers and sisters who stay at home. Why do they stay at home? Have they been to school at all? Can they read, write and count? Share experiences.

How many of the school children have helped those at home? Ask them to tell stories about what they did for children at home. How can they do better next time? What games were best for teaching counting and number skills? What games were best for teaching letters, reading and writing? Did anyone think of new games for teaching these skills?

Have any of the children carried out any of the suggested activities in such a way that it has made a difference at home? in the community?

We can ask the following questions:

- Do people in the neighbourhood (including the older children) know why play is important for young children? Does the school teach why play is important for young children and how the quality of children's play can be improved? Are older children encouraged to play with the younger ones? Are they allowed time and materials for this kind of activity? Do adults in the community show more interest in children's play? Do they understand the need to help and provide materials and play places?
- What materials have the older children collected? What toys and playthings have they made? What songs, games and stories have they collected or made up?
- Have teachers and health workers noticed young children using any new toys, playing any new games?
- Can the older children tell if the toys, games and play areas they have made are well used? Are play areas well-organised, safe and kept clean and tidy?

USING THIS SHEET

Many different people are interested in improving play facilities for younger children, including parents, school teachers, health workers at home and in clinics, youth leaders, preschool groups and community workers.

- Craftsmen and parents can provide skills and labour;
- School teachers can help children to raise money for some materials;
- Headmasters can help make arrangements for the school to be used for playgroups, or even give older children special opportunities to make toys for younger ones;
- Headmasters can arrange the timetable so that older children can do many of these activities for children in lower classes;
- Local women's groups, religious groups, and political and cultural organisations can explain to parents and others why children need to play.

All of these people can be helped by older children.

This sheet should be used together with **Playing with Young Children** (Sheet 1.1), which talks about why children need to play and develop, and how older children can help. **Playing with Babies** (Sheet 1.6) will also be helpful.

UNDERSTANDING CHILDREN'S FEELINGS

THE IDEA

Children need healthy bodies. But they have other different needs. Their other needs are to do with their **feelings**. Often these are difficult to understand because we cannot see and hear them, and children sometimes do not talk about them. If children can begin to understand some of these feelings, they can grow up well and help others to do the same.

A Story About Feelings

John woke up one morning crying. Mary heard him, woke up and ran to him. She picked him up and found he had wet himself. She changed his clothes and hugged him. He laughed and began to sing and make happy noises. After helping her mother, Mary went to school.

After her lessons, Mary went out to play. One girl had a ball and they all played with it except Anne. She refused to play and stood in a corner. Then she caught the ball and would not give it back. Some children started to punch and kick her so she began to cry. The teacher came out. She sent the other children away and explained to Anne that she must give the ball back to the other children. Mary took Anne's hand to show she was her friend. Then Anne felt happier and played with the others.

Where and how these activities have been used

Understanding why a younger child is crying or why an older child is sad or naughty involves an ability to "get inside other people". Once we begin to want to understand others ... we are on a road which leads to better citizenship - towards talking over differences without violence.

That is why this sheet is always one of the first to be translated and adapted. It is also specially relevant in situations where many young children (often now in camps) have been exposed to violence which has affected their behaviour, e.g. in Lebanon, Mozambique, Thailand and Pakistan (refugee camps), or with street children in Brazil or the Philippines.

A special book with pictures and questions on this theme has been produced for Ethiopia, but the idea, text and pictures can be used elsewhere. Contact Child-to-Child.

Child-to-Child is at present preparing a set of activity sheets to help children in especially difficult circumstances. These include children who have experienced war and disaster, children who are at risk in the home (from drugs, alcohol, etc.), children who have been bereaved, and children who do not live in their family home (e.g. children who live on the street, in a refugee camp, in an institution).

As the children were walking home, they saw a dirty boy with uncut hair. The children called him names and laughed at him. An older boy came along and saw that the little boy was hurt and crying. He took the little boy's hand, and asked him where he came from. The poor boy said that he had no parents. The people he lived with were cruel to him. The older boy said he would try to help him. The other children were ashamed because they had been cruel.

Mary wanted to tell her mother about the dirty child when she got home. Her mother was tired and told her to go away. Mary began to cry. Her baby brother John came to her and put his arms around her. He began to cry too, so Mary picked him up and went outside. She forgot about herself and made him play. Then Mary's mother called to her. She left John and he ran after a butterfly.

Suddenly, John saw that he was alone. He began to cry and call for his sister. Mary came back. She picked him up and showed him some chickens. John forgot his tears and chased the chickens away from the food pot.

This shows the feelings of children in every day, natural situations. A story like this helps to show:

- **feelings themselves**, like love, fear, happiness;
- **signs of feelings**, like laughing (happiness), crying (fear), shouting (anger);
- **causes of feelings**, like cruelty, love;
- how children can **understand and help**, and make other children forget their fear or unhappiness.

Our Feelings

Many Different Feelings. All children experience feelings. Even when they are very young, children have many **different** feelings. Of course these feelings grow as the child grows. At first, a child feels content and secure close to his mother. She feeds him, keeps him warm and protects him. Sometimes he is happy, content and trusting. Other times he is unhappy, afraid or angry. As he grows older, his feelings are shared with other people. He can learn to recognise and understand feelings that he and other children experience.

Different Situations, Different Feelings. Sometimes children experience feelings when they are **alone**. For example, when a child is alone in a strange place, he could be afraid, or he might just be curious. At other times, children experience feelings when they are **with other people**. For example, when a mother is annoyed with her children for breaking something she has told them not to touch, they can be afraid or unhappy, guilty or resentful.

Different Children, Different Feelings. Different children can have different feelings. The same happening or the same thing can make each child show different feelings or emotions. For example, when they see animals some children want to play with them, because they feel love and affection. Other children may run away and scream, because they are afraid, or don't like the animals. Other children will simply take no notice of the animals, because they feel indifferent.

Signs of Feelings

Often children cannot tell us what they feel. But we must try to understand their feelings from the signs they show. The way a child behaves can show us what he is feeling. For example, a child who seems selfish, angry and unfriendly, may be unhappy because he does not get enough attention or because he needs affection.

Sometimes one sign can mean many things. For example, a child who laughs may be happy. Or he may be embarrassed or nervous or surprised. A child who cries may be angry. Or he may be afraid, or even frustrated.

Children can be helped to notice signs of feelings in themselves and other children and begin to understand feelings so that they can help and comfort their brothers and sisters, or their friends.

What Causes These Feelings?

Everything in everyday life causes some feeling. Sometimes children can tell what causes their feelings. For example, a child can say he is happy because he has been given something nice to eat.

But often, children do not know what makes them have their feelings. The **causes** of feelings can be **many and not very clear**. For example, if you ask children why they are crying, sometimes they will tell you that it is because their toy has been taken by another child or because their mother has scolded them. But often children are not sure why they feel the way they do. Children can be destructive, for example, breaking plants, throwing stones, killing small animals. If you ask them why, they will not be able to tell you. Perhaps they are unhappy because their mother has sent them out of the house. Perhaps they want to hurt something because someone has hurt them. Perhaps they are afraid.

It can be helpful if a grown up tries to explain to older children what some of the possible causes of different feelings are. In this way, children may begin to understand feelings in themselves and in other people and help by giving attention and comfort.

Understanding and Helping

If children begin to notice feelings and take an interest in them, they may learn about them in themselves and in other people. This will help them to develop as individuals and as members of their community. Children learn to understand themselves and others through living in their **own homes** with their **own families**. They **imitate** and copy people around them before they even know what they are doing. For example, a girl is more likely to shout at her brother if her parents often shout at her or each other.

Giving Comfort. In some situations, children can help one another even better than grown-ups. If a child understands that another child who seems 'naughty' or 'bad' may have feelings like fear and pain, or may need affection or company, he can sympathise or understand his feelings. He can give the child comfort and friendship.

Children often pick up their brother or sister, or come close to them, and put their arms around them to carry and talk to them. These are different ways of comforting, of showing understanding and of helping. Comfort can also be given with words of kindness, praise and affection.

Another way to comfort is to make younger children forget their anxiety (unhappiness, worry) by showing them something different.

In this way the younger child will think of something else. If a child is crying, the older child can say, 'Look at that bird over there.' or, 'Come with me and I'll show you a new game'.

Understanding Differences. Children can also try to understand differences in people's feelings. People and children are not all the same and do not all have the same feelings. Each person, each child, is different.

If a child has a different feeling, it does not mean that he or she is wrong or bad, but only that they are different. Children should be encouraged to understand and accept differences. For example, if a little girl is afraid of the dark, an older child who is not must not laugh at her, or tease her, or make her more frightened. **He must try to understand, and help her to understand why she does not need to be afraid.**

ACTIVITIES

Make Up Stories

Make up a story like the one at the beginning of this sheet, to explain feelings, possible causes and the signs of different feelings. What help can be given in each case? Ask the children to find other feelings within their own experience at home and at school.

Talk About Feelings

Ask questions like, 'What makes you laugh?' 'Why do you cry?' 'What makes you most angry?' Compare the responses of the children: they have different feelings about different situations.

Guessing the Feelings

Children could use a sentence like, 'What are you doing?' Each child, or the teacher or group leader, could say the sentence in different ways. The others have to guess what different feelings (anger, fear or surprise, for example) are shown in the way the sentence is said.

Some children can make pictures of situations where different feelings are shown, and the others can try to guess which feeling is shown in the picture. Pictures could show, for example, a dog running away from a stone (fear); a child taking something from another

who is crying (anger); a child with a glove puppet laughing (fun, joy); a chicken running and flapping its wings with a child chasing it. Can the children talk about the difference between the feelings themselves, and the causes of those feelings?

Children can be asked to mime a simple situation and show feelings. For example, a boy is lost. How does he feel? Or a little girl has torn her new dress. What does she do? Or a child snatches something from another. How does the loser react? The other children can watch and try to guess and talk about the feelings. **Then they can also say how they can help.**

FOLLOW-UP

Have the children understood that it is important to be aware of their own feelings and the feelings of others? Discuss an event which has taken place in the class or in the playground when people have shown different feelings. What were those feelings? How did different children react? Did any of them try to help?

Ask the children to describe what they would do if they saw another child who was:

• angry and destructive;
• crying and afraid;
• quiet and alone, apparently unhappy.

Can the children think of ways of helping others to feel better:

• at home;
• at school;
• in the community?

USING THIS SHEET

Although **teachers, group leaders, Scout and Guide leaders, or play groups** can practise these activities, children learn the most important things about their feelings **at home. Women' clubs** and **institutes**, and **religious groups** can show how much children model themselves on members of their family. If they understand about their children's feelings and behaviour, **mothers** can help children to help one another even better than teachers.

HELPING CHILDREN WHO DO NOT GO TO SCHOOL

THE IDEA

In many countries more than half the children under fifteen do not go to school at all, or leave school very early. They stay at home to look after the younger ones, or to work in the house or the fields. Although the situation varies from country to country, the majority of them are girls.

Schoolchildren can help those who are not at school by sharing their activities with them. They can play simple reading or counting games with them, and pass on simple health ideas learned in school. Children who do not go to school have much to share with those who do. The child at school must look on the child out of school as a friend and partner, not as one who is less important or who knows less.

The stories in this sheet show how children who have not gone to school can help themselves and be helped by other children.

Mohammed's Story

Mohammed was a farmer's son. He came into the city and worked for a rich family. One of his tasks was to take one of the younger children to school. But Mohammed decided that he too needed to learn to read and write. With the help of the older children in the family, he taught himself, using first the simple books of the younger children, and then the books of older friends. Later the family he worked for paid for his schooling, and he was able to go to university.

Where and how these activities have been used

This sheet is particularly important in countries where not all children go to school or where many children drop out early (or are kept away from school to help in the home). Often this second group may have begun to learn how to read and count but may have forgotten.

Parents and other adults need, whenever possible, to help school children use this sheet. They can help them find and make reading and counting material. In **Uganda** and **Zimbabwe** and in some states in **India**, children are being encouraged to write their own simple books which can then be used for reading practice.

Remember when using this sheet that out-of-school children are not second-class children. They have much to teach as well as much to learn. They often have very interesting stories to tell and important experiences to share. **Together** children in school and out-of-school can take health action and solve health problems.

During International Literacy Year (1990), UNICEF among others adopted this approach in promoting literacy.

Kamala and Subira's Story

Kamala and Subira became close friends. As soon as Kamala had learned to read she had to leave school, to look after two little boys at home. Subira was luckier. She stayed on at school and is now in the sixth class. But every day when she comes home, she talks with Kamala and helps her with her reading. They go out together in the street, and play at recognising all the writing on the shops and on the advertisements. Next year, Kamala will join a special evening class and continue her studies. She hopes one day to become a teacher of young children.

What Children Can Do Together

There are many things that children who are in school can do to help children who are not at school, including:

* talking, and sharing ideas;
* helping with counting, reading and writing;
* sharing knowledge, especially about health.

ACTIVITIES

Talking Together

Children can tell each other stories. Children who go to school can read stories to their friends. If the child at home knows some good stories, the schoolchild can write them down. They can then read them together, and then make pictures about them. Remember that **talking** about things helps **reading** about them.

Children can share '**what happened today**.' Children from school can talk about some of the things that happened at school, and some of the things they have learned. Children at home can tell about what happened at home and in the neighbourhood while their friends were at school.

Learning to Count, Read and Write

Children who cannot count, read, or write often feel unhappy, especially if there are many other children in the community who can. By teaching them some simple things, we can help them to be less 'different' from others, and also show them that they can learn new things easily. Then they will have some of the skills they will need when they are older.

Schoolchildren can teach their friends to *count*:

* to learn to count the numbers from one to ten;
* to be able to recognise and write them;
* to add and subtract simple sums;
* to use small amounts of money, and count the change.

Remember: always use real objects when teaching others to count or add or subtract. Use stones, sticks, real or copied coins.

They can teach their friends to begin *reading* and *writing*. Write on the ground if there is no paper or slate, and help them:

* to learn the alphabet;
* to recognise and write the letters;
* to write their name;
* to recognise and write the names of other people in the family;
* to read numbers and signs in the street (if they live in town);
* to read or even write some simple names of objects around the house which are used every day.

Later on in this sheet there are some simple number and reading games that children can make.

Schoolchildren can try to help their friends to **learn anything else which they want to learn**, for example how to write a short letter, how to address and post the letter, how to use the library (if they live in town), how to get to different places. In this way, children who are not at school can feel less alone and can look after their own families better when they grow up.

Passing on Health Messages

The child in school and the child at home can, if they work together, help to improve the health of younger children and the whole family. The child in school may learn very important health messages, and many of these are described in other Child-to-Child activity sheets. In each one, there are ways for the children to work together, so that all the children can take part in community health activities. In this way, **the school-child and the child who stays at home can together help to improve the health of the whole community.**

What Children Can Do Together	Using Activity Sheet
Make toys and play with the young ones;	Playing with Younger Children (No 1.1)
Protect water sources and keep drinking water clean at home;	Children's Stools and Hygiene (No 3.3)
See that little children use the latrine and wash their hands;	Clean, Safe Water (No 3.4)
Identify health problems in their community;	Our Neighbourhood (No 3.5)
Make their homes and surroundings safer;	Preventing Accidents (No 4.1)
Learn to make and give the **Special Drink** when they see that a child is ill with diarrhoea;	Caring for Children with Diarrhoea (No 6.1)
Inform all the families near them when the immunisation team is due to arrive.	Immunisation (No 6.4)

Making Number and Counting Games

Number Games. Play number games like this (or make up another one like it):

Draw squares on the ground like this, and number them. Throw the right number of stones into the right space. Then learn to copy and write the numbers in the sand, or with chalk or on paper.

Practise finding numbers together in the streets, finding and telling where people live, collecting car numbers. Think of other ways to play with and use numbers you see in the street.

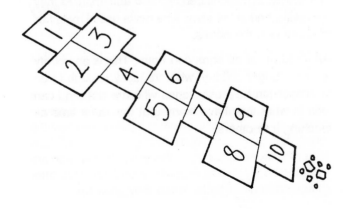

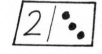

Make dominoes, and match the dots with the numbers.

Counting Games.

* sing counting songs: use familiar ones or make your own;
* count fingers and toes, backwards as well as forward;
* count familiar objects (like stones and leaves), and things around us (like animals, plants and people);
* count animals in the evening, count produce for market;
* play shop, learn to give change (paper money can be made at school), and then go shopping together.

Make Reading and Writing Games

Alphabet Games. Make an alphabet book at school, perhaps with cloth. Or make a set of cards with a letter on each one. Put a picture of a word beginning with that letter on a small card. Use capital letters as well as small ones. Children can learn which letters make their names and the names of their friends. They can choose the cards which spell the names. They can practise writing the letters on the ground with a small stick, or on small cards.

Reading and Writing Games. Label and read the names of parts of the body, and familiar objects in the house and garden. Make messages and act them out to each other. Read signs in the shops and around town. The child who is at school can help the child at home to write his first letter.

Make a picture book for baby. The school child can make it at school. The child who is at home can read it to baby, and that way he will learn too.

FOLLOW-UP

Find out how many of the children have younger brothers and sisters, or older brothers and sisters who stay at home. Why do they stay at home? Have they been to school at all? Can they read, write and count? Share experiences.

How many of the schoolchildren have helped those at home? Ask them to tell stories about what they did for children at home. How can they do better next time? What games were best for teaching counting and number skills? What games were best for teaching letters, reading, writing? Did anyone think of new games for teaching these skills?

USING THIS SHEET

It is not easy to teach others to read and write, or to teach health ideas so they are clearly understood. If children want to help those who are not at school, they will have to continue for a long time. They will need help and ideas and encouragement from others. **Youth leaders, religious leaders, community workers** and especially **teachers** can help in many different ways. They can:

* **discuss** with children how they can help others at home;
* help them to **plan** the help they can give;
* show them how to **make** educational materials;
* **talk about** what they are doing with others who are not at school, and how they can do better.

At school, perhaps some lesson time can be used for developing language and reading games for non-schoolchildren. Materials for reading and counting games can be made during art and craft time for example, or even during the reading or maths lesson. In this way, schoolchildren can use and improve their own skills, and at the same time make useful materials to share with the others.

All children of all ages can help. This is an activity where younger children who are lucky enough to go to school\can help older ones who are not, and can look at what they have learned at the same time as teaching it to others.

A PLACE TO PLAY

THE IDEA

Play helps children to grow and learn. When they play, they learn to use different parts of their bodies so that they become stronger and more skilful. They exercise their mind. They learn to share and cooperate with each other, and to use language. Many children need better places to play, especially in crowded towns, but also in country areas. Older children can help to make play places for younger children. They can find new places, or improve the place where children play already by making it safer and more interesting.

All children need to be active. They like to run and play tag. They like to climb and slide, to swing and jump. This kind of play is not a waste of time. It is very important because it helps children to:

* use different parts of the body, especially eyes and hands, together;
* use the voice and learn to use language, so that they can communicate with others;
* try out new actions and activities;
* use their imaginations and solve problems;
* learn to share and cooperate with others.

In this way, they learn new skills and find out for themselves about new things. All this helps at school, and makes it easier for children to learn.

Children need a safe and interesting place to play, whether this is at home or at school, or somewhere else in the neighbourhood. Older children can help to organise play places. They can:

* provide ideas about how to start and organise a play area;
* collect materials;
* make equipment and places to store play materials;
* play with and help younger children at play.

Where and how these activities have been used

Adults and youths need to help older children use this sheet. Making playgrounds can be initiated by early childhood education centres (as in Kenya) based on local schools. Primary school children (helped by parents) can make and maintain playgrounds for pre-school groups on the same site. The safety aspect is very important and primary school children cannot have the sole responsibility for this, as they may not know whether or not playground equipment is safe.

Teachers Colleges, as in Nigeria, often have playgroups within their campuses. Students can make play areas and at the same time learn to watch young children and record how they develop.

Youth groups, particularly in slum areas of cities, where it is most difficult to provide children with safe places to play need to take action, as they have done in India and Indonesia. This is also an ideal opportunity to encourage disabled children to join in the games of ordinary children but again discrete supervision is advisable.

ACTIVITIES

Provide a Place to Play

Older children can help organise play areas in different places:

- at home they can talk to mother and father about setting aside a special place for children's play materials and equipment;
- at school they can discuss with the teacher or head teacher how to set up play areas. They can organise and help care for materials and equipment. They may be able to persuade the head teacher that the school grounds can be used as a neighbourhood play centre after school hours;
- at clinics and other meeting places, children can organise and care for equipment and materials for children attending the clinic;
- in the neighbourhood, they can look for sites which are safe, and which are suitable for children's play.

> *Many children play under the two big trees near Sunil's village. So the children in the local youth group have taken on the job of improving the play area there. They have cut the dead branches from the tree, and hung ropes with tyres on them from the strong branches. They have made steps in difficult places so that children can climb the trees. They have cleared the high grass, and every few days they go round to pick up rubbish and make sure that there is no glass or sharp metal which could cut the younger children who play there. The place is safe now, and even more fun to play in.*

Choosing a Play Area

Children probably already have a place where they play. Is it safe? Is it big enough for plenty of activity? How can it be improved to make it safer? Would it be better to make a new place?

Can an existing play area be made more interesting? For example, one place might have a stream, but lack trees for climbing and swinging. A flat, open area in the city might also lack trees. Both places can be improved by making some climbing equipment.

Collect and Organise Play Materials

All communities are rich in materials for play activities. These may be scrap materials like bits of wood, polystyrene and metal, matchboxes, plastic containers and tins, old tyres, waste paper and packaging. Or they can be things that are grown, like gourds, coconuts, seeds and seedpods, cornstalks and grasses, or dye from local plants. Sand, stones, charcoal and clay make good play material too. All are free.

Activity sheets on Playing with Younger Children (No 1.1), and Toys and Games for Young Children (No 1.2) give plenty of ideas for making toys from these materials. Or let the younger children use their imagination, and find ways of using these materials.

> *Fermian is an old man who lives just outside a big city. He has more land than other people and has opened a simple play school in his garden for young children. Many people help him. A child who has left school comes each day to help look after the younger children. She is only fifteen, but she likes working with children. Fermian's own grandchildren come along when they are not at school, play with the children, and help to keep the place tidy.*
>
> *Other parents help by bringing play materials. One is a carpenter and brings left-over bits of wood. Another is a printer, and brings end bits of paper in many sizes and colours. Older children at school work with their teacher to collect scrap materials like wire and bottle tops, cartons, beer cans and scraps of material. Sometimes they make playthings like balls, hoops and ropes, building blocks and puppets, puzzles and games, posters and drums. The children at the play centre use the toys and games, and often make their own, as well as singing songs and making up stories. Sometimes they play letter and counting games. At times, old Fermian himself comes out and children gather around him to hear stories.*

Older children can help to collect materials for play. They can also help to store and care for them. Can a special place - a shed or lockable box - for children's play materials be set aside? How can older children help to organise and look after the materials? They can approach shopkeepers and describe to them what materials they could help provide (old boxes, blocks, empty packets, ends of cloth or paper, for example). Some shopkeepers might even be prepared to collect and keep such things for the children.

Make Equipment

Decide what natural materials can be used to make play equipment. For example, the soil itself can be used for making slides. Fallen trees and steep banks are good places to climb and slide. Large stones or the ends of poles can be placed so that children have difficulty stepping from one to another.

Trees have many different uses. They can be used for climbing, perhaps with a few steps built into difficult places. Or simple swings made from rope and old tyres can be hung from strong branches. A long thick rope with a series of knots about one foot apart is good for climbing up into the tree. Perhaps you can build a slide coming down out of the tree.

AS-23

> *Our school is in a crowded city area. It has three shifts, and there are always children in the playground behind the school waiting to go in, or waiting for brothers and sisters to come out. Last year, students in the Youth Service came and built a swing and a bridge, and some stepping poles. We liked them, but they got broken.*
>
> *My friend Bambany and I went to see our head teacher. 'Why don't we build a playground outside the school?' we asked. 'It could have swings and poles and a play place for the little ones.' The head teacher helped us and so did Bambany's father. They showed us how to build the equipment, and how to make it safe.*
>
> *We built the play area for the younger children, and collected some things for them to play with. We take turns to look after the little ones after school. We organise a special play time for them on Saturday when school ends early. We have taught the younger ones to clear up and put things away in a box. Many children use our playground now.*

Trees can also provide shade for younger children playing with water and sand. Cut an old tyre in half and fill it with water. Old tyres can also be used for tunnels. Provide materials that float (wood, plastic) or sink (stones, metal). Provide hollow reeds and containers of different sizes. Use the other half of the tyre for sand and in it put bits of wood, containers, gourds. Put a box full of other materials for making games and toys nearby.

Where there are no trees, children can still climb if they have a climbing frame. Make a see-saw, or balancing board from odd bits of wood.

Supervise the Play Area and Help Younger Children

> *In our country there is a tradition of community self-help. In our village called Karatina, the local councillor called a meeting. The villagers decided to buy land to use as a playground. One man who was too old to farm, offered to sell one acre of his land. Our parents raised some money, and a number of the marketeers and big farmers helped too. Enough money was collected to buy the land, to clear the ground, fence it off and make it safe. A small shed with a lock was built in one corner for storing play equipment and materials.*
>
> *Today one corner of the acre plot is used as a play space for the little children. On the rest of it, a football field and a volleyball pitch have been marked out by the older children. They have also made nets and posts. They organise football and volleyball league games for the younger children, and help to referee. They help to supervise the younger children, and make sure that the play equipment is repaired or replaced when needed, and locked away in the shed at the end of the day.*

Older children can help younger ones by:

*   organising some of their games;
*   giving them good ideas about how to use equipment and materials;
*   giving out equipment and later collecting it and putting it away;
*   organising the repair and replacement of equipment and materials, and teaching younger children to notice and report weaknesses;
*   supervising their play to make sure they are safe;
*   giving first aid and getting help when an accident happens (see Sheet No 4.1, Preventing Accidents).

FOLLOW-UP

Have the older children helped to make a play area in the neighbourhood? at home? at school? If they have not, why not? If they have, then:

*   count how many children use the play place during a fixed period of time (one week, for example);
*   find out which children use it, and what for;
*   ask them how much they use it, and what else they would like to have in it;
*   check to see whether the equipment is cared for, and how new ideas and activities are introduced;
*   ask how many of the older children supervise play activities or referee games.

USING THIS SHEET

Teachers and head teachers can organise older children, encourage them, and be concerned with safety. The school might be willing to set aside ground for an improved play area for all children. Making play equipment and materials might be included in craft lessons. Teachers in training can start a play area near their own college or teaching practice school, after surveying community needs.

Community and youth group leaders can discuss these ideas, how better play areas can be organised. They can help older children by teaching useful skills in refereeing, making equipment and first aid. They can also help to provide resources, help secure land and finance.

Parents and others in the community can provide specialist skills and labour, help in organisation and supervision and contribute materials.

Local media, including press and radio, can explain ideas about better play, and report on progress and success of play area projects.

This sheet can be used together with Playing with Younger Children (Sheet No 1.1) and Toys and Games for Young Children (Sheet No 1.2).

PLAYING WITH BABIES

THE IDEA

A baby's brain develops very fast during the first two years of its life. Of course all babies must have the love and security which comes from being held close to their mother. But children need stimulation as well as love and good food to help their brains grow well. Stimulation is provided by playing with children, talking with them and thus helping them to use their bodies and minds as much as possible. Older children can learn how babies develop and how to play with them in different ways and at different ages and so help them develop.

A Baby's Brain Must Grow and Develop

A baby cow or sheep is born with its brain and limbs well developed so that it can stand and follow its mother a few hours after its birth.

The human baby has a much larger brain, but it is not fully developed at birth. It goes on growing, especially during the first two years of the baby's life. After this time, it grows much more slowly. During these first two years, children need food, love and stimulation to help their brains grow as fast and as well as possible. If children do not have enough food, love and stimulation in these years, it can affect their future lives.

In South America, a study was made of three groups of poor children. One group had good health care but not enough food. Their mental development did not improve and they did not grow well. A second group had plenty of food and good health care but very little stimulation. They grew well but their mental development did not improve. A third group received good health care, good food and a stimulating home and loving environment. The children in this group grew well and their mental development was as good as any in the country.

Where and how these activities have been used

The ideas in this sheet are important everywhere and for every future mother and father (and that means nearly every child). The future health of children depends on adequate stimulation and good play helps to provide this.

Although all parents love and care for their children, not all stimulate them as much as they should (specially when they have to work hard). Sometimes working mothers give young babies over to child-minders who do not try or do not know how to play with them. This is why other children need to help.

We tried asking these questions to older children and even college students in **Namibia, Sierra Leone** and **Britain**:

At what age should you start playing with a baby? Why?
How and how often should you do it?
When should you start talking to babies?
How and why?

We were very worried by many of the answers we received. Do you know what the right answers are? Do you think that the young people you know would all give the right answers

This sheet is about stimulation - but remember that good food and freedom from disease are also important
(*See* **Section 2 on Nutrition.**)

Love is Important - But Not Enough

All over the world families love and care for their children, but unless they play with them and stimulate them something will be missing in their development. This is where older children can play an important part. They need to know how babies develop and how to help them and play with them in different ways at different ages. Remember: Every child is different and babies develop at different rates. Babies who have not had enough to eat or who have been ill need extra help and play.

Mother Comes First

But love and comfort, at first, come before play. In the first three months of life the baby is sleeping and feeding, close and warm, next to its mother. She carries it close to her by day and it sleeps with her at night. This gives a feeling of security and belonging which is the basis for all future development, whether it is physical or social or emotional.

How to Stimulate Children

There are many things to do and games to play with young children at different ages and stages of development.

Play from birth to 3 months
During this time the baby develops very quickly. Watch the baby. Ask the mother if you can play with it. Hold the baby. Talk to it. Sing to it. Gently rub its cheek. It will turn its head towards you. Put your finger in its hand. The baby will hold it. After about 6 weeks it may begin to smile. If you move a bright object like a flower or a spoon it may turn its head to look at it.

Older children can have more and more contact with their younger brothers and sisters after the first three months. Here are some useful ideas. There are many others. **Remember:** Babies love to hear your voice. Talk and sing to the baby when it's awake.

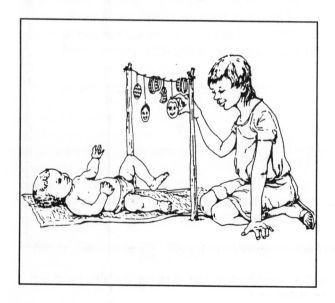

Play between 3 months and 6 months
(1) Hang a mobile made of circles cut out of cardboard on which are drawn faces and bright patterns near where it lies. If this is difficult to make, use any small light moving objects.

(2) Tie or hang objects like spoons close to where it lies so that it can reach and hold on to them.

(3) Make a sound with a spoon and tin or clap your hands so that it will look to see where the sound comes from.

(4) Cut a smooth ring out of bamboo, let the baby reach for it and take it to its mouth; be sure it is clean.

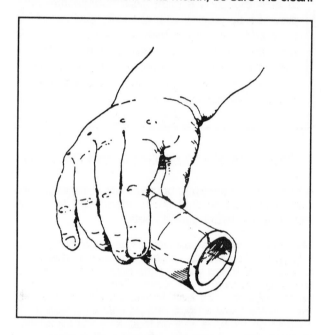

WARNING: All babies put things in their mouths. Be careful what you give them.

(5) Find or make a smooth object and give it to the baby to hold. You will see that the baby drops it when you offer it a second one.

(6) Find games that make it smile and coo. These baby sounds are the very beginnings of speech. When you carry the baby about tell it the names of objects.

Play between 6 months and 9 months
(1) Help the baby to sit up for games. Support it if needed. Talk to it while you play. Call its name or sing a song from different places in the room and see if it can turn its head to find you.

(2) Begin to teach the baby to drink from a clean cup.

(3) Make the baby a rattle to shake or give it a spoon to bang.

(4) Hang some of its toys on pieces of string near where it lies so that it can just reach them.

(5) Give the baby two, then three and four smooth objects. Encourage it to pass or give them to you or pass them from one hand to another.

(6) Give it a block or a tin and it will enjoy throwing it on the floor and then looking for it. It will do this again and again.

Play between 9 months and 12 months
(1) Play games to encourage it to crawl, stand and walk. For example, pretend you are a mother animal and it is a small one. Hold its hand. Take it for a walk. Show it things and talk about them.

(2) Get the child to give you a hug, clap its hands, or wave 'Good-bye', and so practise all the skills it has learnt. Hand it objects that it can hold between its finger and thumb. Watch out! By now it loves throwing things, not just dropping them. Make a soft ball out of grass or cloth to throw.

(3) Give it two objects and you hold two more. Bang yours together. Can it copy you? Make clay or mud animals for it to hold. Get the child to imitate their noises.

(4) Give it a box and things of different sizes to put in and take out of it.

(5) Hide something under a cup or piece of cloth as it watches. See if it can find it.

(6) Tell it stories and sing songs with actions. Sing songs you learnt when you were small.

(7) Make a doll and tell stories about it.

Play between 12 months and 15 months
(1) When the child can walk, let it run and jump into your arms for a hug. See if it can walk a few steps backwards. Watch that it does not hurt itself. It will learn to climb up stairs and steps but will need help getting down. At first it will come down backwards.

(2) Make a toy on wheels that the child can push as it walks, like a box with wheels and handle.

(3) Help it use a crayon to scribble on paper. Make drawings in sand or mud with your stick or finger and talk about them.

(4) Roll a ball to the child and get it to roll it back.

(5) Put one object on top of another. See if it can copy you. Let it make things with bricks and blocks. Wrap a brick in paper. Let it unwrap it.

(6) Encourage it to feed itself with a spoon. Talk to it. Encourage it to fetch things and take them to its mother. This shows how much it understands. Encourage it to name things around.

Making a Record

When you have a new baby take a sheet of paper or use the middle pages of an exercise book. Put its name and the date it was born at the top. Then mark the sheet of paper into 4 sections across and 13 sections down the page as is partly shown in the diagram. The sections across are the weeks in the month; 1, 2, 3 or 4. The sections down are the months 3-15. Label the sections 3 months, 4 months, 5 months, 6 months, etc. up to 15 months in the left hand side. Each week ask your mother and write down the new things your own baby can do, e.g. at 4 months and 2 weeks he first lifted his head to look, at 10 months and 3 weeks he said his first word clearly - MAMA. You may like to decorate it around the edges and take it home for your mother to hang it up for all the family to see. In school, with your teacher's help, you can display it and explain to other children how you observed the exciting development of your baby.

Remember: because one child learns to talk or walk quicker than another, it does not mean that child will always be ahead.

Baby's Development Card

Month	Week 1	Week 2	Week 3	Week 4
3	Baby turns eyes to look when I clap	Baby grasps wooden brick	Baby finds his mouth with his thumb	
4		Baby takes bamboo ring to his mouth		
5	Baby drops a brick and takes a second one		Baby makes cooing sounds	Baby puts toe in his mouth
13	Baby takes 2 steps alone	Baby throws a ball		
14		Baby runs 6 steps and jumps into my arms		Baby scribbles with a crayon
15			Baby climbs 3 stairs, I help him down	Baby fetches a spoon when I asked

Name: _____   Date of birth: _____

ACTIVITIES

Activities in School

Every child in school needs to learn about the development of babies and why it is important to play with them.

Children in upper classes in primary schools need to be encouraged to:

* *Discuss* the need for play with babies and how far the need is being met.
* *Make cards* for each baby born in the family. Compare the cards to see how babies develop at different rates.
* *Collect* suitable materials for making toys.

Children can also develop activities in many different school lessons. They can:

* Design toys in *Mathematics* lessons.
* Make them in *Handwork* lessons.
* Write about their younger brothers and sisters in *Language* lessons.

Activities out of School

With the childminders. School children can talk to childminders - especially those who do not go to school. They can:

* Discuss with them about playing with babies of different ages.
* Show them different ways of playing.
* Collect play materials for them and with them.
* Invite the childminders to school to tell about the babies they care for.

With older people. Older people (often grandmothers) often look after babies with great affection. Ask them to make things, sing songs and tell stories to babies so that you can learn from them too.

Sometimes fathers and mothers with skills can be persuaded to make things (like wooden blocks or dolls) specially for babies.

FOLLOW-UP

Find out and test how far older children understand the development of babies and how they can help. Use this information to test other material - e.g. Adamu walks at 10 months. He was born on 10 December. In what month did he start walking?

Children can:

* *Collect and show* toys made for babies at different ages.
* *Describe* the different kinds of play they have tried with babies.
* *Observe and list.* What objects and toys does baby play with at home? Have any new things been provided?

USING THIS SHEET

Teachers can develop these activities - in health lessons, in other lessons and by example as parents.

Teachers in college and in-service training can learn about play and make and record observations on individual children of their own or in the community. Colleges can have a special place where mothers can bring their young babies to play. Students can work and play with them.

Health workers can work with schools and youth groups.

Women's groups and mothers' groups can spread the message and develop toys.

Non-formal teachers in religious groups and parents' classes can spread the ideas.

Curriculum workers can ensure that this vital knowledge is incorporated in school programmes.

This sheet can be used together with Playing with Younger Children (Sheet 1.1) and Toys and Games for Young Children (Sheet 1.2).

SEE HOW THEY GROW

THE IDEA

All children need to grow steadily so that they can become big, strong, bright adults. Children do not grow steadily when they do not get enough of the right kind of food or when they are ill. It is important to check children's growth regularly. For small children, weight gain as shown on a weight chart is the best sign of good growth. If they put on the right amount of weight in the right space of time, they are growing well. If weight gain is not regular, action needs to be taken.

Healthy seedlings grow into healthy plants. Healthy children grow into bright, strong adults. Healthy children grow and gain weight. It is impossible to tell from looking at a child if he or she is growing as they should but you can see if they are gaining weight steadily on the weight chart. Are they moving up month by month? To grow, a child must eat enough food of the right kind (*see* Sheet 2.1, **Healthy Food**). A child who does not eat enough food of the right kind may get malnourished. A malnourished child cannot grow well and his or her brain may not develop fully.

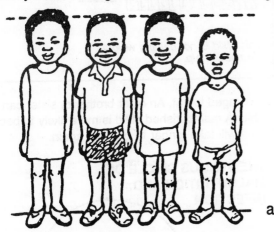

a.

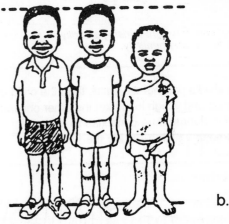

b.

In some countries, one child in four is too small for his age (a), in others, it may be as many as one in three (b).

Where and how these activities have been used

The very close links between nutrition, health and psycho-social development are being increasingly stressed and this means that early detection of malnutrition is of crucial importance. This is why the road-to-health chart described in this sheet is now being used throughout the world by thousands of health workers and nearly every family has a chart for each child.

Health workers often fill in these charts for mothers who do not understand the quite difficult concepts of measurement and graphs very well.

Child-to-Child activities (particularly those based on school) encourage children to help their parents fill in the chart and to understand growth monitoring when they themselves become parents. Weighing, measuring and graphing are essential tools in mathematics - linking these with child health (described in Gibbs and Mutunga, *Health into Maths*) makes maths real and useful. That is why this sheet will be widely used in **all** countries in **Asia**, **Africa** and **Latin America** where the road-to-health charts are used.

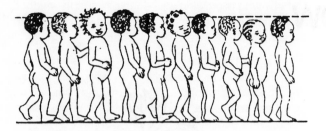

Average well-nourished children at 18 months. There is some variation, some are children of large, tall parents, some of small, short parents.

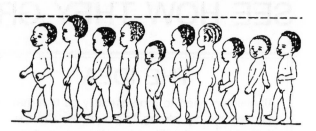

Average children at 18 months in many countries. There is much more variation in size due to illness and the scarcity of good food.

Not all children gain weight at the same rate and not all children weigh the same at birth.

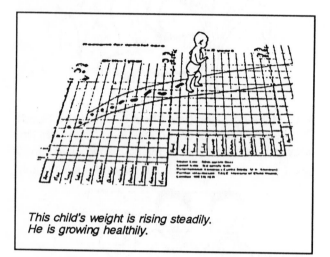

This child's weight is rising steadily. He is growing healthily.

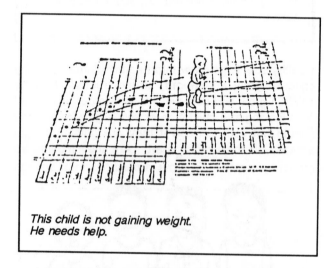

This child is not gaining weight. He needs help.

If the child's parents are small, then the child may also be small and weigh less than the other children but he is not in danger if he continues to gain weight steadily and keeps walking beside the line.

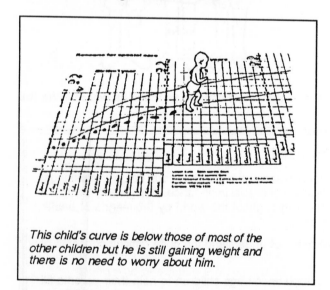

This child's curve is below those of most of the other children but he is still gaining weight and there is no need to worry about him.

A child who is ill may lose weight and become weak. He may not want to eat and so loses even more weight and becomes even weaker. A weak child cannot fight disease very well so he becomes ill again sooner and then loses even more weight. An ill child needs to be

encouraged to eat. An older brother or sister can help in this. A malnourished child is more likely to become ill and will take longer to get well again.

THE VICIOUS CIRCLE OF MALNUTRITION AND INFECTION

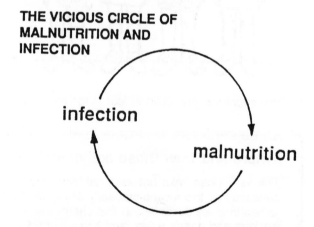

After a child has been ill, he needs extra food to help him catch up and regain his lost weight. He needs to eat extra food for two to three weeks. He needs to eat more often until his weight returns to normal. A child has a small stomach and can only eat a small amount of food at a time. Discuss with the children why a child with an infection does not eat well and can easily get malnourished and why a malnourished child often gets a more severe infection.

A child may be malnourished because:

- not enough of the right kind of food is available;
- there is not enough awareness of what a child needs to grow healthily;
- he may have been ill or so unhappy that he does not wish to eat.

Different solutions are needed in each case.

Cause of Malnutrition	Solutions
The child is ill	Immunization. Hygiene. Good food. Extra food to allow him to catch up. Presence of an adult who shows him regular love and attention.
Not enough food available	Better sharing within the family and between families in the community. More frequent meals. High-energy and protective foods. Longer breast feeding. Avoid bottle feeding.
Poor knowledge of good feeding habits	Education about good eating habits and communal food production. Hygiene and protective measures. Ensuring that the message is spread throughout the community, particularly to the poorer families. Encouraging children to eat when they are ill.

Small Children Have Small Stomachs So Feed Them Often

All the Porridge a Small child needs to eat in One Day - (900 mls)

When Divided Into 3 Meals = Each Meal is TOO MUCH for a Small Child's Stomach

OR All the Porridge a Small child needs to eat in one day - (900 mls)

When Divided Into 5 Meals = Each Meal is JUST RIGHT for a Small Child's Stomach

A baby who is growing well doubles its birth-weight by five to six months, triples it by about 18 months and quadruples it by three to four years.

If the weight of a small baby stops increasing for more than two weeks or the weight of an older child for more than one or two months, this is a sign of trouble, and if he actually loses weight he has probably had an illness and should see a health worker.

GOOD Means the child is growing well

With extra care he is now gaining weight and out of danger

DANGER Find out why and advise

GOOD

VERY DANGEROUS May be ill needs extra care

With extra care he is now gaining weight and out of danger

ACTIVITIES

FINDING OUT

1. The children can measure the weight and height of all the children in the class. Are the taller ones always heavier than the smaller ones. What is the average height/weight of the class? Of the girls? Of the boys?

2. If the children have brothers and sisters, can they weigh them? How many dots have been marked on their charts? Can they carry them? Are they heavier or lighter than their brothers and sisters? Are they older or younger?

3. The children can find out about the eating habits of their community. They can keep a record of what foods are eaten and how often:

   a) over 2 months;
   b) over 6 months;
   c) over 1 year,

   and write a report. When were the foods different? When was more eaten? When less?

4. When do people eat special foods? What kinds of foods? and why? Can they think of other activities in the community to do with food?

5. The children can keep a record of what:

   a) a six-month-old child eats in a week;
   b) an 18-month-old child eats in a week;
   c) a three-year-old child eats in a week.

   Are they eating well? Would the children change the foods? How?

6. The children can record which foods are available when.

7. In a month, what proportion of the class gained weight, lost weight and remained the same?

DOING

1. The children can grow good foods like vegetables in the school yard, in small pots, near their homes. They can look after the plants together and share the products.

2. The children can find out in which houses there is an ill child. Can they help the family by:

   • encouraging the child to eat more;
   • doing little jobs for the mother to give her more time for cooking and feeding the child;
   • bringing him good things to eat.

3. Mark the place on a corncob where the circumference is 12.5 cm (or 13.5 in a community where there is little malnutrition). Let the children put a finger and thumb around the cob at the mark until they get used to the feel of it. They can then go and check children between 1 and 5 years of age to see if their midarm circumference is large enough.

4. With the health worker's help, they can copy the growth chart of children who are growing well. Do they know other children who are not growing well? Copy the chart of a brother or sister and compare it. What happens on the chart when the child is ill?

FOLLOW UP

1. Can the children together plot weight onto a weight chart? Each child can plot another child's weight. Guide them to discuss what the curve means.

2. Can the children sort out different weight charts into those which are:

   • growing well;
   • not growing too well;
   • are in danger.

3. Can they plan the right action to take if the curve is not good?

4. Can the children make up a story to explain the growth curve of a particular child? They can tell the story to others in the community.

5. The children can make up a drama or a puppet show about two families, one with children who are growing well and one with children who are not. Why is this so? What can the families do? Can they help each other?

6. The children can make up posters about eating good food and staying well. They may use some of the ideas in this sheet.

7. The children can make up songs about normal weight gain (e.g. a baby who is growing well doubles its birth weight by about 5 to 6 months).

A STORY: WHAT MADE THE CHILD ILL?

"He's got malaria again. He's so ill and weak. He seems to get it so often."

"But the other children don't get it so often - and when they do, they get better quickly! Was he ill before?"

"Yes, he had diarrhoea - he was sick - he couldn't eat. It left him weak."

"Has he always been weak and often sick?"

"Yes! He was always ill. One thing after the other. More than the other children."

"Even when he was a baby?"

"Yes - and I don't know why. The other babies only had breast milk. We always gave him the best. We bought him bottled milk - from the time he was small."

This sheet should be used in conjunction with the sheets on **Nutrition** (2.1, 2.2, 2.3), **Children's Stools and Hygiene** (3.3), **Clean, Safe Water** (3.4), **Worms** (6.3) and **Immunisation** (6.4).

FEEDING YOUNG CHILDREN:
Healthy Food

THE IDEA

Breastmilk is the best food for young babies but they soon need to eat extra foods to help meet their **energy, body-building and protective** requirements. They need to eat a **mixture** of foods to grow well, to be active and to learn properly. Children who are growing well are ill less often. Young children need to eat a lot of food. A two-year-old child needs to eat about half as much food as an adult.

Meals for Healthy Growth

Breastmilk for babies

Breastmilk nourishes the baby and protects him against sickness. It is best if a child can be breastfed until he is big enough to be able to share the family meal (two-years-old if possible). In any case, a child should never stop receiving his mother's milk very suddenly, especially if the child is very young (less than one-year-old). Sometimes this occurs when the child is sick or because the mother has a new baby. **This is very dangerous.**

Because breastmilk is so important for child survival and healthy growth there is a special activity sheet on breastfeeding (Sheet No 2.4).

First foods for young babies

For the first 4-6 months of a baby's life, breastmilk alone is enough for good growth. After this time other foods must be given as well. The first food given is often porridge made from a cereal like millet or maize.

After 6 months the baby can gradually be given other foods mixed with the porridge.

Every community has its own traditional first foods for babies. Children can find out which foods are used in their own area.

Giving a baby new foods will sometimes be difficult because the taste and feel of these foods will be different from breastmilk. The new food needs to be made soft and given a little at a time and many times a day, until the baby gets used to it and can eat enough. Patience, love and play are all important in helping the child to learn to eat enough of the new foods. Feeding may take some time. Talking and keeping the child interested and happy (try singing songs) may encourage the child to eat more.

It is very important that food for small children is **prepared cleanly. Remember** the rules of good hygiene described in Activity Sheets 3.3, 3.4, 3.5, 6.3.

Where and how these activities have been used

This sheet has recently been revised to bring it in line with recent WHO recommendations and needs to be studied very carefully by teachers and health workers. Some of the information it contains may be a little different to that which is found in older books on nutrition, e.g. there is much less emphasis on the importance of protein and food groups, so some teaching may have to change.

The topic healthy food is central in every health education and Child-to-Child programme and is taught in **every country** which uses the approach. Many different ways of teaching it are used but **two** lessons from experience are worth mentioning:

(i) *Teaching older children and mothers at the same time.* In many countries such as **Egypt** and **Jordan**, nutrition messages are given over the radio to mothers and in school to children to take back home - in this way it becomes easier for change to take place.

(ii) *Practising what we preach in schools.* For example: serving nutritious meals to school children (**Lesotho**); children monitoring food sellers (**Uganda**); children setting up their own stalls to sell nutritious snacks (**India**).

How to choose foods to add to children's porridge

For good growth children need to eat a **mixture** of foods.

Foods like sorghum, millet, rice, maize, cassava, potato and plantain all provide **energy**. They form the main part of our meals and are called **staple** foods. These are often made into soft porridges for babies.

Small amounts of body-building, protective and energy-rich foods need to be added to this porridge made from staple foods.

How can we increase the amount of energy that a young child eats? Fats and oils are very rich in energy. One spoonful of oil or fat provides **twice** as much energy as one spoon of cereal flour.

The **staple foods together with fats/oil** are the main source of **energy** in our diets. **If we do not get enough energy from these foods, body-building proteins will be used for energy instead of for growth and repair.**

Cereal staples provide useful amounts of body-building protein as well as energy. But young children need extra protein for good growth and recovery from illness. Most children get this extra protein from foods like beans, peas, lentils and groundnuts. Meat, fish, milk and other animal foods also provide protein but are not always available and may be expensive. However, if you include even a very small amount of these animal foods in the meals for young children this will greatly improve healthy growth. For example, red meat and small dried fish provide the iron which is essential for making the child's blood.

It is very important to include protective foods in children's meals to provide vitamins and minerals needed for healthy growth. Vitamin A from red palm oil and dark green leafy vegetables and orange and yellow fruits and vegetables like paw paw, mango and carrots is essential to protect children's eyesight and increase resistance to illnesses like diarrhoea and chest infections.

Ideas on growing plant foods like vegetables, fruits and cereals can be found in Activity Sheet 2.3.

The food square below left will help you to choose the right mixtures of foods for children's porridge. We have put breastmilk in the centre of the food square because it is so important for healthy growth during the first two years of life. Try to give each child something from each section each day. You can also include other low cost foods available in your area, e.g. a porridge from Nigeria may be made from sorghum (millet) supplemented with a small amount of beans, spinach and sunflower oil.

Recipe for a meal for a small child*

	raw weight in grams	approximate local measure
Sorghum flour	40g	2 tablespoons
Bean flour	20g	1$^1/_2$ tablespoons
Red palm oil	5g	1 teaspoon
Spinach	30g	about 5 leaves
Onion, to taste	5g	1 teaspoon

*When cooked this will provide about 1 cup (250ml) of food.

The food square to help choose good mixtures of foods for feeding young children

Staple foods	Body-building foods
Millet	Beans, peas, lentils,
Maize	groundnuts, milk,
	yoghurt, curd cheese,
Potato	fish (fresh, dried,
	canned), meat (fresh,
Cassava	canned), chicken, eggs

breast milk

Protective foods	Energy-rich foods
Dark green leaves,	Red palm oil, ground nut
pumpkin, tomatoes,	oil, sunflower oil, butter,
carrots, oranges,	ghee, margarine, lard,
limes and other yellow	cooking fat, sesame
or orange fruits and	seeds, coconut cream,
vegetables	sugar, avocado pear

Many people know that children need body-building and protective foods to grow; and they know that energy foods are important for activity. Some people do not know that energy foods are also essential for growth. Many children stop growing well when they are about 6-12 months old. Often this is because they do not obtain enough energy from their food.

Young children cannot get enough energy from thin porridges made from cereal flour like maize or millet. This is because the flour swells up when it is mixed with water and cooked. A child's stomach will only hold about one cupful of food and this amount of thin porridge will not provide enough energy to grow. Thicker porridge made with less water provides more energy but can be difficult for a young child to swallow. Children need energy-rich meals.

Another reason why young children may not get enough energy is because they are not fed often enough. Children are often fed only once or twice a day. This is not enough. **Small children need to have meals and snacks at least 4 to 5 times a day.**

Small Children Have Small Stomachs So Feed Them Often

All the Porridge a small child needs to eat in One Day - (900 mls)

When Divided Into 3 Meals = Each Meal is TOO MUCH for a Small Child's Stomach

OR

All the Porridge a small child needs to eat in one day - (900 mls)

When Divided Into 5 Meals = Each Meal is JUST RIGHT for a Small Child's Stomach

Sick children may not want to eat - this is very dangerous. Sick children need to be encouraged to eat and drink as often as possible. A child who has been ill needs extra food. He can be fed at least 6 times a day until he gets back the weight he lost during the illness. Feeding sick children can be difficult and take the mother's precious time. Older children and grandparents can help feed young children in their family.

Children with diarrhoea and chest infections need to eat soft foods which are easy to eat, taste good and are free from germs.

In some communities, porridge is traditionally soured or fermented. During fermentation, food becomes more acid which is why it tastes sour. This prevents the growth of germs which cause diarrhoea. This means that a mother can safely prepare soured porridge once a day and use it to feed her child several times during the day. Young children like the taste of soured porridges which encourages them to eat more. Soured porridges stay soft even when cool and are easier for a sick child to swallow.

Children can find out from older members of the community more about the traditional use of soured porridges for feeding children.

Preparation of energy-rich meals

When porridges have been cooked, they are bulky and on their own do not provide enough energy. It is therefore important to add more concentrated energy foods to these porridges. Oils and fats contain the most concentrated energy but sugar is also a good source.

Other foods such as groundnuts, soybeans, sesame seeds, sunflower seeds and avocado pear are all rich sources of energy.

A small amount (1 teaspoon) of energy-rich food should be added to every meal for a child.

Using germinated cereal flour to increase the energy of porridge

In some communities cereals are allowed to sprout (germinate) before they are dried and ground into flour. For example, in Tanzania sorghum (millet) is germinated and in India wheat, rice and maize have all been used successfully. In many places people are now using this flour to add to children's porridge. They do this because a spoonful of this germinated flour will thin down a thick porridge enough to allow a child to swallow it without adding extra water. This will help the young child get more energy from the porridge.

ACTIVITIES

Finding out how food makes the body grow properly.

Children can be helped to understand the connection between food and growing by observing the growth of animals - two caterpillars, for example. (Fly larvae, or any other larvae found locally, could also be used for this). To one, give plenty of the right kind of leaves (find a caterpillar on a leaf and give it plenty of that kind of leaf); to another give almost nothing, or the wrong kind of leaf. After several days, compare the size of the two caterpillars. The one which has been well fed is the bigger. Why?

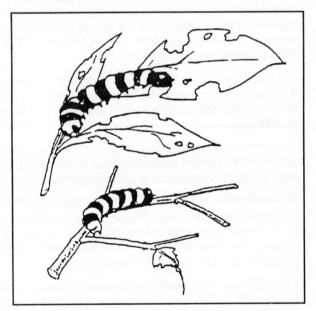

Understanding that a baby needs his mother's milk, but in addition must have other foods after the age of four months.

If an older child has a newborn in his family, he can tell the others how the baby is fed and how the mother knows if it is growing well. Let someone else describe an older baby of 6 to 9 months: how big is it? what does it eat? When does it eat and what foods are prepared especially for the baby.

Children can find out how old they and their brothers and sisters were when their mothers stopped breastfeeding them. They could then work out the average duration of breastfeeding in their area and discuss this with a local health worker.

Children can also find out what first foods are fed to babies and the age at which the child first starts to eat the usual family meals.

The health worker or nursing sister can explain to older children what can happen when small children do not have enough of the right mixture of foods.

Understanding good mixtures of foods for feeding small children. They can visit the market and discuss the different kinds of foods, their correct names, the cost, and the best way to prepare the foods for feeding small children. Costing and weighing amounts of foods for a child's meal could be part of the mathematics or science lesson. The teacher can help children decide which foods are the cheapest sources of concentrated energy. Children can learn about many useful plant foods by helping to grow them in a school vegetable garden.

Children can make a poster of a food square to include the low cost foods available in their area and use their food square to make up recipes for good meals for small children.

Understanding that a small child must have at least four or five meals each day. A small child needs to eat about half as much as an adult. To get enough food, if he was only given cereals like maize, cassava, rice or sorghum, he would need to eat between 8 and 12 cupfuls of cooked food each day. This is very bulky.

Older children can cook two cups of dry cereal. Once it is cooked and put on a plate, they can decide if a little brother or sister of two years can eat that much food at one time.

If germinated flour is commonly used in the area. Children can add one spoonful of this flour to a cup of thick porridge and watch the porridge getting thinner.

If a child only has 3 meals a day ... Many children only have 3 meals a day. This is not enough. Snack foods are a good way of increasing the number of times a child eats in a day. Snack foods are quickly prepared and can be carried around with you.

Schoolchildren may need help in selecting snackfoods to promote healthy growth without wasting money for example on fizzy (soft) drinks. Good snackfoods include fried beancakes, peanut butter/paste on a biscuit, a handful of roasted groundnuts, a banana or slice of avocado pear.

Understanding how to feed children when they are not well. Children who have fever or other illnesses need more food than children who are well. Ask the older children to talk about a brother or sister who has been ill. Did the child eat less? Did he become thin?

We need to encourage children who are ill to eat and drink as often as possible. Just as soon as the child

is better, he will need to eat even more food than usual. When a child is ill, he should have sugar in his drinks and he should drink often. He must be helped when he is too ill to eat and drink (*see* Sheet No. 6.2, **Caring for Children Who Are Sick**).

There are often months in the year when young children have more frequent illness e.g. diarrhoea, chest infection and malaria during and after the rainy season. These months may also be the time when grown up members of the family are very busy in their food gardens and farms. Children can discuss this. They can make a local calendar showing the months when there is most sickness in their young brothers and sisters and also showing the busy times for growing food.

FOLLOW-UP

Have the children understood the idea? Here are some examples of the kind of questions that should be asked:

- What is a good diet?
- Choose two high-energy foods from the following list: peppers, cooking oil, oranges, cassava, wheat, sugar.
- How many meals per day should children between the ages of two and five eat?
- After illness, do children need to eat less, more or the same amount of food?
- A two-year-old child has rice (or millet, or cassava, or plantain or maize) twice each day. How can the child's feeding be improved?
- What is the best food for babies?

It is also important to know that these ideas are having some effect upon the health of children in the community. Two good ways to check up on this are:

- the weight of children under five should increase every month (older children can check the weight of younger brothers and sisters); and
- the arm circumference of children between one and five years should be in the green area when measured with the Shakir strip (*see* Sheet 2.2).

USING THIS SHEET

Some of these activities can be used with younger children, some with older. They can be introduced by health workers at the school or clinic, by teachers, by Guide, Scout and other Youth Leaders, and by community and pre-school workers.

This sheet should be used together with Sheet No 2.2, **Feeding Young Children: How do we know if they are eating enough?** and Sheet No 2.3, **Growing Vegetables.**

FEEDING YOUNG CHILDREN:
How do we know if they are eating enough?

THE IDEA

Children must have enough of the right kind of food for healthy growth and to fight infection

Many children are not getting enough of the right foods. These children can develop normally if they are helped soon enough. There are three simple ways of finding out if an infant or young child is not getting enough good food:

- by knowing how **to recognise the signs** of having too little good food;
- by taking young children **to be weighed regularly** at the clinic;
- by **measuring** the upper arm of children under five years of age.

The young child needs good mixtures of foods for proper growth and development and to fight infection. Meals for young children made from staple foods (e.g. maize) also need bodybuilding supplements, protective

Enough of the Right Foods

Sheet No. 2.1, **Feeding Young Children: Healthy Food**, underlines the importance of feeding babies and young children **enough** of the **right** foods so that they can grow properly and are able to fight disease. At first, a child only needs its mother's milk but after the age of four to six months, babies need other foods as well. By the time they are two-years-old, young children need to be eating about half as much as adults. They can only eat a small amount at any one time, because their stomachs are small. They must therefore be fed small meals four times or more each day.

ENOUGH

"Children like chickens should always be pecking!"

Where and how these activities have been used

This activity is important in **every country**. Even in richer countries some malnourished children can be found. However, the identification of malnourished children must be very carefully monitored. The public measuring and exposure of malnourished children and the shaming of these children and their families is to be avoided at all cost.

Experience in using the activity suggests two approaches:

(i) The children taking part in surveys need to be closely supported and organised by **health workers**. Thus health workers may encourage children to measure arm circumferences but only when closely supervised (**Zambia**);

(ii) Children **learn the signs of malnutrition in schools** and **learn to measure each other and to "get the feel" of different arm circumferences**. They then make use of this knowledge and skill at home - reporting informally to the teacher or health worker when they find something which worries them (**India, Nigeria**). This is also a very important way of giving them understanding and skills they will use as adults.

supplements and energy-rich supplements. The foodsquare to help choose good mixtures of foods for feeding young children is shown in Activity Sheet 2.1.

Children who do not eat enough of these good mixtures of foods become **malnourished** or **undernourished** and are frequently ill.

When a child is malnourished, it is always **serious**. He is less strong than a healthy child, less active, less interested in things and therefore less able to think and to learn. He is less able to **resist infections**, he becomes ill more often, and he is in danger of becoming **steadily weaker and dying.**

If babies or young children do not eat enough good mixtures of foods and nobody knows how to help them, they will become very ill. These children may look very thin with loose, wrinkled skin, or may look swollen with cracked (broken) and peeling (coming off) skin.

This is why it is very important to recognise babies and young children who are not eating enough from the earliest stage. It is important also to learn how to help them. If these children are well fed, they will grow and develop normally.

Simple Ways to Recognise Children Who Are Not Eating Enough

☞ *Learn to look for signs*
By looking carefully, we can recognise signs in babies and young children who are not eating enough. Such children will:

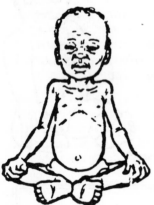

- look unhappy and not smile much;
- cry a lot;
- make few sounds or not talk a lot;
- play little and become less active than usual;
- seem quite sleepy;
- get more illnesses;
- stop growing and often lose weight and become thinner;
- eat less than usual because they are not hungry.

What causes a child to be malnourished?
Children who have an illness such as diarrhoea or measles often lose weight because they become weak and less able to eat so that they are not able to eat enough. (Activity Sheet No. 6.2 gives ideas on how to care for children who are sick.)

Children may not eat enough good mixtures of foods because their families are too poor and cannot buy enough of the food supplements. Mothers may not know about good food mixtures. Many mothers are very busy and need help to find time to feed their children frequently.

What Can We Do for Babies and Young Children?

Watch them for **changes in mood:** they may stop smiling, making happy noises or playing.

Watch them for **changes in activity:** they may move about less, roll over and crawl less, and want to sleep more. They may not learn to sit up.

Watch them for **changes in appearance:** they may get thinner and look unhappy.

☞ *Weigh babies and young children*
Up to the age of five, children must be weighed regularly to make sure that they are gaining weight properly. Babies should be weighed each month. The health worker will note the baby's weight gain each time he or she is weighed. If the weight gain is not enough, the baby may be undernourished and need a change in feeding.

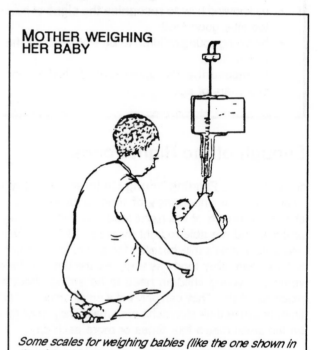

MOTHER WEIGHING HER BABY

Some scales for weighing babies (like the one shown in the picture) have a large spring and show the weight on the baby's Road to Health Growth Chart.

☞ *Measure the child's arm*
It is very simple to identify undernourished children by measuring around the upper arm, between the shoulder and the elbow, with a special measure called the Shakir strip.

- **Making a Shakir strip**

The strip can be made from strong paper, thick plastic, or a rope, a strip from around a plastic bottle, or fibre from plants. It is important that the material does not stretch and this can be checked by pulling it beside a ruler.

The strip should be about 1 cm wide and about 40 cm long.

Whatever material is being used, put a mark near one end (0), then at 5 cm, 12.5 cm, 13.5 cm

UP TO 40 centimeters

GREEN = NUTRITION O.K.

GREEN

13.5 cms

YELLOW

12.5 cms

RED = MALNOURISHED

RED

0 cms

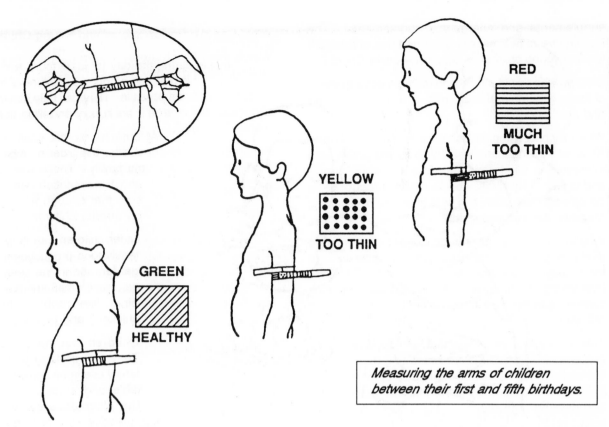

GREEN

HEALTHY

YELLOW

TOO THIN

RED

MUCH TOO THIN

Measuring the arms of children between their first and fifth birthdays.

and finally 20 cm from the 0 mark. It is very important to get the marks at 12.5 cm and 13.5 cm in exactly the right places.

• Using the strip

The measurement around the middle of the upper arm (between the elbow and the shoulder) changes very little between a child's first and fifth birthday. Feel your own arm, that of a five-year-old child and that of an infant about one year old. In the one-year-old, there is more fat than muscle; in the five-year-old, more muscle than fat.

In healthy children, the measurement is more than 13.5 cm. When the strip is put around their arm, the zero (0) mark reaches the green part of the strip. If the zero mark reaches the yellow part, the child is too thin; if it reaches the red part, the child is much too thin and may be undernourished.

ACTIVITIES

Children can discuss. Do they know children who are undernourished? Do they have very swollen bellies? Is their skin dry and cracked? Are their limbs very thin?

Teachers, health workers and Guide or Scout leaders can show drawings or posters of children who are undernourished.

Children can make a Shakir strip. Measure carefully.

Children can learn to use the strip. They can practise measuring around maize cobs, bottles, wooden poles and small trees. In school, they can measure around the arms of their friends. Because they are older than five years, the zero mark should always be in the green part. At home, children can show their mothers how to use the strip on younger brothers and sisters.

Children can find out. They can visit the health worker who can tell them about how much incorrect feeding and undernourishment there is in the community, and about how dangerous it is. The health worker can demonstrate how babies are weighed and checked at the clinic. (Get a sample of the clinic weight card and examine it.)

Children can measure the heights of their younger brothers and sisters. They can mark the heights on a wall at home. If the child's name and the date are written against the mark, the child can be measured six months or a year later. The older children can observe the growth of the younger ones. (Weighing and measuring activities like this can be used for part of the mathematics or science lesson.)

Children can find out how mothers in their community know when their babies are getting thinner. Some mothers put strings around the babies' arms, legs or hips. These strings need changing as the baby grows.

meals during the day (at least four), and that his diet has as good a mixture of foods as possible. They can help him to eat if he is not hungry (try telling stories).

At family meals, little ones usually eat after the older members of the family. Those who know about malnutrition can make sure that enough food is left for smaller children.

Older children can help with family food production in the garden and in the field, and can raise small animals and birds like rabbits, ducks, chickens and pigeons.

Children can make a play. They can pretend that in a family everyone comes to the table and enjoys the food. The older ones eat quickly and greedily. There is nothing left for the youngest child. He is sad and cries. In a second family, the older children make sure that the younger ones get enough food. The baby is happy and laughs.

Older children can help mother by feeding their younger brothers and sisters.

Children can pass the message. By stories, songs, plays, puppet theatres, posters and games, children can join the fight for good feeding. They can encourage mothers and other relatives to take babies and young children to the clinic for regular weighing. They can explain the Shakir strip. They can take part in health campaigns, including exhibitions, drama and songs, where they show how to find out if babies are getting enough of the right foods.

Children can help an undernourished child. If they find a child who is undernourished, with a mid-upper arm measurement less than 12.5 cm (i.e. in the red area of the strip), or in danger of becoming malnourished (i.e. between 12.5 and 13.5 cm - in the yellow area of the strip), they can warn parents, the health worker or the teacher. If the child is a younger brother or sister, they can encourage their mother to take the child straight away to the clinic or health worker.

Children can help a smaller brother or sister who is undernourished. Mothers can take small children to the clinic, and older children can go with them. The health worker will give advice about a balanced diet (*see* Activity Sheet 2.1).

The older child can follow up later, at home, by helping mother to feed the child: to make sure that he has enough food, that he is given a number of smaller

FOLLOW-UP

Have the children kept a record of the heights of younger brothers and sisters? Have they accompanied mother to the under-five clinic to see how a baby's weight gain is checked and recorded?

Have the children measured the arms of their brothers and sisters using the Shakir strip? Have they checked any other small children in the school or neighbourhood? How many children did they find with measurements in the green part of the strip? in the yellow part? in the red part? What did they do about it? What difficulties did they find? What did they do about them?

USING THIS SHEET

Everyone in the community must look out for children who are too thin and must try to help. It is not easy to persuade mothers to change the way they feed their children. Their own poverty may make it difficult. This is why as many people as possible in the community must understand and help. There are many things older children can do.

This sheet should be used together with **Feeding Young Children: Healthy Food (Sheet No. 2.1).**

GROWING VEGETABLES

THE IDEA

Vegetables are good for our health. Together with meat, fruit and wild plants, fresh food grown in our garden helps to make us strong and healthy. For healthy minds and bodies, children need to eat different kinds of food each day, including vegetables. Children can improve their own health and that of others by growing a variety of vegetables, at school and at home.

To be healthy, we need to eat good mixtures of foods:

Body-building foods (e.g. beans, peas and other legumes, groundnuts, meat, fish, eggs, milk, insects). Although meat and fish are very rich in protein, we can get enough protein for our needs from plants, like legumes, or milk and eggs.

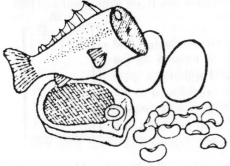

Staple foods (e.g. rice, maize, millet, cassava, potatoes, bananas) and **energy-rich foods** (e.g. oils, fats, sugars, sunflower and sesame seeds, coconut cream, avocado pear).

Protective foods which contain minerals (e.g. iron) or vitamins (e.g. vitamin A, vitamin C). Dark green, leafy vegetables, like spinach, are rich in iron and vitamins, and orange and yellow fruits and vegetables like mangoes, tomatoes, berries and carrots, contain many vitamins.

Where and how these activities have been used

Children love to watch seeds grow but nobody likes working for long hours in somebody's garden. Thus this sheet is important and interesting but can also be misused, since one danger of Child-to-Child activities is that children can be exploited by adults to do work which they (the adults) prefer not to do.

The great majority of Child-to-Child programmes using this activity are well aware of this danger and by contrast give the children who take part in them a lot of interest and fun. Here we give a few examples from many programmes.

In **Jamaica**, some rural schools encourage children to start gardens at home (not in school) and brothers and sisters cooperate and compete with others for the best vegetable patch.

In **Uganda**, teachers' colleges and the schools round them have vegetable gardens - and older children are paired with younger ones in tending them.

In **Indonesia**, plants are grown in the classroom with groups of children responsible for their care.

In **Zimbabwe**, several schools in **Mashonaland West** have started a food production project, including the growing of vegetables.

Although we have grouped foods into energy, body-building and protective foods, remember that some plants, such as beans and other legumes, are very rich in both energy and body-building foods.

Some energy, body-building and protective foods are expensive to buy but alternatives can be grown quite cheaply in gardens and containers (e.g. plant pots, old tins, etc.), and may be collected free from the wild.

Grow:

Energy foods: cereals (e.g. millet, sorghum, rice, maize and wheat), roots and tubers (e.g. potatoes, cassava or manioc) and some fruits (e.g. avocado).

Body-building foods: pulses (e.g. peas, beans, lentils).

Protective foods: dark green, leafy vegetables (e.g. spinach, rape, amaranthus) and some fruits (e.g. tomatoes, pumpkins, oranges, papaya, guava, lemon, pineapple and mango).

Collect:

Wild fruits, berries, nuts, seeds, roots, leaves and insects.

Take care, however, and only collect things which are safe to eat. Many people in the village will be able to advise you about the fruits and insects which are poisonous to eat.

Kumar's story

Kumar and his family lived in a shanty town near a big city. Kumar always felt tired and weak and he looked pale. Kumar went to school but he was too tired to work at his lessons and too weak to play with his friends.

*Finally Kumar went to see the health worker who told him that he had hookworm which had given him anaemia, a disease which is caused by a lack of **iron** in the body.*

Kumar does not eat meat very often and does not like green vegetables. The health worker treated the hook worm, gave Kumar some iron pills and told him to eat lots of dark green, leafy vegetables to make himself strong. Kumar and his family grew green, leafy vegetables in some tin boxes around the compound. They all ate a handful of these vegetables many times each week and Kumar became stronger and stronger. After six months, he was playing games with his friends. The next year, Kumar was chosen for the football team.

Dark green, leafy vegetables, cereals, legumes and meat contain **iron** which is needed to make blood in order to prevent anaemia.

Remember that eating foods which contain vitamin C, e.g. an orange, will help the body absorb the iron from plant foods like dark green, leafy vegetables.

ACTIVITIES

The children can **visit**:

- Local farms and gardens to find out what vegetables, fruits and cereals are grown there and how many crops a year can be grown of each;
- A local market to find out what crops are sold and where they come from. Why some are sold fresh when others are dried for sale.

They can **find out**:

- Which vegetables or fruits grow well at which time of year;
- Whether or not the price of important foods varies with the time of year.

The children can collect a leaf from each of the wild plants growing locally and discuss with members of the community which are the best to eat and why. They can also discuss which are safe to eat and how to prepare them.

Groups of children can **design and display** charts to include all the food plants used within the local community, the ones found at the local farms, gardens and market. They can show which ones are imported from other regions and which grow wild.

The children can answer the question: Many people do not eat meat. How do their bodies grow and stay healthy? The children can discuss the possibility of having enough variety of food when they only eat the food crops grown in their village, town or region.

The children can **plan**, with the help of the local health worker or their teacher, their meals for three days using only locally grown food with no meat. Are there any food crops that we could grow in our gardens to improve our diet and make it more varied and interesting?

The children can discuss the following questions with their friends:

- Which leafy vegetables have you eaten in the last seven days?
- Which of them grow in your country?
- Do any of them not grow in your country?
- Do small children in the family get them?

They can draw and name the leafy vegetables which grow in their area.

The children can find out if there is a vitamin deficiency in the area and if there are any vegetables or fruits which can be grown to make up this deficiency.

Sangay's story

Sangay lives with his parents in a village high up in the mountains. The family always eat a lot of rice and some meat and Sangay always got his share but his mother never gave him any green, leafy vegetables or any yellow fruit or vegetables. When Sangay was five he found it difficult to see in the evening. This was due to too little vitamin A. His sister who was two had measles. She also had too little vitamin A in her diet and due to the lack of vitamin A and the measles, she went blind.

Green, leafy vegetables and yellow fruit contain vitamin A which helps to keep our eyes healthy. Sangay's sister went blind because she ate too little vitamin A.

The children can work with the health worker and find out how many people suffer from blindness and anaemia (ask the health worker how to recognise the symptoms of anaemia) in the community. They can ask questions such as:

*   At what age did the person go blind or were they born blind?
*   Why did they go blind?
*   Are they blind in one or both eyes?
*   Is anyone in their family suffering from anaemia?
*   Do they eat dark green, leafy vegetables? If so, which and how often?
*   Do they eat red and yellow fruits? If so, which and how often?

Growing good food is fun.

It is exciting to plan a garden, to decide which plants to grow and to learn how to grow them. It is very satisfying, and healthy too, to eat your very own fruit and vegetables.

BUT to make a garden is a lot of work, so get it right from the start. Invite agricultural extension workers, local farmers, teachers, parents and friends to give advice on how to plan your garden and the best way to grow food plants in your area. If enough people are interested, you could plan a community garden.

MAKING THE GARDEN

Follow these steps:

1. The place
Answer these questions before you decide where to put the garden:

*   Do you have flat or slightly sloping land?
*   Do you have soil which is well-drained, deep and fertile?
*   What kind of soil do you have? Is it loam, sandy or clay? This will affect the water content of the soil and how it is watered.
*   Do you have enough water from a nearby stream, river or well? Plants need water regularly.
*   Do you have land which has at least six hours of sunshine each day?
*   Do you have land free from large trees and rocks?
*   Do you need a fence to keep out goats, cattle, chickens, other animals and people?
*   Do you need a place for your garden which is near your house or school, so that it can be easily looked after?

(If you live in a windy place then your garden will need shelter. If you live in a place where it rains throughout the year, then another source of water is not so important.)

2. The plan
Here you are, at work in your garden. Draw a map to show: the water source, the fence and nearest buildings. As you move through steps 2-6, you can add to your map the seed bed, pathways, the rows of vegetables, the crop areas, fruit trees, compost heap and tool store, etc.

Ask as many people as possible for advice so that you can decide which are the best food crops to grow. What are the traditional crops grown locally? What are the traditional patterns of cropping? Why? Try to grow crops from each food group. For example the garden can include maize and sweet potatoes (staple), groundnuts (energy) and beans (body-building), pumpkins, carrots and spinach (protective). Perhaps each group of children can grow some easy and some difficult crops. Crops like pumpkins can be planted a few at a time so that they are not all harvested at once. The planting of the crops can be planned for year-round production taking seasonal changes into account and times such as the school holidays.

3. The garden
Prepare the garden. If you are using a seedbed this can be done while the seedlings are growing:

- Clear the weeds;
- Dig over the soil, add compost or manure (animal waste);
- Mark out the pathways and rows for the vegetables.

Children, did you find out about and make the local kind of fencing to protect the garden from animals? What local methods are used to protect seeds and seedlings from birds and other garden pests?

Make sure that there is a good water supply to the garden or all the work may be wasted.

4. The seedbed
Having found out where to get the best seeds locally (use local seeds where possible) and which of these seeds need to be planted in seedbeds (tomatoes, cabbage, aubergine and peppers, for example), the preparation can begin.

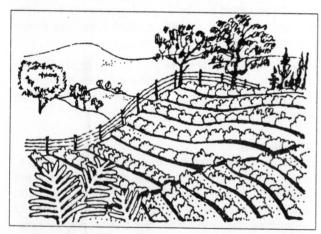

Seeds can be started in boxes or trays, but seedbeds are the cheapest and work just as well. Carefully prepare fine soil which has been mixed with local compost and well-watered. Use the local method of shading seedlings from the sun which will dry them

up. Find out how often the seedlings need to be watered as they grow and the best time of day to do it. It is important to avoid watering when it is very hot as the water will evaporate but the water should not be allowed to rot the plants. Find out how long they need to stay in the seedbed before transplanting.

This is a good time to study how seeds grow into plants in Biology!

5. Transplanting
What advice did you get on the way to move small plants from the seedbed into the garden, i.e. transplanting?

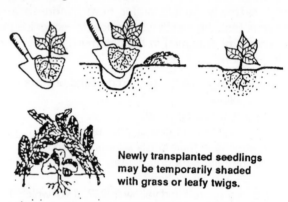

Newly transplanted seedlings may be temporarily shaded with grass or leafy twigs.

Children should first find out the local spacing of plants, both in and between rows. Young plants will need both water and shade immediately.

6. Direct sowing and planting
Sow the seeds of spinach, carrots and groundnuts, beans and maize in the garden soil where they are to grow. The larger the seed the deeper it must be buried in the soil.

Children should remember the advice given on planting depth and distances. What did the agricultural extension officer have to say about the growing of crops like sweet potatoes from both their root tubers and stem cuttings? What are the traditional methods of planting local varieties of sweet potato?

Did you remember to put these on your map - seedbed, pathways, named rows of vegetables and crop areas?

Let the children ask the agricultural extension officer about crop rotation. What are the advantages of crop rotation and which crops should follow which in the vegetable garden?

7. Containers

Many plants, like tomatoes, can grow very well in plant pots, old tins or other containers. The children can collect containers, have holes knocked in the bottom of them and broken pot or stones added for drainage. Soil and compost should be placed in the container and as long as it is big enough for the plant, and the plant is taken care of, it should grow very well there.

8. Pest control

The children need to watch out for pests (insects, moths, larvae, slugs, snails, locusts, etc.) An important way of protecting against harmful pests is to make sure the plants are healthy. Some gardeners use poison to kill pests but others do not want poisons on their plants so they pick them off by hand (give them to the chickens), wash them away with soapy water or plant flowers like marigolds amongst their vegetables. What other methods for preventing insects and disease are used locally? The children can try to guess what it is about marigolds that the pests do not like.

Remember, not all animals are pests. A single toad can eat at least 10,000 insects in one season. Earthworms are very important for the fertilization of the soil. Many useful insects help the gardener by pollinating plants and eating harmful insects and other pests, so find out which local animals are your friends and KNOW YOUR ENEMIES!

The children can now discuss the question - What are the most important things needed for strong and healthy plant growth?

This would also be a good time to introduce the study of some insects and other garden animals in the Biology lesson!

9. Food, light, space and water

Plants take their food and water out of the soil through their roots. Plant food can be added to the soil as manure (animal waste), compost (decayed leaves, weeds, kitchen waste, wood ash) and fertilizer (chemicals, which are usually made in a factory). Children can find out about the plant foods used on local farms and gardens. Where do farmers and gardeners get them from?

Children can compare the growth of one seedling in a pot of garden soil mixed with compost with the growth of another grown in sand with no compost. Water the seedlings and see how they grow. What happens to the two plants and why?

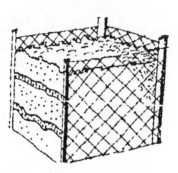

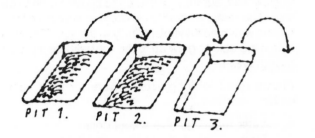

PIT 1.   PIT 2.   PIT 3.

Children can discuss what they think would happen to themselves if they, like one of these plants, went without food for one month.

Although young seedlings have to be protected from strong sunlight, green plants generally need light to live and too much shade is not good for them. Remember that plants, like people, do not like to be overcrowded. If plants do not get enough food, light and water, they do not grow well and become sick and may die.

Mulching is placing grass and plant cuttings on the ground around plants. Is mulching used by local people? How does it help to keep the water in the soil?

Water from washing and bathing is useful for plants grown outside the home. Water, good soil, sunshine and open space all combine together to give ideal growing conditions for many plants.

Children can design their own experiment to compare the growth of plants in wet soil with the growth of plants in dry soil. Do the experiment and explain what happens.

Plants, like people, need space, light, food and water to grow well, but they also need to be anchored in the soil. The roots, as they grow down in search of food, air and water, hold the plant firmly in the soil. The leafy stems are able to grow up to the light without the plant falling over.

Plants need looking after - Care for your plants daily:

• Water regularly, give a cool drink;
• Remove weeds, give space and light;
• Keep 'thinned' out, give more space;
• Put compost or mulch around them, give food and save water;
• Look for pests and diseases. Give them protection, ask the agricultural extension worker for help.

The children can design a chart to compare the daily care of young children and plants which are to grow up strong and healthy.

Remember garden tools need to be kept clean and carried carefully to avoid accidents!

10. Picking the crops
The best part - your plants are ready to eat. Harvest them!

Some crops, like tomatoes, can be picked just before they are ripe. You are then sure to harvest them before the thief! Most fruits continue to ripen after being picked. Investigate how each crop is picked and treated after picking. How are they traditionally stored? The extension worker should know the best methods of storage. This is very important as it allows the food to be eaten throughout the year.

> **Remember!**
> Grow crops in containers for fun, decoration and food!
> Grow a fun plant, sugar cane, bananas, coffee, paw-paw, etc.
> Grow a selection of herbs for use in cooking, perfumes, medicine.
> Plan a menu for the day and cook a 'balanced meal' from the food grown.

FOLLOW UP

Children can be asked, after several months, to discuss with the other children what they have done in their gardens and what they would like to do next.

A competition can be organised to judge the best school garden, house garden, plants in containers or vegetables.

A display can be mounted of the vegetables and fruit grown. Plant and develop more gardens.

Celebrate a harvest festival!

USING THIS SHEET

Some of these activities can be used with younger children, some with older. They can be introduced by agricultural extension workers at a school or clinic, by teachers, by guides, scouts or other youth leaders and by community or preschool workers.

This sheet should be used together with **Feeding young children: Healthy food** (Sheet 2.1) and **Feeding young children: How do we know if they are eating enough?** (Sheet 2.2).

OUR TEETH

THE IDEA

Each person gets two sets of teeth. The second set are permanent teeth and must last for a whole lifetime. If we let them get rotten, or if our gums are diseased, we can suffer much pain and may lose our teeth. We can prevent tooth decay and gum disease by taking less sugary food and drink. We should also clean our teeth carefully several times each day.

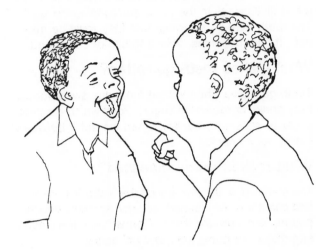

Why do we need teeth?

We need teeth for:

* biting and chewing our food;
* smiling and looking good: a person with shining whole teeth looks happy and attractive.

Having good healthy teeth allows people to eat a wide variety of foods. We have two different kinds of teeth because our teeth have two main tasks - biting and chewing. Our front teeth are for biting food and the back ones are for chewing it. Good teeth can give pleasure as we bite into foods.

Clean, strong and shining teeth make you look attractive and help you to speak clearly.

Children should understand that they get two sets of teeth in their life. The first set begins to fall out between the ages of five and eight years. The second set is their last set, and they will get no more! It is important to look after both sets very carefully.

Where and how these activities have been used

Despite the great importance of this topic, many health education programmes do not include oral hygiene. In fact, oral hygiene is not possible without some oral health education. Nonetheless, this activity sheet is important in nearly all Child-to-Child health programmes but a particular priority in urban areas in many countries.

It is a very popular activity with children because of the many opportunities for fun provided by the topic. No child who has watched a tooth being eaten away in a glass of sweet fizzy drink will ever forget it!

In addition to the many health programmes which include units on teeth, there are certain programmes which have concentrated on dental health and used the Child-to-Child approach with great success.

In Delhi (India), the "smiling teeth" a preventive dental health programme began in 1987 to improve oral hygiene, health knowledge and the children's self-esteem. The Child-to-Child approach was used and the teachers involved were given special training to use this approach. They found it so effective that they began to use it with other subjects too. This has also increased their confidence and satisfaction.

In Chiang Mai (Thailand), an oral hygiene programme has been introduced in the schools and this includes the Child-to-Child approach. Ten and eleven-year-olds supervise the oral hygiene of the younger pupils. There are competitions for the healthiest mouths.

Similarly, in Bhutan, the younger children are monitored by older ones.

What happens when teeth go rotten?

Some children's teeth decay. They get brown and black holes which look ugly. The holes are small at first, but if they are not filled by a dental worker, they turn into big holes which can hurt. These children often have toothache, bad breath and may even have a boil or abscess in the gums surrounding the teeth. The teeth may be so rotten that they must be taken out. It then becomes difficult to bite or chew food.

What makes teeth go rotten?

Teeth get holes when we eat too many sweet foods, fizzy drinks or too much sugar. Food which contains sugar is especially harmful when we eat it between meals, as a snack.

What makes gums diseased?

The gums cover the jaw around the teeth. When teeth and gums are not cleaned properly, something called **plaque** forms around them. Germs live in the plaque and make our gums sore and unhealthy.

How can we look after our teeth?

Children should understand the importance of caring for their teeth. They should brush their teeth every day with a brush or a brushstick. They should not eat too much sugar, sweet food or fizzy drinks which may rot teeth. Remember too, for young babies, mother's milk is best for building healthy teeth from the start.

How best can we look after our gums?

If the gums are diseased the teeth can become loose and later drop out. So children should keep their gums healthy by cleaning teeth and gums properly to get rid of plaque. Germs in the plaque can make the gums soft and they may bleed. If the gums bleed, they are not being cleaned properly.

> **Remember!**
> Healthy gums do not bleed!

ACTIVITIES

Children can observe

Children can look at the teeth of:
- their younger brothers and sisters;
- older children;
- babies;
- children of the same age;
- adults including older people.

Encourage them to count the number of teeth in a person's mouth.

- Do all children have the same number of teeth?
- How many teeth do babies have when they are born? (They usually have none.)
- When do the first teeth usually appear in most babies? (They usually appear at about 3-4 months.)
- How many do they have when they are two years old? (Most children have about twenty 'milk' teeth when they are two.)
- When do the first set of teeth start to fall out? (Permanent teeth begin to appear at about the age of six, and push out the milk teeth.)
- What is the greatest number of teeth in a mouth? (An adult has 32 permanent teeth.)

While the children are looking at teeth, do they notice that some teeth are black? Do they notice that some teeth have holes in them? Such teeth have decay. They are rotting. Have any holes been filled by the dental worker? What do they look like? What are they filled with? Have they talked to any older people who have lost many teeth?

Children can keep a record

How many children brush their teeth, how often, when, how? Who has lost a tooth? Why? Who has had a filling in a tooth? Keep a record for several months, for each child.

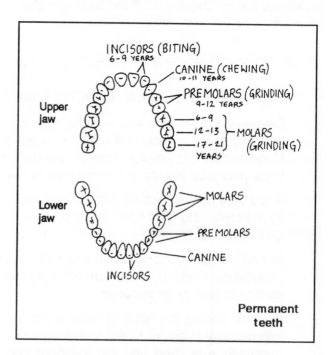

Permanent teeth

Do children recognise that there are different kinds of teeth? What other things do they notice? They could make drawings to show the number and arrangements of teeth in the top and bottom jaws.

Children can experiment

A lot of sweet food, like cakes, fizzy drinks and sweets, is not good for teeth. Here is a simple experiment.

Find two teeth (use teeth from children whose first set is falling out). Drop one in a fizzy drink and the other in water. Leave them for about two weeks. The tooth in the fizzy drink gets soft and you can scrape some of it off with a sharp instrument. The tooth in the water does not get soft.

Children can discuss

At school, the observations of children can be discussed and recorded. Children should be able to say why teeth are important. Can they imagine what it is like to have no teeth? What problems has a person with no teeth?

Discuss the different kinds of teeth. Children can find the jobs of the different teeth (biting or chewing).

Children can bring teeth of different animals to school. Children can look for the skulls of dead animals. Are the teeth of animals different? How are they different? Why are they different? (Do the children understand that some animals, like dogs, eat meat, while other animals, like cows, eat grass. Sharp teeth are for biting and chewing. Short, flat teeth are for grinding and chewing.)

Which animals have sharp teeth? (Dogs and cats, mice and rats will have some very sharp teeth for biting things.) Which ones have more grinding teeth? (Cows, goats and sheep, which chew a lot of grass, have large flat molars for grinding up the food.)

Have they noticed gaps in some children's mouths? Has the first set of teeth fallen out? How many teeth have fallen out?

Did they notice holes in some teeth? Has the hole been filled by a dental worker? Can they suggest a local pain killer to put on a rotting tooth, or on the gum near it, to stop the pain? This does not stop the tooth from rotting.

The children can discuss why they think it is necessary to brush teeth every day. They could also say when they think teeth should be brushed. (They should be brushed at the same time as the children wash their faces, that is, in the morning and last thing at night before going to sleep.)

Ask if any children have smaller baby brothers and sisters who are bottle fed. Sometimes older brothers and sisters give sugary water in a bottle to the baby. This is not good for the teeth because the sugar in the liquid rots the teeth when the baby sucks the bottle. Children should understand that mother's milk is the best food for building strong and healthy teeth.

Children can make and use a brushstick

Each child can make a brushstick, which looks like this:

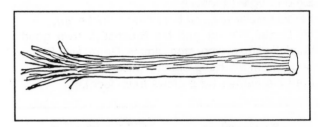

- use the twig of a tree; is there any tree used locally which is especially good for making brushsticks?
- chew on one end of the twig and use the fibres as a brush.

Tooth brushes can be used if they are available. Practise using the stick or toothbrush. It must clean all the surfaces of the teeth and the children should brush from side to side.

The children can bring their brushsticks or toothbrushes to school each day and brush their teeth together before class.

They can make a brushstick for a younger brother or sister at home and teach them how to brush their teeth well.

Children can make 'toothpaste'

The children can learn to make a kind of toothpaste or toothpowder, by mixing salt and bicarbonate of soda (from the chemist or market) in equal amounts. Just

SODA

SALT

plain salt can also be used to clean teeth. To make it stick, wet the brush or stick before putting it in the powder.

In some areas, fluoride is put in the community's drinking water so that everyone will have stronger teeth. Fluoride toothpaste should be used if available. The children should discuss this with the health worker.

Children can make a play

The children can do a sketch or puppet play about their teeth. The characters could be as follows:

Jimmy Germ (the gum thief);
Simon Sugar (a rotter);
Sammy Molar (a good but rather stupid man);
Mr Dental Worker and Ms Brushstick (two good, helpful people who stop Jimmy Germ and Simon Sugar from attacking Sammy Molar);
Fred the Farmer (who grows fresh food).

Here is an outline plot which can be developed by teachers and children.

1. Sammy Molar tells Mr Dental Worker what it is like to be a tooth. He says how frightened he is of Jimmy Germ and Simon Sugar.

2. Jimmy Germ and Simon Sugar appear and tell the audience how they plan to rot Simon Molar and make his gums so weak he will fall out.

3. Mr Dental Worker and Ms Brushstick discuss how to stop them from attacking Sammy Molar.

4. Sammy Molar gets covered in sweet food by Simon Sugar. Sammy Molar starts to go bad. Jimmy Germ attacks his gums. Sammy cannot stand up well.

5. Sammy Molar describes his problems to Mr Dental Worker who explains the importance of not eating too much sweet food and cleaning his teeth.

6. Mr Dental Worker introduces Sammy to Fred the Farmer. He tells Sammy about foods that will not hurt him. Simon Sugar is very angry.

7. Sammy then visits Ms Brushstick who drives out Jimmy Germ.

8. Simon and Jimmy quarrel and blame each other.

Children can make a check list of good tooth care. They can make a list of do's and don'ts for looking after teeth and gums. This list might include the following:

DO

- Brush our teeth and gums every day
- Brush our teeth before going to bed
- Eat healthy food
- Teach younger brothers and sisters to brush their teeth
- Have a brush or brushstick for each person in the family

and so on...

DON'T

- Let our teeth rot
- Forget to brush our teeth
- Drink sugary drinks
- Eat many sweets or a lot of sugar
- Use broken sticks, charcoal or other hard materials for cleaning teeth

and so on...

FOLLOW-UP

The check list suggested above will test how much the children understand about caring for their teeth.

It is important to know whether they are looking after their teeth better. This may be clear if records are kept of the children's toothbrushing habits over a period, of say, six months. The results could be compared to see if there have been any improvements.

USING THIS SHEET

The idea of strong, clean and healthy teeth can be introduced to children by a number of people:

- by dental workers during a visit to a school;
- by teachers at various levels of primary school - teeth are a good topic for work in health and/or science lessons;
- by Scout, Guide, community and health workers in out-of-school groups;
- by a drama group or puppet theatre in a short drama or puppet play.

LOOKING AFTER OUR EYES

THE IDEA

Eyes may become sore, infected or even blind if we do not care for them. This means keeping eyes and faces clean and free from flies, eating foods that are rich in vitamin A, and looking after eyes which have become infected or are threatened by disease.

The Eye

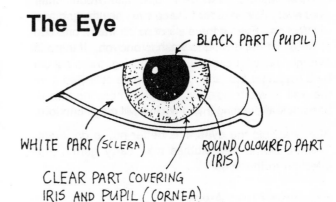

BLACK PART (PUPIL)

WHITE PART (SCLERA)

ROUND COLOURED PART (IRIS)

CLEAR PART COVERING IRIS AND PUPIL (CORNEA)

Sight is important because we use our eyes for almost everything we do. Sometimes, eyes cannot do their job because they are not properly looked after. Many eye problems are caused by:

- dirty faces which attract flies and germs;
- not eating enough food with vitamin A;
- a disease which can make us blind.

There are three ways to keep our eyes healthy and to prevent eye infections and perhaps blindness:

- keep eyes and faces clean and free from flies;
- eat food which is rich in vitamin A;
- look after eyes which are infected or diseased.

If you look at an eye, you will see:

- the round, coloured part (iris);
- the black, centre part (pupil);
- the clear part (cornea) which covers the iris and pupil;
- the white part (sclera).

The pupil lets in light, like a window, so that we can see. The eyelid helps to protect the eye itself, and keeps out light when we sleep. Tears, carried by the eyelid across the eye, wash away dirt and help to keep our eyes clean. That is why we blink. Eyelashes help to keep out dust, dirt and flies.

If an eye is healthy, the white part is clear, and the eye seems to shine.

Where and how these activities have been used

In most countries (particularly in the tropics) it is very important for children to learn to keep the eyes of younger ones clean. The Child-to-Child story book, Flies, emphasises this in an amusing way.

There are often areas within countries where blindness and eye disease is particularly serious in communities. In this case, children can act as health workers to survey problems and persuade families to seek treatment from health centres.

It is possible to design entire Child-to-Child projects around the care of eyes and the prevention of eye disease. Components of such a project would be:

- An identification of eye conditions in a local area (often certain specific areas are affected).
- An enquiry into how these may be caused or treated.
- Campaigns specifically designed: (a) to improve hygiene;
       (b) to improve nutrition;
       (c) to emphasise treatment ...... related to this condition.

A very successful Child-to-Child project, organised in **Tirupati, India,** in conjunction with the Royal Commonwealth Society for the Blind, concerned xerophthalmia which can cause blindness and is due to lack of vitamin A. The children learnt:

- Why vitamin A is important.
- Which foods are rich in vitamin A.
- How to recognise the signs of a vitamin A deficiency.
- What to do when someone has a vitamin A deficiency.

Keeping Eyes Clean

Washing the Face and Eyes

Children should wash their faces and around their eyes every day, in order to keep eyes healthy and free of infection. Even if there is not much water, one cup of water for each child to wash is enough. If there is enough water for cattle and for cooking, there should be a cupful for the face. Water can be collected from the well or water-hole, or, if it rains, from the roof (a banana leaf draining into a bucket will catch enough).

After washing the eyes, it is better not to dry them. Towels, cloths and clothes may carry germs and infection to the eyes.

Keeping Flies Away

It is very important to keep flies away from the face and eyes. Flies like to feed on dirty eyes and will carry germs into the eye which can cause infection.

It is difficult for babies and younger children to keep flies away from their eyes. Older children can:

* wash young ones' faces and eyes;
* keep animals which bring flies away from the house as much as possible;
* bury rubbish and faeces and dirty things that flies walk on.

Eating Good Food

Young children may become blind if they do not eat enough foods which have plenty of vitamin A. The first danger sign is when a child cannot see as well as healthy children in the dark (night blindness). If they still do not get food rich in vitamin A, the cornea may become cloudy and scarred, causing complete blindness.

Such blindness can be prevented by regularly eating certain foods with plenty of vitamin A, such as:

* **dark green,** leafy vegetables (e.g. spinach);
* **red and yellow** coloured fruits and vegetables (e.g. tomatoes, carrots and paw-paw);
* **red** palm oil.

Diseases Causing Blindness

Blindness can be the result of a disease.

Measles. A well-nourished child can fight diseases such as measles which cause blindness (*see* Sheet No. 2.1, **Feeding Young Children: Healthy Food**). If a baby has measles it may feel more comfortable in a dark place for a few days. Feed the baby carefully with food that has plenty of vitamin A, and comfort it. Better still, get a vitamin A capsule from the health worker, as soon as you know it is measles. Watch the eyes. If they become sore with redness and pus, the child should be taken to the health worker.

Remember: It is easier to prevent measles. Get immunisation for the baby.

Trachoma is an eye disease spread by flies and direct contact. It can be treated with the right ointment, but the easiest way to prevent blindness from trachoma is to keep children's eyes clean. Wash carefully and often. Keep flies away.

Remember: Complications of trachoma can cause blindness. Help to prevent it when the child is young. Get medical help as quickly as possible to stop the eye going blind.

River Blindness is caused by tiny worms, spread by small black flies that bite. In areas where river blindness is a problem, there is little children can do directly. In these areas, there will be local health programmes to fight the disease, and children should know about them.

Eye Infections

Keeping eyes and faces clean helps to stop infections of the eye which might be dangerous. What can children do if their eyes do become infected?

* If something like a bit of dirt or sand enters the eye, do not leave it there. Infection and permanent damage may result later. Do not rub the eye. Visit the health worker to check for damage and to make sure that the dirt is out.

* If the eyes are red or sticky with pus, or swollen, clean them very carefully. Use a small piece of clean cloth and burn or bury it afterwards. Or use a clean finger, but always wash your hands immediately afterwards. Eye infection can easily be spread to others.

* If the eye is red, sticky or swollen, go to the local health worker or drug store as soon as possible. An ointment may be necessary. Take care when putting the ointment on. Ask advice about how to do this.

* If there is a little painful red lump on the edge of the eyelid, this may be a stye. Styes are not dangerous but can be very painful. Bathing with warm clean water can help ease the pain.

Blindness

If we do not prevent infections, fight diseases which can cause blindness and eat a healthy balanced diet, we may become blind ourselves. Some children are born blind. Others' eyes are blinded by accident, infection, disease, or poor diet.

We know that a person is blind if they cannot count fingers held three metres away from their eyes. That person will probably need help, and there are many ways in which children can be useful.

ACTIVITIES

Observing how the eye works. Stand in a room with sunlight coming in. (Don't ever look DIRECTLY at the sun.) One child can shade one eye with a piece of card. Another child can observe the size of the eye's pupil when it is in shadow. The first child can then remove the card quickly so that his friend can see how the size of the pupil changes when it comes into the sunlight. In this way, children can observe how the pupil lets light into the eye and helps us see.

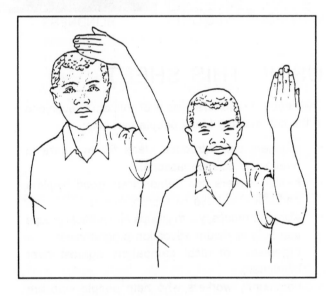

Children can look at each other's eyes and draw what they see. They should notice and label the three main parts of the eye.

Ask the children to notice how a healthy eye looks. Is the white part clear? Does the eye shine?

Getting rid of flies. Children can do many things to fight flies. First, they can find out where the flies come

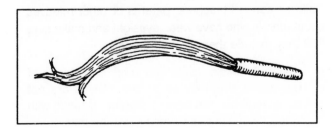

from. They can draw a plan of an area in the community and mark where the flies gather. Do they notice that they gather near animals? They can help to keep animals away from the house, wherever possible. They should also notice that excreta and rubbish attract flies. Encourage children to bury these.

> Older children can compose songs and rhymes using a theme such as:
>
> *Brush the flies*
> *From babies' eyes.*
> *Keep them away,*
> *Don't let them stay!*

They can also make fly swats for use at home using palm leaves, bamboo and other local material.

Older children can help children who are already blind by finding out where they live in the community. Does anyone help them? Older children can help to guide them to school. They can read them books, talk to them, help them to learn and include them in games and activities as often as possible. They can find out whether there are local facilities for the blind or for those who can only see a little. Do mobile eye clinics visit their area?

Children can help most of all by keeping eyes clean.

Keeping eyes clean. Older children can help younger ones at home to wash their faces and eyes every day. Help to collect water which is needed for washing the face and eyes. Each child should have clean water. Why? Remember not to use a cloth or towel for drying the eyes. Why not?

Older children can work in pairs and inspect each other's eyes every day. Have they washed their faces and eyes - the faces and eyes of younger brothers and sisters at home?

Getting enough vitamin A. Children can learn to identify local foods that are rich in vitamin A. Such foods can help to prevent blindness. Draw colourful charts, pictures and posters of these foods. Collect and show local 'spinach-type' foods, or other dark green, leafy vegetables. Say which foods eaten at home contain vitamin A. Are they eaten regularly?

Teachers and extension workers can help children to make a garden to grow some of these plants. Older children can grow some near their home. Waste water from cooking and washing can be used to water these plants if rain is scarce.

It is very important that children who see and hear well always play with those who do not.

Understanding what it is like to be blind. One child can tie a cloth around the eyes of another. The second child can try to move around without being able to use his eyes. The first child can help him. Several objects can be put in a deep bag. Children can place their hands inside and try to tell what the objects are without being able to see them. Try to work with a blindfold over the face.

Children can find out if there are blind people in the community. Find out if there is a special school or an eye clinic nearby. Children can try to find out what caused the blindness by asking when the person became blind. A health worker can also help with information.

Perhaps the children can identify:

* a person who has been blind from birth;
* a person who became blind in the first few weeks of life (possibly because of an infection from the mother);
* a child who became blind between one and six years of age (perhaps because of lack of vitamin A, measles or a severe infection);
* a person who became blind as an adult (perhaps because of trachoma or river blindness);
* an older person who is blind because cataracts are covering the pupil of the eye.

Children could make a chart to show some common local problems and put it up in the classroom and the local clinic.

NOT ALL CHILDREN HAVE THE SAME DIFFICULTIES

FOLLOW-UP

Children can keep records to show that they have inspected their brothers' and sisters' eyes each day and helped them to wash.

Each child could write a story about helping another with an infected eye or poor eyesight. Or they could make a play - let one child act having measles and the others can mime or describe what they did to help.

A competition can be held to draw a clear map showing where flies live locally.

Each class in a school could keep a record of numbers of children with eye problems. Do the problems get less when children are older and cleaner?

Ask the children if they know any children who cannot see well. Are they doing anything to help? What are they doing?

GOOD EYES

GLASSES CAN HELP

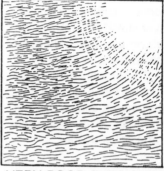

VERY POOR EYESIGHT

BLINDNESS

USING THIS SHEET

The health of children's eyes is of concern to everyone in the community. Many people can help:

* teachers can introduce ideas for eye care in health and science lessons;
* health workers can demonstrate good hygiene and talk about eye care programmes;
* women's groups, youth groups and political groups can help to mount education programmes;
* organisers of local campaigns against river blindness;
* community workers who help people who are already blind;
* older children can tell younger ones about eyes, and why they must be clean, how they can wash their eyes, and how they can kill flies;
* Scouts, Guides, children's groups and youth groups can carry out projects in cooperation with adults which will help to improve the health of eyes in the community.

Children can tell teachers, parents or other relatives about friends who have weak eyesight and make sure that they include them in their games.

CHILDREN'S STOOLS AND HYGIENE

THE IDEA

Diarrhoea, typhoid, cholera, polio and some other diseases are caused by germs present in stools. These germs can pass from one person to another on the hands, in dust, in food and drinks, and on flies. Getting rid of stools in a safe way, and washing after defaecation and before eating can help prevent the spread of these diseases.

Diarrhoea is Dangerous

Children have diarrhoea when they pass frequent, watery stools. They may also vomit and have a swollen belly with cramps. Diarrhoea is caused by germs which live in dust, stale food, dirty water, and human stools. Through the diarrhoea, the body tries to 'wash out' the bad germs.

Diarrhoea is a frequent cause of death in young children. They die from **dehydration** when they lose large amounts of fluid (water and salt) from their bodies because of the diarrhoea, and this is not replaced.

How to tell when a child is dehydrated and how to prepare a **Special Drink** to replace fluids lost is described in Sheet No. 6.1, **Caring for Children with Diarrhoea**. Diarrhoea can often be prevented by proper feeding (*see* Sheet No. 2.1, **Feeding Young Children: Healthy Food**). But the most important way we can help to prevent diarrhoea and other dangerous diseases is by keeping ourselves, and the places where we live and play, clean.

Stools are Dangerous

Many people know that stools are dirty, but they may not know that the germs in stools can cause diseases. Diarrhoea, worms, cholera, typhoid and polio are spread when germs are passed from our stools to hands and clothes, to the water we drink and the food we eat, making us ill.

By being careful when we pass stools, by keeping our hands and bodies clean after a bowel movement, and by cleaning up any stools which are dropped in places where we live and play, we can help to prevent the germs that cause these diseases from spreading. Animal stools are also dangerous.

Where and how these activities have been used

All health programmes emphasise sanitation but not all have found ways of involving children in ways which are interesting and amusing as well as useful.

This sheet on little children's stools does this. Here children can present new knowledge "we learnt at school" which is almost certainly not known by parents and other children.

ASK THE QUESTION:

We all know that adults' stools have dangerous germs in them - but what about little children's stools? Are they:

> The same as adults' stools?
> Less dangerous?
> More dangerous?

Check the sheet for the answer. Did you know it? How many others got it right?

Once children understand the problem, there are many kinds of action they can take at home or together at school. Doing this for younger children makes them much more conscious of their own hygiene.

Some children in a village in **Pachod (India)** have gradually changed the defaecation habits of the village. The children went from house to house explaining to the women and the other children the importance of defaecating far from the water supply and where they live and covering faeces with earth to prevent the spread of disease. These good health habits have now spread to other villages in the area.

Why Children's Hygiene is Important

- Many people think that children's stools are harmless, but this is wrong. A child's stool has perhaps five or six times as many germs as the stool of an adult. When the small child has diarrhoea, the stool is especially dangerous for all members of the family.

- Babies have no control over their bowels and may pass their stools in many different places both inside and outside the house. This is not only dirty but very dangerous because germs from these stools can spread easily to the rest of the family and neighbours.

- When they are older (about 2-3 years) and have learned control of their bowels, children will copy what they see others doing. If they see others in the family defaecate in the field or in the garden, or squat in an alley or by the side of the road, they will copy them because all children want to grow up and be like the others.

- Young children spend a lot of time crawling and sitting on the ground. They often put things into their mouths. And so they pick up germs in the dust from any stools that are lying on the ground around them.

- It is very easy for anyone taking care of a young child to spread germs from the stools. Germs can be spread on our hands from wiping a child's bottom, to food, cooking dishes, the furniture, clothing or the hands of other people. These germs can end up by getting into the mouth of another child or adult, and making them ill.

What Can We Do to Stop the Spread of Germs?

Children can learn good hygiene habits which prevent the spread of germs causing diarrhoea and other illnesses. Older children can *discuss* effective preventive measures.

Use a Latrine
Whenever possible, use a latrine for bowel movements, and not the field or compound. Help younger children to use the latrine properly. Cover the latrine hole, keep the latrine clean. When a latrine is not available, stools should be buried to keep off flies.

Keep Hands and Bodies Clean
Use water and ashes or soap, if available, to wash hands, bottom and soiled cloth. If the soiled cloth cannot be washed, or leaves have been used for wiping the bottom, bury them or throw them in the latrine. Clean a child's bottom and hands if they are dirty.

Keep the Place Clean

Clean up and bury stools dropped on the floor or in the yard. As often as possible (even four times a day) check to see that the places where young children play, crawl and sit are clean. Wash spoons, dishes and things that young children have played with.

Remember: KEEP CLEAN AND USE A LATRINE

How Can We Improve Small Children's Hygiene?

Older children can help small children to learn good, clean bowel habits.

Teach Younger Ones to use a Latrine

Where there is a latrine, the older child can encourage the small one to say **when** he needs to go. The older child can then take the younger one to the latrine.

If there is no latrine, older children can help young ones learn to pass their stools in the right places by taking them with them to the woods, the fields or elsewhere to relieve themselves.

Encourage good hygiene habits such as:

*   cleaning the bottom;
*   washing hands after using the latrine;
*   covering the latrine hole to keep flies away;
*   closing the door of the latrine after use.

For girls it is particularly important that they wipe themselves properly after passing stools. If a little girl wipes her bottom with a forward movement, there is a risk that a part of the stool will be taken to where it can enter the body and even reach the bladder. This is an important cause of bladder infection in little girls. If she wipes backward, some of the stool may be left on the little girl's bottom, from where her clothes may become soiled. It is best to wipe only very gently, and neither too far forward, nor too far backward.

Provide a Suitable Latrine

When a household has one latrine, it is often made for adults. It is some distance from the house; the foot plates are far apart; and the hole is too large, too dark, and too deep for a small child. It is a dark and frightening place for small children, even if an older child goes with them. They would rather pass their stools in a corner of the house or just outside the door, where there is light and the security of having someone older nearby.

Small children need a latrine built specially for them. It should have a small foot plate, with a small hole, and be near the house.

A child's latrine can easily be built. Here is a picture of the kind of latrine that is suited to young children.

The hole is about 1.5m deep. The plate is about 2m wide, about a meter long, and about 4cm thick. The hole is no more than 10cm in diameter. The latrine can be located in the courtyard beyond the back door of the house. A wooden cover is kept over the hole. After each use a small amount of water is used to wash off the plate so as to avoid attracting flies.

A basin and soap, if possible, are nearby so that someone can clean the children after they use the latrine, or show them how to wash their hands after cleaning their bottom. The latrine will last for two to three years before the pit fills up. When it does, a new pit can be dug, if there is still a small child in the house.

But even if a child's latrine is not built there are ways of helping to keep children's stools safe. Children can be taught to pass their stools on a banana leaf which can be immediately dropped into the adult latrine.

ACTIVITIES

Discuss. Talk about the way to teach younger children to keep clean and use the latrine, and why this is important.

Older children can discuss some things which help the germs to spread. Examples would be:

- taking a piece of cloth, wiping the bottom, and leaving the cloth lying around;
- simply holding the child out bare-bottomed over the floor or the ground.

Practise good hygiene. Practise good habits at school: use the latrine; keep it clean; keep hands clean after using the latrine; wash hands before taking food.

Why do some children not use a latrine? Ask them to explain. Discuss these reasons and agree on ways of encouraging use of the latrine.

Build a child-size latrine. Older children can build a child-size latrine in the school compound as an example, measure the pit and make a mould for the plate.

A teacher or other adult needs to supervise the children who do the construction themselves. Parents can help by providing the materials - sand, cement, wood, etc.

The children can be grouped according to the places from which they come. In class, they can develop plans for helping each other build child-size latrines at their homes. A progress chart in class can show each home with a small child. Put a tick when a latrine is built at that home and another when the small child has learned to use it. This may be done for boys and girls separately.

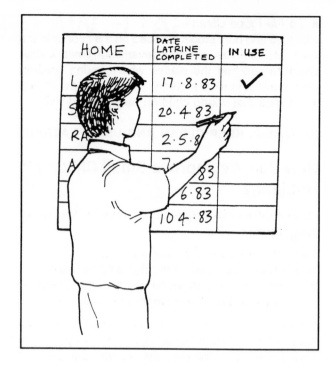

WHAT'S WRONG HERE?

FOLLOW-UP

Ask the children questions:

- What causes diarrhoea?
- How can diarrhoea be prevented?
- Why is it important to be especially careful about younger children's stools?
- What are some of the good hygiene habits which can help to stop the spread of germs?

Does the school now have a latrine? and a place to wash hands? What about at home? How many families have a special latrine or a special place for little children to defaecate? Have the children helped to make the special latrine? Have the children helped younger brothers or sisters to learn better hygiene? Ask them to describe what they did.

USING THIS SHEET

Teachers and health workers can emphasise the importance of keeping clean and using latrines, to prevent the spread of diarrhoea. Science lessons can be used for learning more about germs - what they are and how they spread sickness.

Teachers and parents can work with older children to plan and build the child-size latrine.

Children at school, and through Scout, Guide, and religious groups can spread the ideas of good hygiene - good food, clean water, and keeping clean - especially by their own good example. They can teach younger ones how to use a latrine and how to keep themselves clean, and help to build suitable child-size latrines where they are needed.

CLEAN, SAFE WATER

THE IDEA

Every living thing needs water to live, but dirty water can make us ill. We must be careful to keep water clean and safe: where it is found; when we carry it home; and when we store it and use it.

Water is Our Friend

Water is our best friend. Without it, animals and humans become weak and die. In many countries where there is not enough rain, there is not enough water and people suffer. Water is always precious. We must use it carefully and keep it clean.

Dirty Water Can Be an Enemy

Even when there is enough water, if it is not clean and safe, it can be our worst enemy. Babies and young children especially need clean drinking water because dirty water which has germs in it makes them ill. Some of the illnesses caused by dirty water are diarrhoea, dysentery, cholera, typhoid, jaundice, worms and, in some countries, bilharzia.

Germs and dirt which cause disease can get into the water:

• at the source;
• when we collect it and carry it home;
• when we store it and use it at home.

Sometimes water looks clean but it is not good to drink because it has germs in it.

IF THE GERMS ARE IN THE WATER, THE WATER IS NOT SAFE!

Where and how these activities have been used

This is one of the most popular and most used sheets in all programmes round the world. Its accompanying Child-to-Child reader, *Dirty Water,* has been very widely translated and adapted, e.g. into Arabic, Spanish, Nepali, Chinese, Indonesian and other languages.

It is very frequently used (as in Bunumbu, Sierra Leone) as the basis for a project by children with the community in a way which establishes links between the child, the family and the community and between knowledge acquired at school and put into practice immediately outside of school. Activities relating to this topic can involve various subjects across the school curriculum, e.g.:

- mapping water source;
- calculating water use;
- story writing;
- analysing water purity.

Experience from using this sheet suggests:

(i) Be realistic - water is precious, time is limited and activities should not suggest action (such as boiling all water where firewood is scarce) which is not possible;

(ii) Emphasise setting a good example - when children at school or in their home practice good water habits (e.g. covering pots, using ladles), their example often teaches better than words.

Some children, in an area of Nigeria, where guinea worm was very common, built a wall around the water hole to stop infected people walking into the water and leaving eggs there. With the help of the village tailor they made filters for each family to filter the water and remove any crustaceans carrying eggs from the drinking water. They were thus able to greatly reduce the number of people who had guinea worm.

AS-59

Keeping Water Clean and Safe

We get water from many sources. Water comes from springs, rivers, ponds and wells. It is collected from these places as well as from rain or taps. There are many things that we can do to keep water clean and safe where we find it. It is also important to keep it clean when we carry it home, and when we store it. Here are some ways of keeping water clean.

Storing Water

Use a clean cloth (keep it well-washed and dried) and place it over the empty storage container. Tie it in place if necessary. Pour water carried from the well or stream through the cloth to remove dirt, dust and insects. If the water is allowed to stand for a while, many impurities will sink to the bottom. Strong sunlight will also destroy many germs in water stored in a transparent container.

SAND FILTER

FINE SAND →
COARSE SAND →
PEBBLES →
WIRE SCREEN →

WHERE WATER IS FOUND

DON'T

- Let people or animals bathe, urinate or pass stools in or near water;
- Let people wash clothes or throw rubbish into the water;
- Let people use a dirty container to draw water.

DO

- Where there is more than one place to get water, try and keep the cleanest one for drinking water.
- Where there are taps and wells with safe water, try to use these.
- Always use a clean container - clean on the inside **and** on the outside - for drinking water.

WHEN WATER IS COLLECTED AND CARRIED HOME

DON'T

- Use a dirty container;
- Let things fall into the water, or put branches of trees or other things into the water;
- Touch the water with dirty hands.

DO

- Always use a clean container for water.
- Cover the container.
- Be careful not to spill water so that it carries dirt back into the well.

WHERE WATER IS STORED

DON'T

- Let flies, dust, dirt and other objects fall in;
- Put dirty cups, hands or ladles into it;
- Let a sick person share the family drinking cup, or put left-over water back into the storage container.

DO

- Always use a clean container for storing water.
- Keep the storage container covered so that nothing can fall in.
- Always use a clean ladle for taking water.
- Keep a separate water storage container and ladle for people who are ill.

Drinking Water

If the water has been kept clean, it is probably safe for drinking. If you know that the water has been made safe by chemicals, you can certainly drink it safely.

If you are not sure that it is safe, the water can be made safe by boiling. It is especially important to use boiled water for babies, very young children and sick people. Remember to put it in a clean container and to keep it covered. You can also make or buy a special filter which removes some of the dangerous substances from the water. Ask your health workers about filters.

Always use a clean glass, cup or gourd for taking drinking water.

ACTIVITIES

Children can discuss. Why is water important? List all the things you can do with water, at home, in the community, in hospitals, on farms, in the whole country. For which of these do we like to have clean water?

Is water which is clear or which has a good taste always safe, clean drinking water? (The answer is no. Why?) How do germs get into water?

In what ways can water help us? In what ways can water harm us? Do some of the children often have an upset stomach or diarrhoea? Are there other people in the family who do? What about the babies? What do you think might have caused this illness?

Children can find out.

In the community. In small groups, go to see the sources of water in the village and make a map to show where they are. Find out which sources are clean and well looked after, and which are dirty. If the source is dirty, what is making it dirty? Watch how people draw water and how they carry it home. Is the water kept clean and safe? Discuss what you have seen with the other children.

At school. Make a list of illnesses that can be spread through unsafe water, and find out about them. Find out more about water at the school. Where does the water come from? Are the toilets near the water source? How often is the water container cleaned? Are cups used? Are ladles used? Are cups and ladles washed before and after use? Is there somewhere to wash hands before eating and drinking?

At home. Make a list of all the containers used for water. Make a list of people in the family who had an illness which comes from dirty water. Who collects the water for the home? Can you help them? Who keeps the water clean and protected? Is the water container covered? Is there a ladle?

Find out from the health worker what is the best way to get clean drinking water in the community.

Children can help. Children can help to keep water clean and to take care of it. They can discover activities which are suitable for their age, and can do them alone or in teams or pairs. Here are some examples of the kinds of things they can do.

At the source of the water. Help to keep the **water supply** clean. Explain to little children that they must not urinate in the water, or pass stools around the edge of the water. Collect up rubbish and other objects from around the edge of the water, and take them away.

Where there is a **tap** help people to use it. This may mean helping old people to fetch and carry water.

Where there is a **well**, the surroundings must always be kept clean. If there are stones, help to build a small wall around the well.

Check to see if the **rope and the container** are clean. Help to make a support to hang them up so that they do not lie on the ground. If there is no cover for the well, help to make one if possible.

When people collect water and take it home. Explain that the containers they use must be clean. If the water at the source is not clean, explain to people that they should filter or boil the water.

At home. Explain to younger children that they should not put their hands or dirty objects into the water. Help to keep the container where the water is stored clean and covered. Help younger ones to use a ladle to get water out of the storage container and teach them to put the cover back on the water when they have finished.

Children can make up stories.

Here are some ideas for stories:

The Child Who Grew Small

A child goes down to the river to fetch water and falls asleep on the river bank. While he is asleep he dreams he has become very tiny. Then all the dirt in or near the water becomes, to him, very frightening. He battles his way through it and at last wakes up ... and decides to try and stop the pollution of his water supply.

The children can be asked to think what would happen if they were very small and the dirty things were very big. What would become big? How would they feel?

The Water Dirtiers

Some powerful and selfish people in the community make the village water source dirty with their animals, or by throwing rubbish into it. What can children do? How can they get help from older people in the village?

The End of a Happy Life

This is the story told by the germ family about their very happy life in and around the water source. Life becomes less and less comfortable when children begin to keep their water clean. In the end, the germ family is forced to move to a new and dirtier place.

Children can show what they can do to make the germ family's life more difficult.

Children can make pictures and friezes. All these stories are very good subjects for pictures the children can make in groups. Some children can paint the background and others can add different things onto the pictures by sticking them on. Use cloth or leaves or stones or any other kind of material to make the pictures more interesting.

A **frieze** is a series of pictures which tell a story. Different children can draw the pictures and others can write the story underneath. A group picture or frieze can tell a story, or it could be about a topic or sequence like 'safe water', or 'collecting clean, safe water and bringing it home'.

Children can make up plays, mimes, dances, or puppet plays. These stories and others can also be dramatised. Children can be animals, insects, even things, as well as people. In the Water Dirtiers story, for instance, children can be Grown-Up People, Cows, Flies, Children, Germs, a Fence the villagers put up around the water supply, and even the Water Supply itself. The other two stories are both excellent for turning into mime or dances or puppet plays.

Children can make posters, games and puzzles. Here are some very simple ideas that can be used for posters, but there are many others. These pictures (above right) and others like them can be used to make:

- cards for matching (picture with text);
- dominoes;
- fit-together puzzles.

DON'T MAKE OUR WATER DIRTY

Children can pass the message. Children can pass the message to other children at school, or to children who do not go to school, to parents and family members, and to the community. They can sing songs, tell stories, make plays, posters and games for playing with younger children.

FOLLOW-UP

Children can be asked, after several months, to discuss with the other children what they have remembered, what they have done to make water cleaner and safer, what more they can do.

Is the place where water is collected cleaner? Has all the rubbish been taken away? Are water containers always clean, especially on the outside? Do more children wash their hands after defaecating and before eating? How many people are still getting illnesses from unsafe water?

USING THIS SHEET

Health and community workers can tell people the best way of getting clean drinking water in their area, and explain how clean water is important in first aid.

Women and children who collect and use water can understand the importance of keeping water clean and how we can do this.

Teachers, in many lessons - geography, maths, language, science - can use the idea of clean water as a source for discussion, and for projects, for example on map-making, disease prevention, filtration, and pollution .

Children at school, in Scouts and Guides and other youth groups can help keep the environment, and especially our water, clean.

This sheet should be used together with **Caring for Children with Diarrhoea** (Sheet 6.1).

OUR NEIGHBOURHOOD

THE IDEA

The health and safety of everyone in the community can get better when:

- people in the community **understand** better what the community health and safety problems are, and how they are caused;
- people **communicate** with one another, and discuss what they can do to make their lives better;
- people **take action** to improve community health and safety.

VILLAGE HEALTH MAP

Children are important members of the community, and there are many things they can do to make their neighbourhood a healthier and safer place. They can:

- find out what helps or prevents children from growing up safe and healthy;
- find out about health care resources and services in the community;
- think of ways of helping families in the community to improve the health and safety of their children;
- take direct action to improve community health and welfare;
- pass on ideas about good health and safety to their own families, and to younger children.

Children can join together in groups such as 'Health Scouts' to make the community healthier.

1. My house - *prevent accidents*
2. Market - *keep clean*
3. Stream - *clear snails*
4. Well - *fence off*
5. High grass - *cut down*
6. School - *sweep classrooms*
7. Kitchen - *kill flies*
8. School garden - *grow vegetables*
9. Main road - *remember safety drill.*

Where and how these activities have been used

This sheet (very widely used) emphasises how important it is for Child-to-Child activities to be based on important skills needed for finding-out about people and places, such as:

- making and reading maps;
- learning about people and how they live together;
- understanding about customs within society;
- learning how to talk with people and find out information from them;
- learning how to record this information.

In many countries, schools decide to be Child-to-Child schools and the cleanliness established in them makes a good starting point for improving the hygiene and health practices of the whole community.

This sheet is very important in establishing links between health education and the community where knowledge should be applied. It also helps the child to become aware of the structure, problems and resources of the community and especially what can be done. At the same time the child is gaining surveying and mathematical skills and learning to relate these to real life situations.

Child-to-Child activities are based on spreading health messages ... but spreading messages depends on understanding **where** they need to go; **who** needs to receive the the messages and **how** they can be helped to understand them.

On the basis of this, a Child-to-Child workshop met in 1979, in Uganda, to plan a book, *Health into Social Studies*. That book is now in production.

ACTIVITIES

Mapping the Community

In order to show ways to help make the community a healthier and safer place, the children can make a map of their neighbourhood, using copies of maps or making their own. They can identify places where accidents might happen, or which might be a source of disease. They can mark on the map things like:

- places where animals and insects that spread diseases live;
- places where accidents can easily happen to young children;
- places where water is collected, and where food is bought and sold, which need to be kept clean and clear of animals;
- places where rubbish is dumped.

They can also show on the map where there is a clinic and/or a health worker.

Younger children may find it difficult to make a map. They can draw a picture of the school, or their home, or the way to school, and show where there might be danger.

WHO HAS BEEN IMMUNISED				
Names	BCG	DPT 1 2 3	POLIO 1 2 3	MEASLES
1. ANDERSON	✓	✓✓✓	✓✓✓	✓
2. KAMALA	✓	✓	✓	
3. ZOOM	✓			✓
4. JAMES	✓			✓
5. PADMA	✓	✓✓	✓	

BCG — PROTECTS AGAINST TUBERCULOSIS
DPT 3 DOSES — PROTECTS AGAINST DIPTHERIA, WHOOPING COUGH AND TETANUS
POLIO 3 DOSES — PROTECTS AGAINST POLIO
MEASLES — PROTECTS AGAINST MEASLES

Identify Health and Safety Needs

Find out more about the health of babies and young children in the community.

- How many of the children, how many of their brothers and sisters, have been fully immunised? Talk about immunisation. What does it mean? Why is it needed? Who does it? Where? Make an immunisation record chart for children in the group (*see* Sheet No 6.4, **Immunisation**).
- How many children, or others in their families, have been sick with measles, diarrhoea, or pneumonia during the past year? (*See* Sheet No 6.4, as well as Sheet No 6.1, **Caring for Children with Diarrhoea**, and Sheet No 6.7, **Coughs, Colds, Pneumonia**).
- What are the other most common illnesses among children in the neighbourhood?

- What are the most common accidents among children? Where do they happen - at home? at school? on the road? (*See* Sheet No 4.1, **Preventing Accidents**, and Sheet No 4.2, Road Safety.)

Identify Health Services and Other Resources

On their map, the children will have marked the health clinic, if there is one. They can visit the nearest clinic or hospital and find out, for example:

- the times it is open;
- if there are special times for children under five years of age;
- if there are special times for immunisation.

Look at one of the health record cards, and ask the health worker to talk about the most difficult health problems in the community. Ask them to explain more about immunisation. Find out what accidents happen most often in the neighbourhood.

In any community there are often other people with different kinds of health knowledge. For example, some people know how to make herb teas, some women help at childbirth, someone may have been trained in first aid for accidents, several people may be trained health workers, some may be clinic or hospital sisters, medical assistants and so forth.

Children can:

- Find out and make a list of all the people in the neighbourhood who may have special health knowledge: where they can be found; what their special health knowledge is; and who to go to with a particular health problem.

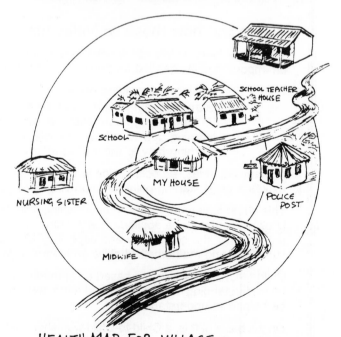

HEALTH MAP FOR VILLAGE
The Circles represent each hour's walk from school or home.

- Find out about local medicines. What plans are used? Who knows how to make up the medicine? When is it used? Grandparents and older people in the community may know about traditional medicines.
- Discuss what to do in case of an accident or bad illness, especially at night. Who is the best person to go to? Is there an ambulance service? Where is the nearest police post? What is the best thing to do in case of an emergency?
- Make a 'health service' map of the community, or add this additional information to the 'health needs' map. Mark where to go for help, and when and where special clinics are held.

What Can Children Do?

Children can take action themselves to help their families to improve their general health and safety. Many ideas for ways in which children can help have been suggested in other activity sheets (Sheet No 6.4, **Immunisation**, Sheet No 3.3, **Children's Stools and Hygiene**, Sheet No 3.4, **Clean, Safe Water**, Sheet No 4.1, **Preventing Accidents**, for example).

Passing the Message

At school, children can tell other children about health problems and resources. They can try to make their school a healthier and safer place by passing the message about things like:

- using latrines and practising good hygiene;
- playing safely and preventing accidents;
- keeping the school and playground free of places where mosquitoes can breed.

Children can pass the health and safety messages to other children in the school in many different ways:

- Write books or reading cards for younger children;
- Draw posters and help younger ones to talk about them;
- Make up health games to play with smaller children;
- Make plays and puppet shows, songs and dances;
- Organise the children into teams to compete in cleaning-up activities.

In the community, children can pass the message to families and neighbours.

- Hold an open day at the school, with posters on the wall about immunisation, maps of health needs and resources, and plays about road safety and accident prevention, for example.
- Make posters about immunisation - why it should be done, where it can be done and the times - to put up around the market or community centre.
- A group of children can 'adopt' a newborn baby in the neighbourhood, and make a vaccination card to remind the mother when the baby is to be immunised. Check to see that it is done.
- Another way to pass the message about immunisation is for the children to visit families to tell them the correct time and place for the immunisation clinic. Each child can be responsible for several families.

Taking Action

Children can talk with their teachers about what action they can take together to improve health and safety in the community. Direct action might include:

- helping to clean up the source of community drinking water (Sheet No 3.4);
- working to make sure that each family in the neighbourhood has a latrine (Sheet No 3.3);
- setting up a plan to help a disabled child (Sheet No 5.1);
- setting aside time for a road safety campaign at school, and around the neighbourhood (Sheet No 4.2);

- helping all children in the school to make sure that their families have all been properly immunised (Sheet No 6.4), starting with any children in the group, or in their families, who have not been immunised;
- learning some simple first aid to be used in case of an accident (Sheet No 4.1).

Health Scouts

In some areas, children can form special groups of *Health Scouts*. Health Scouts can have special uniforms, songs or flags. Health Workers can work with Health Scouts and devise special tests and badges to show that they have acquired special skills. Health Scouts can work closely with health workers finding out information and spreading ideas. In some countries, special groups of 'Accident' or 'Safety Scouts' may be set up.

Each older child can be a health leader for a few households, and tell the health worker where help is needed, or pass on information from the health worker to the household.

Remember: Children as a group can help the community even if there are no Health Scouts.

What Can Other People Do?

Find out which people in the community might be able to help, including:

- teachers and headmasters, parent/teacher associations;
- health workers;
- council members, local government officials;
- farmers and agricultural officers.

Who else might help?

The children can hold a council meeting to discuss community health and safety problems. They can play the parts of different people in the community, including policemen, older people, community workers, students and youth group members, as well as those mentioned above. They can discuss and make a list of community health and safety problems. Then they can make suggestions for ways of solving these problems. At the same meeting they can discuss who they should pass their ideas on to.

FOLLOW-UP

Look at the neighbourhood and health needs map a few months later to see if there have been any changes for the better or for the worse. Have the children themselves been responsible for any of the changes, for any of the improvements? Who else has been working to make things better?

Have the children used any of the skills they have learned in any of their other lessons: using maps in

geography, for example, or their knowledge of water borne diseases in science lessons?

Make another immunisation survey of the children and their families. Have they all been correctly immunised? Is anything being done to help those who have not yet been immunised?

Review what to do and where to go for help in case of an emergency, especially at night.

If Health Scouts have been organised, ask the group to keep a record of what has been done. Examine the record regularly.

USING THIS SHEET

Teachers can introduce these activities during health, science or other suitable lessons on the timetable, or during after-school activities like Young Farmers' Clubs.

Headmasters can support the teachers by setting aside time for surveys and direct action campaigns, so that children and the community understand how important these activities are.

Youth leaders and community workers can use these activities as part of a larger programme of working in the community, assisted by community health workers who can provide the necessary professional advice and support.

Children have the most important role in passing the message and taking direct action, through friends and families, and through organised groups like Scouts, Guides and youth brigades. By mounting health and safety campaigns - like 'Find the Mosquito Larvae', 'Fly Catching', 'A Clean School and Playground' and 'Roads Aren't Playgrounds' - they can do a great deal to improve the health and safety of everyone in the school and community.

PREVENTING ACCIDENTS

THE IDEA

In some places, as many as two children in a school die each year because of accidents. Many more will be injured. **These accidents need not happen.** Children can help to reduce the number and seriousness of accidents by practising safety at home, out-of-doors and on the road. Children can learn to spot the most common dangers, and understand how these dangers can be avoided or prevented. They should always watch out for the safety of others, particularly smaller children.

Children can also be prepared to help when an accident happens.

Children can talk about the accidents which they have seen happen most often in their community. Different sorts of accidents happen to children who live in different places - in towns, in villages, in rural areas. Identify accidents which have happened in the last six months at home, on the road, anywhere out-of-doors and discuss **why** they happened.

At Home

*   **burns** from cooking pots or lamps, electrical appliances, hot food, boiling water, steam, hot fat (scalds), strong acid or corrosives (like battery acid) which damage the skin;
*   **cuts** from broken glass, rusty pins, rough wood or sharp knives and axes;
*   **obstruction (prevention) of breathing** from swallowing small objects like coins, buttons and nuts;
*   **poisoning** from eating or drinking harmful things;
*   **internal (inside) bleeding** from swallowing sharp objects like razor blades;
*   **electric shock** from touching a broken electrical appliance or electrical wire.

On the Road

*   **death** or injuries like heavy **bleeding, broken bones** and **damage to main organs** of the body (liver, lungs, brain) (*see* Sheet 4.2, **Road Safety**).

In the Playground or Out-of-Doors

*   **burns, cuts and broken bones;**
*   **poisoning** from eating certain plants and berries;
*   **bites** from animals and snakes and **stings** from bees and other insects;
*   **drowning** in open water or wells.

Where and how these activities have been used

This sheet and the accompanying story book, *Accidents,* are very widely used round the world (particularly in areas where there are special dangers to children from people living very close together). In fact, this activity is usually among the first introduced in new Child-to-Child programmes because accidents are a very common cause of death and injury among children world-wide.

Activities are easy to introduce (campaigns, surveys, drama, one-to-one responsibility for younger children, safety committees, etc) and fun for children to take part in. There are few problems in adapting content to different countries and no difficulty in anyone accepting the message, which is one of recognising and avoiding danger for oneself and others. Many accidents can, in fact, be avoided with a little care and foresight and the children soon learn to recognise danger, especially for the younger ones.

Activities are reported from places as different and far apart as Nepal and Denmark, India and Mexico, **Nigeria** and **Indonesia**.

It is also important for them to learn what to do should an accident occur (*see* Sheet No. 4.3, **First Aid**).

Preventing Accidents from Happening

At Home

Danger from Burns. Accidents at home often involve fire, and children can be badly burned. If their hands are burned, they may never be able to hold a pencil or a tool; if their feet are burned they may not be able to walk properly. There are many ways to prevent burns at home:

- Watch babies and young children very carefully. Do not let them go near the fire.
- Raise the family cooking stove, or make an open cooking fire on a raised mound of clay instead of directly on the ground.
- Use a thick cloth when touching hot pots.
- Be very careful that the handles of cooking pots are out of reach of babies, and turned so that they are not easily knocked over.
- Put petrol, petrol lamps and matches out of reach of small children.

Danger from Poison. Young children are also often injured or even killed when they eat or drink dangerous things.

- Never put dangerous products (e.g. bleach, plant poison, paraffin or petrol) in a coca-cola or other soft drink bottle. Children can drink them by mistake.
- Keep all medicine and poisons out of reach of children (lock them in a cupboard or trunk, or put them on a high shelf). Label all poisons and medicine carefully. Medicines are particularly dangerous because little children often eat tablets thinking they are sweets.
- Teach young children not to drink out of strange bottles or eat strange fruits and plants which may not be safe.

Danger from Sharp Things. Many cuts can be easily prevented.

- Keep the floor clear of broken glass and nails. Get rid of nails or splinters which stick out.

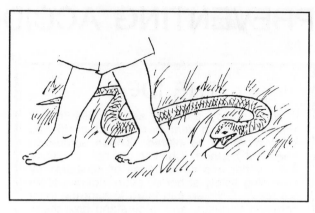

- Keep sharp knives and razors out of the reach of young children.

Older children can identify **other** common accidents which happen at home. How can they be prevented?

In the Neighbourhood

Danger from Snakes. Children can protect themselves from snakebites.

- Recognise which snakes are dangerous and where they live.
- Learn to remain very still if you are close to a snake. Wait for it to go away.
- Clear grass and weeds from the paths most commonly used by children.

Danger when Playing. Children are active and need safe places to play.

- Know the neighbourhood, and avoid dangerous places where there may be machinery, animals, snakes, glass or sharp metal.
- Make wells safe so no one can fall in.
- Play safely. DON'T:
  - climb in dead trees;
  - throw stones and other sharp things;
  - swim in swift-flowing rivers;
  - run while chewing a stick;
  - eat fruits and berries which may be poisonous;
  - play with fire;
  - make animals angry, especially when they have young ones with them.

On the Road

Many children are injured or killed each year by vehicles on the road, especially when they are walking along the road, or when they are trying to cross the road. The special rules for safety on the road are discussed fully in Sheet No 4.2, **Road Safety**.

ACTIVITIES

Be Aware of Danger

Children can record accidents that have happened to members of their families. Make three lists or graphs of accidents which happened at home, on the road, out-of-doors, and decide which kind of accidents happen most often in the community.

Why do you think these accidents happen? If you can discover why they happen, you can also find out how to **prevent them from happening so often**.

Discuss which accidents are most common for children at different ages (and why) - under 2 years, from 2-6 years, after 6 years.

Contact the health centre and ask if children can be given details of all accidents to children over the last 6 months. Make charts or graphs of the accidents that are reported.

WHAT'S WRONG IN THIS PICTURE?

Make pictures which show different dangers at home, in a playground, or at school. Put the good ones on a wall. Let the other children discuss them.

Make a series of drawings to show how an accident might happen:

1. Mother is filling the cooking stove with kerosene.
2. A visitor comes to the house and mother goes to talk to the visitor.
3. A small child, left by himself, picks up the kerosene bottle and drinks from it.

First Aid if an Accident Happens

Children can learn and practice *first aid*. Often schools or youth groups give special first aid classes. However here are some simple measures to practise and remember.

Get Help Quickly

If someone has a bad fall from a tree, or gets badly hurt in a car accident, do not move them. Cover them with a blanket to keep warm and GET HELP QUICKLY.

If someone gets a poisonous bite, do not move the limb which has been bitten. That will only spread the poison around the body. Carry the child and GET HELP QUICKLY. Do not try to treat the bite yourself. It must be done by the health worker.

Cuts and Wounds

With clean hands, wash the wound with soap and boiled water, or hot salt water. Clean out *all* the dirt because wounds that are left dirty can become bad ulcers.

Most small wounds do not need bandages. It is better to leave them to dry in the air so they heal more quickly. If you do use a bandage make sure it is very clean. Keeping the wound clean is better than using things like mud or iodine.

If the wound is really deep, take the person to the health clinic for treatment.

Burns

Put the burned part AT ONCE into cool, clean water for at least ten minutes. If the burn is small probably no other treatment will be needed.

If the burn is very deep or covers a large part of the body, loosely cover it using a clean cloth with a little Vaseline on it and get medical help as soon as possible.

- DON'T break the blisters;
- DON'T remove any clothing sticking to the burned area;
- DON'T put grease, oil, herbs or faeces on the burn.

Remember: if a person's clothes are on fire, you can put out the flames by rolling them in a mat or throwing a blanket over them. Then treat for burns.

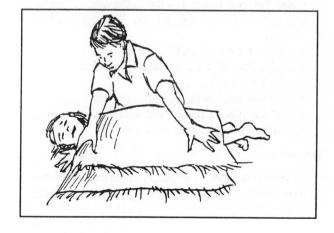

Preventing and Avoiding Accidents

At School

- Look around the classroom; outside the school; around the playground outside. Look for dangers which might cause accidents. Make a list of anything that is not safe, or which might cause an injury. Discuss it with the teacher.
- Have a safety competition or campaign. Organise a project to remove or correct the dangers on the list. The children can help to:
  - mend broken chairs or desks;
  - clear the ground of nails, glass and other sharp objects;
  - cut down tall grass and weeds;
  - explain to younger children the rules of safe play.
- Form groups or teams to be responsible for looking after different parts of the school and playground. Elect a 'Safety Scout' who will lead these groups or teams.
- Discuss the school rules. Which ones have been made to prevent accidents and injury? Are there any rules that should be added?

At Home

- Watch over younger children to make sure they understand simple safety rules. Keep them away from fires. Prevent them from putting things in their mouths, ears or noses. Teach them not to touch medicines or poisons. What else should they know about?

In the Neighbourhood

- Organise a campaign with the theme 'Play Safely'. Make posters. Talk to people. Make up plays and songs for people to see and listen to in the market, outside the health clinic.
- Identify places where it is dangerous to play and discuss how these can be made safer. Take action in a group.
- Encourage the local council to put up warning signs in places which are obviously dangerous.

On the Road

- Children can draw a map. Make it very simple. Show the main roads and footpaths which children use when they come to school. The children can discuss:
  - where they cross the roads;
  - why they cross the roads (is it really necessary?);
  - where accidents have happened;
  - which places have most accidents and why;
  - which places need extra care.

General

- Organise a safety campaign at school, or in the community. Have a campaign for two weeks

against burns, then later have a campaign about safety at play, or road safety.

- Use a variety of different ways to pass the safety message to others, especially younger children.
- Write and act plays, or make a puppet play about why accidents happen, and what can be done to reduce them. Act them at school, or at clinics, or in the market.
- Make posters which show hazards in different places, and warn of the accidents which might result. Put them in classrooms or at the clinic, or in the market. (Perhaps the children could have a poster competition.)
- Make up a song about road safety and teach the song to younger brothers and sisters.

FOLLOW-UP

Have the children carried out a safety campaign? Compare the number of accidents before and after the campaign.

Check to find out if the children remember and practise the road safety rules.

Is the school a safe place for children to work and play?

USING THIS SHEET

Teachers in school and out of school, **Red Cross workers, health workers, Scout and Guide leaders, Young Farmers and other youth leaders, writers** in newspapers, comics and magazines can all help to encourage the idea of safety for children wherever they are.

This sheet should be used together with **Road Safety** (Sheet 4.2) and **First Aid** (Sheet 4.3).

ROAD SAFETY

THE IDEA

Many children are injured or killed because they don't follow the 'rules of the road' when they are walking, or riding a bicycle, especially at night. By being more aware of the dangers on the road, and by following the important rules of the road, children can prevent these accidents from happening, and make sure their young brothers and sisters are safer too.

Why Do Road Accidents Happen?

Talk about why accidents happen on the road before reading any further.

ACTIVITY 1: WHY ACCIDENTS HAPPEN

- Have any children in the group been injured in an accident on the road? Do they know anyone who has? Talk about how the accident happened and how it could have been prevented.
- Talk about what causes accidents on the road. Why do they happen?

- not watching for traffic because the road seems empty;
- taking risks like jumping onto the back of buses or running beside cars;
- not taking special care when they walk on roads at night.

Accidents can happen to children:

When they are walking

- walking or playing near busy roads and not being careful to watch for cars and trucks using the road;
- not looking before they run out into the road: maybe they are chasing a ball, a friend or an animal;

When they are riding bicycles

- when the bicycles are too big or have poor brakes;
- when they put too many people or parcels on the bicycle;
- when they try to show off to their friends by taking their hands off the handlebars or riding in the middle of the road or even zig-zagging along;
- when they don't use hand signals;
- when they ride bicycles at night without proper lights.

Where and how these activities have been used

Road Safety programmes have their place in most school programmes but until the Child-to-Child approach was introduced they had two weaknesses:

(i) They did not cater for out-of-school children. Child-to-Child programmes can fill this gap **either** through scout and health scout programmes, as in **Benin, or** through schools passing on messages from school to out-of-school children, as in **India** (**Gujarat** and **Rajasthan**).

(ii) They only emphasise what children can do for themselves rather than their responsibility for others (the old as well as the young). Child-to-Child programmes have helped to emphasise children's responsibility by encouraging the setting up of Safety Committees to make and teach rules to other children (**India**) and giving older children particular responsibility to teach others and ensure their road safety (**Botswana**).

Sometimes *drivers of vehicles* cause accidents:

*   when they have been drinking alcohol, or are very tired;
*   because they drive too fast, or fail to signal a turn;
*   because their vehicle is overloaded;
*   because the vehicle is not in good mechanical order or the tyres are smooth so that the brakes cannot stop the car in time, or the headlamps do not work.

Roads may be wet and slippery in the rain so that drivers cannot steer properly or stop in time to prevent an accident.

Animals can cause accidents. A chicken or a goat may run into the road, so that the car brakes and swerves, injuring or killing a child.

Road Accidents Can Be Prevented

Every child should know about the most important **rules of the road,** in their own neighbourhood.

On the Road: Roads Aren't Playgrounds

*   Don't play on or near any road where there is traffic.
*   If there is no sidewalk, keep to one side of the road. **Face the traffic** when you are walking.

ACTIVITY 2: DANGERS ON THE ROAD

*   Show that things move at different speeds on the road. One child can be a person walking on a road, others a donkey, a bicycle, a motorbike, a car, a lorry. One at a time, they can move from one line drawn on the ground to a second, some distance away. Who is slowest? Who is fastest? Observe and remember the different speeds. Which ones are the most dangerous?
*   Use the school playground to learn about dangers on the road, and to practise road safety. Draw 'roadways' on the ground similar to those in the neighbourhood. Create 'dangerous' situations by putting a bend in one road, and an intersection in another. Some children can act like bushes or parked vehicles. Other children can pretend to be car or bus drivers, or people riding bicycles along the road. They could drive carefully some of the time, but at others pretend to be bad drivers, speeding up or failing to stop at a light. Children can take turns showing how they would walk along the road, or try to cross the road safely.

ACTIVITY 3: TRAFFIC SURVEY

*   Older children can carry out a survey of traffic movement. Make a chart showing how many people, carts, cars, bikes, donkeys and lorries have passed a certain place over a certain period of time - one hour, for example. Divide the children into teams, so they can survey several different places. Or they could survey the same place at different times. Discuss and compare the charts.

	TIME			
	8 - 9.00	9 - 10.00	10 - 11.00	11 - 12.00
PEDESTRIANS	18	25	14	7
BIKES	22	24	21	23
CARS	7	7	3	8
BUSES	5	2	1	3
TRUCKS + LORRIES	20	15	18	11

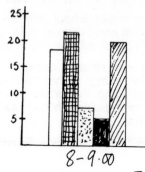

8 - 9.00

TIME

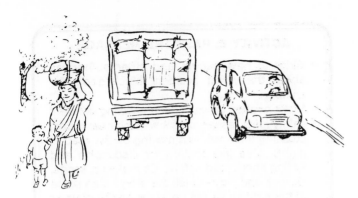

- When you are on or near the road, always **look** AND **listen** for cars and trucks. Don't forget to pay attention to what's going on around you.
- Stay away from heavy machinery, road works, large holes in the road and trenches beside the road. Railway lines are dangerous too.
- Look after younger children on the road.
- Follow the road safety rules, and teach them to other children.

Crossing the Road: Look, Listen and Then Walk

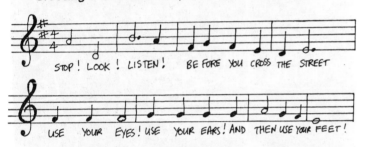

STOP! LOOK! LISTEN! BEFORE YOU CROSS THE STREET

USE YOUR EYES! USE YOUR EARS! AND THEN USE YOUR FEET!

- First, find a safe place to cross - at a corner, at traffic lights or a clear place on the road. **Always cross where you can see for a long distance in both directions, and where drivers can see you.** It is dangerous to cross between or near parked vehicles, at the top of a hill, near thick bushes, or at a curve in the road.

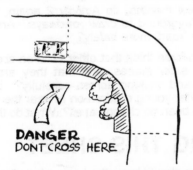

DANGER
DON'T CROSS HERE

- Stop at the edge of the road. Using **eyes and ears,** look for traffic coming, and listen as well. Keep looking and listening until you are sure the road is clear of traffic.
- When no cars are coming **walk, don't run,** straight across the road. **Keep looking and listening while you are crossing.**
- Young children must always cross with an older child or adult.

At Night: Darkness Doubles Danger

- Take special care at night, because it will be difficult for drivers to see you.

- Always wear white clothing or something light-coloured when you are walking or riding along a road at night, so that cars and trucks can see you.
- Walk facing the traffic.
- Use your ears as well as your eyes.

Riding a Bicycle: Concentrate, Look Around, Signal Clearly

- Make sure the bicycle is in good working order, and pay special attention to the brakes, reflectors and lights.
- You must have control of your bicycle at all times.
  - Is the bicycle too big for you?
  - Do you have too many passengers? Are you carrying too many parcels?
  - Do you show off, or take risks?
- Ride at the side of the road, not in the middle.
- While you are riding, concentrate - with both eyes and ears on traffic and people around you. Pay attention to where the other vehicles are, especially if they are turning.
- Signal to other vehicles if you are turning right or left.

Traffic Lights

The rules about traffic lights are different in each place.

ACTIVITY 4: TRAFFIC LIGHTS

Find out what:

- traffic lights are used for;
- the colours mean;
- the rules are for crossing at a traffic light.

Remember: Don't always trust the lights. When crossing at lights, wait until the traffic has stopped before you cross, and always look out for drivers turning.

ACTIVITY 5: HELP EACH OTHER

- Take special care of younger children at accident black spots. Make sure that they know about the dangers at these spots. Older children can 'adopt' younger children to see that they use the road safely on the way to and from school.

ACTIVITY 6: APPLY THE RULES OF THE ROAD

- Ask someone, perhaps a policeman, to come to talk about road safety, and especially about dangerous places in the neighbourhood. Ask if they can bring copies of any road safety materials with them.
- Do Activity 2 (making roadways in the school playground) again. Is there a difference in the way the children behave?

ACTIVITY 7: NEIGHBOURHOOD ROAD SAFETY

- Draw a map of the neighbourhood on the board or a large piece of paper, or in the sand in the playground. Children can discuss:
  - which places they use to cross the roads, on the way to school, on the way to market, on the way to meetings, at other times;
  - where accidents have happened; which places are accident black spots;
  - speed limits on the roads, as well as road signs;
  - which places need extra care;
  - which places are the safest places to cross;
  - how they can help each other, especially the little ones, when walking.

If possible, use information from the survey of traffic movement to help the discussion.

- Discuss road safety around the school:
  - is the school near a main road?
  - is there a fence around the school?
  - what are the dangers from fast-moving traffic?
  - what are the dangers of playing on or near the main road?
  - is there anyone to help young children to cross the road before and after school?

This sheet should be used together with **Preventing Accidents** (Sheet No 4.1).

ACTIVITY 8: PASS THE MESSAGE

- Write to newspapers and other authorities about the worst accident black spots for children.
- Make posters or wall charts showing different safety rules, especially for walking near roads, crossing the road, and moving on the road at night. Use the posters for discussion and writing about road safety. Or make up songs, dances and plays to tell the story. Can some of the posters be put up at the health clinic or the market?
- Remember: Always pass the message to younger boys and girls at home, and teach them about road safety as soon as they begin to walk.

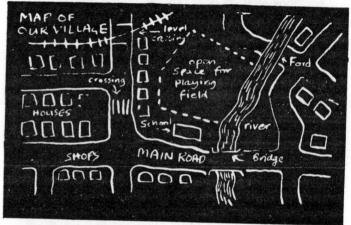

FOLLOW-UP

Review the rules:
- for crossing roads;
- for walking on the road at night;
- for riding a bicycle.

After a few months, do Activity 2 again, using the school playground to draw roadways. Are children using the 'road' more safely?

Do the children think that other children are crossing roads at safer places, and that they are looking, listening and walking across carefully? Is anyone looking after young children on or near the road? Or has there been no change at all? What do they think?

USING THIS SHEET

All children should know the basic rules of road safety. **Teachers and headmasters** can set aside time for road safety activities. Include map-making activities in geography, and letter-writing in language lessons.

Youth group leaders and **religious leaders** can help children outside school to understand and pass the message to others.

Health workers and **police** can help children to understand dangers on the road by talking to groups of children.

Most of all, **children** can help other children by passing the message to others, and helping younger ones to use the roads safely.

FIRST AID

THE IDEA

Most accidents happen at home, at school or in the community. Some injuries are minor, some are serious and can even cause death. Children are often the first people on the scene of an accident. Children need to know how to give effective First Aid. Children can teach others their First Aid skills. Learning about First Aid is interesting and practical and gives children vital and sometimes life-saving knowledge.

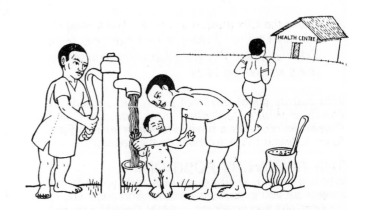

WHAT IS FIRST AID?

First Aid is the first treatment given to a person after an accident. This includes getting medical help when necessary.

The aim of First Aid is to:

• Keep the person alive;
• Help the person to get better.

For example: A man has cut his leg with an axe.

• Keep the man alive: Stop the serious bleeding from the cut.
• Help him to get better: Clean and cover the wound to prevent infection. Comfort the injured man and take him to the health centre.

HOW TO HANDLE AN ACCIDENT: THE SAFE APPROACH

1. Look around at the situation:
    • Are you or any other people in danger?
    • What was the cause of the accident?
    • How many people are injured?

2. Remove the danger to yourself and the injured people. (e.g. In a road accident you should ask someone to stop or control the traffic.)
3. Ask someone to go for help.
4. Look at the injuries and decide what you can do to:
    • Keep the people alive;
    • Help them to get better.
5. Behave calmly and confidently and reassure the injured people.

PRIORITIES FOR FIRST AID

In accidents where many people have been injured, the most seriously injured must be treated first. Remember that the noisiest person may not be the most seriously injured.

The **ABC rule** states the most important priorities to save lives and prevent permanent injury.

A Open the **Airway** (the passage from the mouth and nose to the lungs) and keep it open to allow the person to continue breathing. Check if anything is blocking the airway and remove it if possible.

Where and how these activities have been used

First aid has long been taught to children and was in many ways a Child-to-Child activity long before the Child-to-Child movement was formed. **Red Cross/Crescent** and **Scout, Guide** and other youth movements have always taught first aid and encouraged children within the movements to help each other.

The Child-to-Child approach builds on these activities in two ways. It emphasises:

(i) All older children need to know very simple first aid so that they can use it when necessary and pass it on to others. Try some simple tests on older children in the community. How many know the first aid for (a) a burn and (b) a fall from a tree?

(ii) Children need to pass on knowledge not just to others in their group but also to older children in their community, including those who have not been to school.

B Check the **Breathing**. Place your ear next to the person's mouth and nose. Listen and feel and watch their chest and stomach to check whether they are breathing. If not, give *Mouth-to-Mouth Ventilation*.

C Check the **Circulation** of the blood by feeling for the heart beat. If there is no heart beat, give *External Chest Compression* which pumps the blood around the body.

This activity sheet does not teach the methods of *Mouth-to-Mouth Ventilation* and *External Chest Compression*. Ask a health worker or trained First Aider to teach these methods to the children.

THE RECOVERY POSITION
When a person is **unconscious** they seem to be asleep but you cannot wake them. Someone who is unconscious and breathing properly should be placed in the **Recovery Position** to keep their airway open. This makes sure that vomit and any other liquid will come out of the mouth so that they can breathe easily. Use the Recovery Position if you have to leave the injured person to go for help.

To put a person in the Recovery Position:
1. Put the arms by the person's side.
2. Roll the person over onto their front.
3. Place the arms and legs as shown in the diagram.
4. Make sure that the chin is forward, the head tilted back and that the **person can breathe freely**.
5. If the person has broken bones, move them with great care. Take special care of their back and neck. Use a support like a rolled blanket instead of their arms and legs to keep their chest raised a little off the ground.
6. Get medical help.

head must be pushed back to help him breathe easily.

leg, arms positioned to stop him from rolling onto his face.

This arm stops him rolling on to his back.

BLEEDING
Bleeding can be very mild and last only a short time or very serious and can lead to death.

We need blood to stay alive. Adults have about 4 litres of blood in their bodies. Blood is pumped (pushed) around the body all the time by the heart. Blood travels through two kinds of tubes called **arteries** and **veins**. The heart pumps the blood under pressure around the body through the **arteries**. The blood in the arteries is **bright red** and moves quickly. The

blood travels back to the heart through the **veins**. If someone is bleeding from a **vein**, the blood oozes (comes out slowly) and is **dark red**. If an artery is cut, a person loses blood very quickly. It may spurt out in time with the heart beat. **You must take immediate action to stop the loss of blood. A person can die within three minutes from severe loss of blood.**

FIRST AID
1. Immediately **press the cut tightly** with your hand or the injured person's hand over a clean pad of cloth and **DO NOT LET GO!** If you cannot get a cloth, just use your hand.
2. Sit or lie the injured person down. Raise the injured part above the heart.
3. If the pad becomes soaked with blood, **DON'T** take it off. Put another pad on top of the first one and bind it tightly with a cloth. It should not be too tight. You must be able to fit a finger between the cloth and the skin.
4. Send for the health worker immediately.

SHOCK
This happens when a person has been badly injured or is in great pain. In this state the person is losing blood and liquid from the body. Sometimes a person gets injured and bleeds inside the body without showing any blood outside. Any serious loss of blood or other liquids from the body can cause shock. This is a very serious condition and you need to be able to recognise the signs. When a person is in shock:

- the skin becomes pale or grey;
- the skin feels cold and clammy and sweats a lot;
- the heartbeat speeds up;
- the breathing speeds up and is quick and shallow;
- the person may seem confused.

FIRST AID
To put a person in the Shock Position:

1. Lay the person down.
2. Turn the head to one side.
3. If possible, raise the feet.
4. Loosen the clothing around the neck and waist.
5. Get medical help or carry the person to the health centre in that position.
6. Do not give the person anything to eat or drink.
7. If the person is likely to vomit or becomes unconscious, place them in the Recovery Position.

NEVER USE THE SHOCK POSITION IF A PERSON IS UNCONSCIOUS.

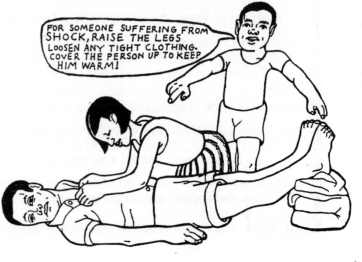

FOR SOMEONE SUFFERING FROM SHOCK, RAISE THE LEGS LOOSEN ANY TIGHT CLOTHING. COVER THE PERSON UP TO KEEP HIM WARM!

HYGIENE RULES

When giving First Aid remember your hygiene rules.

Germs spread diseases. There are germs all around us: in the air, in the water, in the soil, on food, in faeces and in blood. You will have germs on you. It is important to stop germs from spreading. Some germs can cause very serious diseases. These hygiene rules will help protect you and the person you are looking after.

1. Wash or wipe your hands before you help each person.
2. Cover any open cuts and grazes on your hands to prevent the spread of germs.
3. Wash your hands afterwards.

FIRST AID FOR COMMON INJURIES AND ACCIDENTS

WOUNDS

This is an injury which breaks the skin and which allows blood to escape from the body and germs to enter it. If germs are allowed to settle in the wound, the wound may become infected. With small cuts the bleeding will soon stop.

FIRST AID

Most small wounds heal well if you do the following soon after the injury:

1. Wash the wound with very clean (or boiled) water.
2. Wash the germs or any dirt away from the middle of the wound.
3. Dry the surrounding area.
4. Cover the wound and surrounding area with a very clean pad of cloth (not cotton wool or any fluffy material) and bandage it in place. If the wound is small you can apply antiseptic cream.
5. Wash the wound and put on a clean bandage twice a day.
6. If the wound is serious put on a bandage and take the person to the health worker.
7. If the person has not been recently immunised against Tetanus, ask the health worker for an injection against this very serious disease. (*See* Activity Sheet 6.4 on **Immunisation.**)

Objects that get stuck in wounds
1. Don't try to remove the object.
2. Bandage lightly over and around the object with a clean cloth, making sure that the wound is fully covered and protected.
3. Take the person to the health worker. They may also need a Tetanus injection.

Infected wounds
If wounds are not kept clean and dry, germs grow and cause infection. An infected wound is hot, red, swollen and very painful. Pus (a thick yellow liquid) may come out of the wound. If this happens the wound must be covered with a very clean pad and the person must go to the health worker.

Infected wounds must be treated by a health worker in order for them to heal and to prevent further illness.

NOSE BLEEDING

FIRST AID
1. Tell the injured person to sit up and breathe through the mouth.
2. Pinch the soft part of the nose for at least 10 minutes.

3. Tilt the head forward and downwards.
4. If the bleeding doesn't stop take the person to the health worker.

BURNS

Burns are very common in the home. Children and babies are often involved in accidents with burns. These are always very serious and help should be got from the health worker as soon as possible.

A burn is more serious if it covers a large area of the skin or is deep. Burns which cover a medium to large (i.e. 9%) area of the body are a threat to life, especially for very young children. Serious (large) burns will need urgent medical help as the injured person may go into shock.

FIRST AID
1. Remove the person from the source of heat. If a person's clothing is on fire, wrap them in a blanket or roll them on the ground to put out the fire.
2. **Cool the burnt area immediately** using lots of cold, clean water. It may take up to half an hour to cool the burnt area. If the burn is very large put the person into a bath of cold water.
3. **For small burns** (less than the size of a large coin or stamp):
   Keep the burnt area clean and dry and protect it with a loose bandage. If the burn is bigger than a large coin, show it to a health worker.
   For large (serious) burns:
   Cover the burnt area with a dry and very clean piece of cloth and get medical help immediately.
4. If necessary, treat for Shock. If the person is unconscious, put them in the Recovery Position.

Remember :
- **Don't** break the blisters.
- **Don't** remove any clothing which is sticking to the burnt area.
- **Don't** put grease, oil or herbs on the burn.

BROKEN BONES (FRACTURES)

A cracked or broken bone is called a fracture. There are two types of fracture:

- a **closed fracture** where you cannot see the bone;
- an **open fracture** where the bone has broken through the skin and can be seen.

It is important to keep the injured part still, in a fixed position, to prevent any further damage to the body. However, if the person is unconscious, they must FIRST be put into the Recovery Position.

FIRST AID
1. If there is serious bleeding, treat this life-threatening problem first.
2. If the person is unconscious, put them into the Recovery Position.
3. If it is an open fracture, cover the wound with a clean cloth to prevent infection.
4. **To stop the broken bone from moving:**
   - place padding made from soft cloth around the broken bone;
   - support the broken bone by bandaging it to a splint (see below) or a strong part of the body.
5. Try to raise the limb with the broken bone to prevent the limb from swelling.
6. Check for signs of Shock and treat if necessary.
7. Get medical help or transport the person to a health centre, making sure that the broken bone is well supported and cushioned.

Making splints
Splints help to stop the broken bone moving.

1. The splint is made from something which is stiff or does not bend easily. This could be cardboard, many newspapers, thin bamboo matting, etc.
2. Pad the splint with soft cloth.
3. The splint must extend beyond the injured part on either side.
4. Tie it securely with strips of cloth but not so tight as to cut off the blood supply to the injured part. (Never use string or wire!)

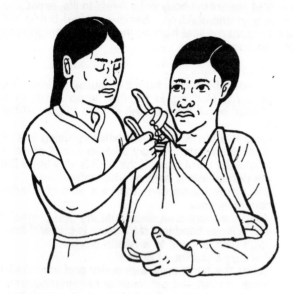

POISON
Many people, especially children, swallow dangerous poison by mistake. There are many different kinds of poison which have different effects on the body. In most cases they cause stomach pain and vomiting.

Some of the most common poisons are: kerosene and petrol; chemicals used for farming, including DDT, insect killers; medicines (any kind when too much is taken by mistake); bleach and cleaning powders; iodine; poisonous leaves and berries.

FIRST AID
1. Give the person plenty to drink, e.g. fresh water or milk. Do not give fizzy or alcoholic drinks.
2. Do not try to make the person vomit.
3. Seek the help of a health worker immediately.
4. If the person is unconscious, put them immediately into the Recovery Position and do not try to give anything to drink.

SNAKE BITES
Most snakes are not poisonous. For example, many countries in Africa have up to 100 types of snakes. No more than 10 of these are poisonous. The health centre may have medicines to treat the different kinds of poisonous snake bites.

FIRST AID
1. Lay the person down and keep them calm and still.
2. Stop the poison spreading by keeping the bitten part still. Try to keep it lower than the heart.
3. Wash the bite with water.
4. If the person becomes unconscious, put them into the Recovery Position.

5. Get the health worker to come.
6. Try to find out what the snake looked like. If possible show it to the health worker.

HEAT EXHAUSTION
A person who works and sweats a lot in hot weather may become pale and weak and perhaps feel faint. The skin is cool and moist. The pulse is rapid and weak. The person may seem confused. This is caused by dehydration. It is a very serious condition.

FIRST AID
1. Lie the person down in a cool place and raise the feet.
2. Give the person plenty to drink. The Oral Rehydration Solution is the best drink to give (see Activity Sheet 6.1).
3. If the person is unconscious put them into the Recovery Position and do not give anything to drink.

HEATSTROKE
Heatstroke is caused when the body temperature gets dangerously high. This may happen in very hot weather. The skin becomes hot and dry. The person has a very high fever and may be unconscious.

FIRST AID
1. Lower the body temperature immediately by:
   - moving the person to a cool place;
   - sponging or wiping the person with cold water and fanning him until the fever drops.
2. Get medical help immediately.

Use the same treatment for fevers.

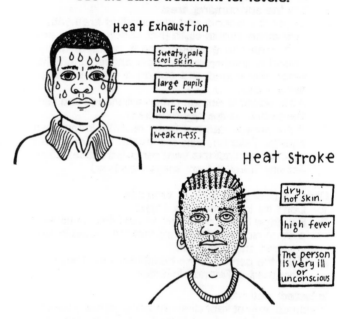

ACTIVITIES

Making a First Aid Kit

People often think that they cannot give First Aid without special First Aid equipment. This is not true. You can always give First Aid using the things you find around you.

It is however a good idea to have a First Aid kit prepared in the school or community. You can make this easily and cheaply.

> ### A Basic First Aid Kit
>
> 12 triangular bandages*
> Antiseptic cream
> Safety pins
> Cotton wool
> A torch
> Sticking plasters
> A thermometer
>
> *each made from a square
> metre of clean cloth cut in half

To make bandages the children can boil the cloth, dry it by hanging it up in the sun and parcel it in clean paper. They can make dressings by covering cotton wool with cloth to make a pad and then sewing this onto strips of cloth. All the First Aid kit can be put into a clean, air-tight container.

The children can discuss how to use this equipment to practise all the First Aid treatments they have learned. For example, in how many ways can you use the triangular bandages? To make pads to stop bleeding, to tie a support for a broken bone, to make a bandage for a wound....and many, many others.

Learning First Aid Skills

It is very important that the children practise the different First Aid treatments many times so that they will feel confident; and know what to do in a real accident. Make this practice as realistic as possible, using First Aid equipment and perhaps red paint for blood.

In learning the First Aid skills, children can:

- **Watch** someone demonstrate the different First Aid treatments one by one and **practise** each one in turn with their friends.
- **Act out different accidents** and give First Aid. Other children can say whether they gave the correct treatment, *e.g. They can pretend to fall from a tree and break their leg; to cut their arm with a knife; to be knocked unconscious by a falling coconut; to be burnt by boiling water; and many more.*
- Discuss when they would use the Shock Position and when they would use the Recovery Position. They can act out examples of each.
- **Learn how to feel a pulse** (heartbeat):
  - place the tips of the fingers gently on the inside of the wrist below the thumb and move them until they can feel the pulse. This is the blood being pumped from the heart around the body.
  - put the thumb and fingers gently around the windpipe, then take the thumb away and feel the pulse through the fingers.
- Count **how many heart beats** they have in a minute. They can run around a field and then feel their pulse. What has happened? They can try finding and counting the pulse on their friends

and adults. The children can make a chart to show their results.

- **Discuss how much blood** adults and children have in their bodies. An adult has about 4 litres of blood in their body. Small children obviously have less blood and so bleeding in them is more serious (e.g. an average sized child of 10 years would have about 3 litres). The children can measure 4 litres of water to see how much it looks like. If possible, mix in some red dye so it looks more like blood. If a person loses more than half a litre of blood it is dangerous. Try pouring half a litre of the red water on the ground to see how big a pool it makes.
- Listen to the story of Violet and Michael and **discuss the First Aid rules.**

> ### A STORY
>
> *Michael and his little sister Violet were walking to school one day, when Violet fell and cut her arm on some sharp metal. The cut was deep and a lot of blood was flowing out of it. Michael acted at once. He pressed the cut on little Violet's arm as tightly as he could, lifting it high above her head. He sent someone to get the health worker. He asked his friend to fetch him two clean cloths and told him to make one into a pad. He strapped the pad onto the arm binding it tightly with another cloth. He knew that the danger was great when the cut was deep and bright red blood was flowing fast. He had acted quickly to stop the flow of the blood.*
>
> *Violet looked very pale; Michael felt her pulse which was very fast. Her breathing was also very quick and shallow. Michael knew that she was in shock. While they waited, Michael lay Violet down with her legs raised and her injured arm well above her head. When the health worker arrived, he said, "Well done, Michael! You have saved Violet's life. You stopped the severe bleeding and you treated her for Shock."*

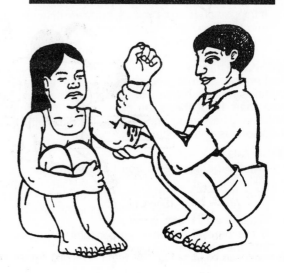

- Make up **other stories** to show the use of First Aid in different situations. Remember the rules about the **Safe Approach**, the **First Aid Priorities** and **Hygiene**. Later children can act out these stories. The stories could be about:

    - *The day my little sister burnt her hand.*
    - *Three accidents on the day of the great storm.*
    - *When baby Rajee drank kerosene.*

- **Practise how to clean wounds**, washing the germs and dirt away from the centre of the wound. Put a drop of ink onto a plate. Try to remove the ink by cleaning from the centre outwards. Remember to fold the cloth to a fresh clean piece each time to wipe the ink. It should be possible to make the plate completely clean!
- **Think of the bones** which could be broken in the body and design ways of supporting these bones. They can collect materials to make splints and practise making and strapping on splints with their friends.
- **Make a stretcher.** A stretcher is used to carry an injured or ill person. It is made usually from very strong cloth and two long poles. A home-made stretcher can be made by rolling two strong poles into the sides of a blanket.
- **Draw pictures** and **act out plays** to show the difference between heat exhaustion and heat stroke and the different ways in which to treat them.

Finding out more

The children can:

- **Do a survey** to find out what kinds of accidents people in the community have had. How many have there been? Why did they happen? What kind of First Aid was given? Was this First Aid correct? Do they know how to do it better? They can make a chart to show the results of their survey.
- **Use the survey** to make a list of all the accidents which have happened in the community and discuss ways of preventing these accidents (*see* Activity Sheet 4.1, **Preventing Accidents**.)
- **Find out the local treatment** for burns and wounds and discuss with a health worker whether these are helpful or harmful.

Passing on First Aid Skills

The children can share their important First Aid knowledge with other children, their families and communities in many ways:

- **Discuss the results of their survey** and decide on the messages and ways in which they can teach others about First Aid.
- **Make up plays, songs, posters and games** to teach about First Aid.
- **Design a First Aid test** which they and other children can take. If they don't pass the first time, they can practise and try again. Special badges can be given when children pass their First Aid test. A simpler test can be designed for the younger children. Each First Aider can always carry two clean triangular bandages with them.
- **Establish a First Aid post** in the school or community. They should keep the First Aid kit always ready.
- **Organise an Open Day** in the school or community to pass on messages about accident prevention and First Aid.

FOLLOW-UP

The children can find out:

- how many of them remember the First Aid rules;
- how many of them have used their First Aid knowledge;
- how many other children and family members have learnt some First Aid;
- if the First Aid post is being maintained and used.

USING THIS SHEET

Children can help by using their First Aid knowledge and passing it on to others. **Teachers** can include these activities in science, health and other lessons and can follow-up later to support the children in their First Aid activities. **Leaders of youth groups**, such as **Scouts**, **Guides** and **Red Cross** can use these activities and introduce First Aid tests for badges. **Health workers** can also carry out these activities with children as good First Aid treatment given by others helps them in their own work.

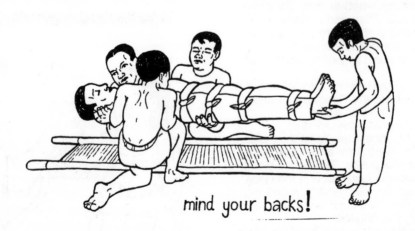

mind your backs!

This sheet can be used together with Preventing Accidents (Sheet No 4.1) and Road Safety (Sheet No 4.2).

CHILDREN WITH DISABILITIES

THE IDEA

Some children cannot walk, or run, or see, or hear, or talk as well as other children. These children are disabled. There are many reasons for this. Even if they cannot do certain things very well, they may be able to do other things as well or better than other children. By learning more about disabilities, children who are not disabled can understand some of the practical problems disabled children have. They can help children with disabilities by being friendly and playing with them.

If there is a disabled child in the group, explain to the child what you are doing and why. This child has a lot of practical experience of disability. Involve him or her as much as possible in giving information and decision-making. Your respect for his knowledge and opinion can do a great deal to build his confidence and self-esteem. Explain that the other children may laugh if they fall over or bump into things, but if they do so they are really laughing at themselves.

Although children usually behave well with a child with a disability, they can sometimes be unkind and tease or bully a child who is different in some way. They may leave him out of their games and other activities, making him feel lonely and miserable. They may be cruel because they are afraid of something they don't understand because it is different. Instead they can see what they have in common, be friends with them and share their play activities. In this way, they can help to make the life of disabled children better and enrich their own. They may gain a good friend!

Able-bodied children can be helped to understand disabled children and to include them in their activities. They can learn that disabled children are like other children in every way except for their disability. For some children the disability is slight, for others it is severe and they have difficulty doing the same things as other children of the same age. They often can do other things as well or better.

Disabled children like to laugh, they like to play, they like to have friends, and they want to learn just like other children. In fact they need to learn even more than others as their disability may prevent them from taking some types of jobs when they are older.

Where and how these activities have been used

Many countries have recognised that **children themselves** can help their disabled friends in ways that adults cannot. For this reason, special projects to rehabilitate the disabled (e.g. in **India, Mexico, Kenya**) have emphasised the Child-to-Child approach.

A very important book, *Disabled Village Children,* by David Werner, gives detailed suggestions of what can be done and equipment which can be made for and with disabled children. It includes a large section on Child-to-Child with many excellent suggestions for activities. The book draws from practical experience in a long-running community-based project for the rehabilitation of disabled children in **Mexico, Project Projimo. The** children learn to deal with disability, work together to overcome their problems and learn skills which will enable them to become as independent as possible.

DIFFERENT KINDS OF DISABILITY

Children can be disabled in several ways.

Physically disabled children often have difficulty moving about. If their legs are weak, they may have trouble walking or sitting, and may need help. Others whose arms and hands are weak may find it difficult to hold things like a cup or a pencil.

Some disabled children may be deaf or blind or have difficulty in seeing clearly or hearing well. Because deaf children cannot hear well they may also have difficulty in learning to speak. They are not "dumb" or stupid. They will learn to communicate with hearing children in many ways if hearing children make the effort to understand them. It is very important for their intellectual development that a means of communication is developed. Sign language is a very good way but every possible means of communication including gestures, speech, lip reading, body language and pictures can help.

Some children may find it difficult to learn and understand things. It may take longer for them to learn. They can learn in small steps but may need a lot of repetition.

Some children may have fits and fall to the ground and shake or appear to stare into space without seeing anything. It can be frightening to see someone with a fit, but the fit will end soon. The child is not in pain and will not die. Keep calm, and make sure that the person having the fit is safe and does not harm himself. Make sure that he cannot bang against anything that might hurt him and put something in his mouth so that he does not bite his tongue. There is no need to be afraid, the condition cannot spread from one person to another.

Children who are disabled cannot do everything like other children. But often there are certain things that they can do better, or at least as well, as the others. For example, a child who uses crutches or a wheelchair may have very strong arms and hands. A child who is blind may be very good at hearing and identifying different sounds. A child who learns very slowly may be very kind and helpful, and a good friend. If we work together we can achieve more than by ourselves. Disabled people are usually very happy to help if we ask them.

The children can do a role-play to illustrate the drawing opposite and give other similar examples.

Not all disabilities prevent people doing what they want to do, living a full life and accomplishing great things. There are many people - teachers, politicians, religious leaders, scientists, writers and many others - who have disabilities. Some artists cannot paint with their hands but use their feet or mouths instead. Some disabled people have very happy family lives and make good parents.

DID YOU KNOW

- There are Olympic Games for people with disabilities.
- An Irish boy who cannot speak has won international prizes for writing books and poetry.
- Franklin Roosevelt, who was President of the USA, had polio and could not stand without help.
- Stevie Wonder, the famous pop singer, is blind.

CAUSES OF DISABILITY

Some people are superstitious about disabilities and think that they are caused by some kind of magic. This is not true. They are not caused by witchcraft and are not a punishment for wrongdoing.

There are several main causes of disability:

- A child can be born deaf, blind or physically or mentally disabled because he did not develop properly before birth.
- Sometimes the birth of a baby is difficult and an injury may occur during the birth.
- A child can become disabled by disease, e.g. polio, measles, leprosy, whooping cough. Polio can cause paralysis, and measles can make children blind, deaf, and mentally disabled. Most diseases which cause disability can be prevented (Activity Sheet No. 6.4, **Immunisation**).
- Children are sometimes disabled by accidents. They may burn themselves, fall out of trees or injure their eyes. Road accidents can damage a child's body forever.
- Young children may become disabled if they have a poor diet and do not get enough food or the right kind of food. In severe cases, they may become blind, or their brain may not develop properly, so they become mentally disabled.

Where possible, let's prevent disability!

I CANNOT OPEN THIS JAR. COULD YOU TRY, ROBERT? YOU HAVE SUCH STRONG ARMS

ALRIGHT, I'll TRY.

HELPING THE DISABLED

If we understand the different kinds of disability, and know how they are caused, it may be easier to mix with children who have a disability and learn how to work and play with them and live better together.

Some important things to remember:

- **Give them equal chances.** Treat them as you treat any other child being as nice or as 'nasty' as you are with others. Help them to have the same chances at school and in play. Children together can discover that life is exciting and fun.

- **Help them gain confidence.** Let them take risks like other children. If they are too protected they will always be afraid.

- **Make them feel wanted.** Concentrate on what the child **can do**, not on what he cannot. For example, a blind child may be very good at singing and a physically disabled child may be very good at maths.

- **When help is needed, let the disabled child help too** with things that they can do and feel proud to have achieved. Disabled children should also have obligations just like any other children.

- **Help them to help themselves and be as independent as possible.** Don't help them with a certain job unless help is really needed. Let them do the things they can do, even if they do them slowly or not very well.

- **Include them in play activities:** children always learn faster if they are helped by the group and if their exercises are made into games. All children learn and develop through play.

This equipment makes these brothers, both with cerebral palsy, mobile. The one sitting down cannot walk, the other can only walk with some support.

A child with weak hands is often fed by someone else but might be able to feed himself with a straw or a spoon or cup that suits his hands. The children may be able to make a suitable cup or spoon.

Rubber tube

strip of tyre tube

Rubber ball

ACTIVITIES

UNDERSTANDING DISABILITIES

Children can understand better some of the practical problems of being disabled by playing some of the following games.

Experiencing Disability

Organise a game of football or tag. Before starting, tie a stick to one child's leg, so that he cannot bend his leg. Some children can try playing on one leg only (hopping). Tie a cloth over the eyes of another child so that he cannot see properly. Can he recognise voices? Can he recognise people by feeling their faces? Can they think of other ways of finding out what it feels like to be disabled?

Let several children play these games. The rest of the children can behave in different ways to those who are 'disabled'. Some help, others laugh; some are friendly, but others ignore them. The children can think of different ways to behave. They can take it in turns to 'be disabled'. How do they feel about the 'disability' and about the way the other children treat them?

Discussing Disability

Look at a picture or a photo or make a drawing of a child with a disability. Talk about disabled children, or older people, in the community. Discussions could include some of the following:

*   Who runs fastest in the class? Who jumps furthest? Why can the others not run as fast or jump as far? Everyone has limitations but sometimes they are more serious and some children can only walk with difficulty or not at all. Let the children work together to find some other limitations that they have and perhaps find ways of overcoming them together. They will see that everyone is good at some things and less good at others.

*   Do you know someone who cannot run or walk like you? Why can't he run or walk properly? Or perhaps you know someone else with another kind of disability. What kind?

*   Do other children play with this child? If not, why not? Do you? Is the child able to play some of the games, or not? Why not?

*   Do other children laugh at this child? Why? What is it like when other children laugh at you?

*   Do you like having friends? Do you like playing with other children? How would you feel if you were disabled and had no friends? Or if you were alone at home all day by yourself?

*   What can disabled children do better than you can? Can you think of a disabled person with very strong arms, or very good hearing, or a very good memory, or who can write, read or draw very well?

*   How can you make life better for children with disabilities? Make a list of things you can do.

*   Do you know of any disabled people who make a valuable contribution to your community?

*   Do you know of any disabled people who have become famous in your country?

*   What does it feel like to have a disability?

The disabled children may be better at certain things and can win certain competitions, e.g. if the child has strong arms he may be able to win a wheel-chair race. He may also be good at arm wrestling.

TAKING ACTION

Making a plan

Sometimes there is a disabled member of the community or a community worker interested in disability, who would be willing to speak to the children.

Children can discuss ways to help a disabled child to be happier and to do more things for themselves. They can list the disabled children they know, and think of ways in which they could help each one of those children. They can make a plan and then form action groups. Whenever possible, disabled children should be members and parents and teachers can help to guide these groups.

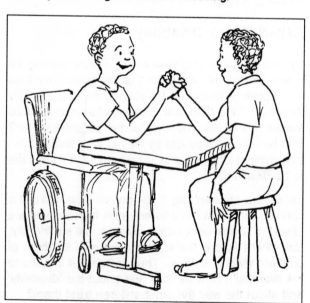

> It is **important** not to forget the disabled child after a little time, or he will feel very abandoned. If a friend becomes disabled, your friendship is even more important to both of you.

Here are some ideas for plans:

- One or more children can make friends with a disabled child, and visit him or her regularly at home, to talk and play with him or her. They can get to know the family and find ways of helping.

- Find a way of getting disabled children to school and home again, if they cannot walk or are blind.

- At school children can find out who has a disability and what kind and they can all work and play together.

- Disabled children need play and adventure like all children. Children who cannot walk can still play guessing games, cards, or singing and clapping games. Sighted children can read to children who are blind. Stronger children can take children whose legs are weak or who cannot walk swimming. They may also enjoy creating a puppet theatre and think of many other things they can do together.

- Make toys or equipment which disabled children can use, and play with them to help them get stronger. A tyre and rope, tied to a strong branch, make a good swing. Some ideas for making a back rest, a floor seat and a trolley can be found in Activity Sheet No. 6.5 about **Polio**.

- Find ways of making exercises to strengthen muscles, to improve hearing, to improve learning and memory into games. Play and doing are the best ways of learning and disabled children will learn faster if the exercises they must do are made into games or useful tasks which can be done at home.

- Give disabled children plenty of encouragement. Listen to them. Give them time to do things. Like all children, they must learn to help themselves. The more independent we become, the happier we are.

Helping children with severe disabilities

Some children have very severe disabilities. They cannot move around or take part in all games. They may like to hear stories, or just have someone touch them and hold their hands. Remember that when children cannot speak or think well it can be difficult to know what they are feeling. They may be lonely and unhappy, and need friends who will visit, laugh with them, talk and play. Severely disabled children may be very intelligent but their intelligence will not develop unless they are stimulated and given the opportunity from an early age. Ways of enabling them to go to school can completely change their lives.

Many children who cannot talk or move well are very intelligent and can think, feel and understand as well or better than other children. Try and find out what they want by looking at them, listening to them and taking notice of them.

Little children with problems

A little child may have a weak back or legs and find it difficult to sit, walk or crawl. Older children can help him to learn through play. For example, if a child cannot crawl, two children can help support the child's weight while he crawls by putting a cloth under him.

Another child can encourage the little child to crawl by holding out a toy or fruit. Play the game every day, so that the little child's arm and leg muscles get stronger and perhaps one day the child will crawl without any help.

FOLLOW-UP

If children have started a project with a disabled child, plenty of time is needed. Once each month, or every two months, the children can discuss:

- what they have been doing;
- what things have worked well;
- what difficulties they have found;
- how they are trying to solve those difficulties.

If they are not doing a special project, they can discuss how they are trying to change the way they think and act towards children with disabilities, both at school and in the community. Disabled children can join in or lead the group discussions.

This sheet can be used together with Sheet No. 6.5, **Polio** and Sheet No. 5.2, **Helping Children Who Do Not See and Hear Well**.

USING THIS SHEET

Teachers can:

- help by giving **all** children an equal chance of learning.
- help children to make a list of those who are disabled and think of the ways to include them in their activities so that they can overcome their difficulties and play together. They could play all the games from the Child-to-Child activity sheets together.
- supervise the play activities of children, to make sure that they include disabled children and that they are sensitive to the feelings of those who are disabled.
- work with parents and health and community workers to help older children to carry out an 'action plan' to include the disabled in all their activities.
- set up groups for parents, teachers, health workers and community workers.

Disabled people themselves can help. They may have their own ideas about what should be done.

Community workers and teachers should find out where there are disabled children who are left alone or ignored at home. The other children can contact them and find ways of playing with them and including them in their activities.

Helping Children Who Do Not See or Hear Well

THE IDEA

Some children cannot see or hear as well as others. If this is discovered early, we can do a lot to overcome the problem. Therefore it is very important to find out if children can see and hear well while they are still young. There are different ways of doing this.

Other children can help to find out whether a child sees and hears properly, and learn to do a lot to help those with sight or hearing problems. **Together** they can overcome their difficulties.

Children who **do not hear or see properly** will not learn as quickly as other children. Sometimes, we do not realise what is wrong with such children. We do not know that they are having difficulties because they do not tell others. They may not even know themselves what the problem is.

Babies who **do not hear** will not learn to talk or understand as early as others so their development may be slower than that of other children. However, if we can communicate with the child in other ways, he will be able to develop more normally. Children with hearing problems may appear shy and quiet and prefer to be alone.

Sometimes **children who do not hear well** seem to be naughty because they do not understand what to do. They do not always respond to sounds or voices. They may fail to answer questions or come when their name is called.

Children who cannot see properly may seem to ignore their friends. They may stumble or fall (*see* Sheet No.3.2, **Looking after Our Eyes**). They may not notice holes in the ground and so trip over.

Understanding what it feels like to have problems hearing and seeing. One way of getting children to think about problems of seeing and hearing is to ask questions like:

* Do you know anyone who does not see or hear well? How do they behave? Are their other senses more developed?
* Do you act differently with these people? What do you do?
* How do you think you would feel if you did not see well? or hear well?
* How many people in your community do not see well? or hear well?

It is very important that children who see and hear well play and learn with those who do not!

Where and how these activities have been used

Children with seeing and hearing difficulties are far more common than we think. Once we know that they exist we can often help the children to lead a normal life. But we must identify these children first.

Many people have criticised the activities in this sheet (although all of them have been developed with children in the field, e.g. in **Mexico** and **Mozambique**). They say children are not doctors or health workers and cannot measure properly. This is not the point. If children (or their teachers) can identify some of their friends who **may** need help, then the health worker can test them more thoroughly and help those who really do have difficulties. If no one cares and no one tries to find out, then no one is helped.

That children should be able to recognise when help from a health worker is needed is a basic principle both of Child-to-Child and primary health care.

We use all our senses to help us understand the world around us. If, however, one of our senses is not working properly, we have to rely on our other senses. Children can play the following games to help them understand the difficulties of children who do not see well and how we can use a different sense when one is not working properly. They can also invent some themselves.

They can play a game in which one child is blindfolded and then tries to recognise his friends by feeling them. A blindfolded child could also try to find his way from one place to another. Let him describe how he feels. Which sense is not working here? Which sense is being used now? Is it as good?

Another game can show how important both hearing and seeing are to us. Children of all ages stand in a circle. One child stands in the middle with his eyes covered. Around his feet are small stones or other objects. Some of the other children try to creep up and steal these objects without being heard. If the child in the middle hears the 'thief' and points to him, the thief has to go out of the game. If a child seems to have more difficulty hearing the 'thief' than the other children, she may have a hearing problem and should see a health worker.

HELPING CHILDREN WHO CANNOT HEAR WELL

Understanding Deafness

Other games can help children realise how difficult it is if one cannot hear well.

* Have one child cover his ears while another tells a funny story to the group in a very quiet voice. One child can pretend to be a teacher, and ask all the children to answer questions about the story. Can the child whose ears are covered answer the questions? How does he feel? Ask him to talk about how he felt when the others laughed.

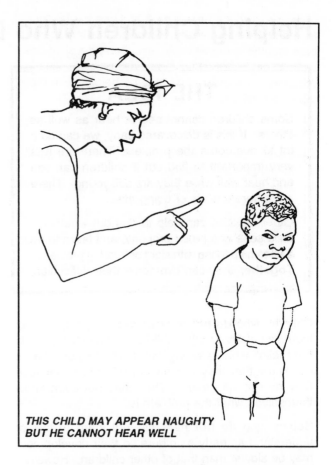

THIS CHILD MAY APPEAR NAUGHTY BUT HE CANNOT HEAR WELL

* Get children to read each other's lips. One child can tell a story in a very quiet voice. The others can sit about one metre from him with hands over their ears. How much of the story did they 'read' from watching his lips?
* Let the children talk about all the sounds they can hear around them. Then let them cover their ears. What can they hear now? How do they feel about it?
* Get the children to make up a sign language. Let them pretend that their partner is deaf and take turns each to use signs to ask for something in the room.

A game for observing if children hear well. Older children can help to find out how well children can hear by playing a game with the younger ones. Let young children about to enter school stand in a semicircle. An older child stands by each younger one. Each older child has a pencil and paper. Another older child stands at the centre of the semicircle. He should be several metres from the younger ones. He then calls out the name of an animal very loudly. Each younger child whispers the name to his helper who writes it down. This is repeated with the names of ten or more animals. Each time the older child says a name, his voice gets quieter, until he is whispering. When the list is finished, the helpers compare their lists to see what the younger children have heard.

If any child hears fewer names than the others, he **may** have a hearing problem. Let him sit in the front of the class where he can **hear** and **see** the teacher's face and the board easily. However, it is important to note that this is not a proper test. Even, if a child does seem to get all the list right, he may still have a hearing problem. The older child may be helping him more than he realises.

Recognise the Signs

Here are some signs which can tell us if a young child is having difficulty hearing:

- He makes normal noises as a baby, but does not learn to speak as he gets older.
- He does not notice voices or noises if he does not see where they are coming from.
- He seems to be disobedient, or is the last person to obey an order or a request.
- He's eyes look cloudy, the ears are infected or liquid or pus is coming out.
- He watches people's lips when they are talking;
- He turns his head in one direction in order to hear;
- He speaks rather loudly and not very clearly; .
- Sometimes he may appear to be quiet and perhaps rude and prefers to be alone;
- He may not do as well at school as he should.

A child who behaves in this way may need help. Young children can be severely deaf without it being recognised and older children can be slightly deaf without it being recognised. What can we do to help them? We need to find ways to meet their needs.

Like any other child, the deaf one learns by watching others and copying what they do. When they are included in family activities, they learn as quickly as other children. If deaf children are left alone, they will not learn.

Children who are born deaf, or who become severely deaf when they are very young, have great difficulty in learning to speak. They cannot hear speech sounds, and so they are not able to copy the sounds. However, some children learn to understand people's speech by watching their lips (lipreading). Others learn to communicate with hand and body signs. Some people make the mistake of thinking that these children who cannot speak are dumb. This is not necessarily so. **Many deaf children are as intelligent as any other children and can learn to speak very well if given the right help.**

Many deaf children can hear *some* sounds. These children can learn to speak more easily if they are helped.

There are a number of ways that older children can be of help to other children who cannot hear properly:

- If they **notice signs of deafness or infection** in the ears of the younger children in the family, they can tell parents, teachers or health workers.
- They can find out how well younger children can hear.
- They can **communicate** with deaf children by learning some sign language or by speaking slowly and directly to deaf children so that they can lipread.

- They can think of ways to **include** children who are deaf in their games and activities.
- They can **understand** that the deaf child can often do as much and sometimes more than children who hear well but that there are some things which the deaf child will find very difficult.

Noticing Deafness

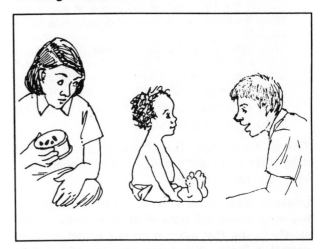

Use this test for young children who do not speak. Sit the child on the ground. Stand about one metre behind him so that he cannot see you. Use a rattle (like seeds in a tin) and gently shake it, first to one side of his head and then the other. Have another child sit in front of him, to check his reaction. If the baby's eyes or head do not move to follow the sound, he may have difficulty hearing.

It is also possible to test in the same way by:

- tapping or stirring a spoon or bowl;
- making a snake hissing sound;
- calling the baby's name softly.

These different sounds have different pitches and the child may only reply to some or them. This means he can only hear certain sounds. Can the baby hear the sound at all? How close do we have to be before he can hear the sound? Can he hear it when it is a gentle noise, or does the sound have to be very loud before he can hear it?

There is another test we can use for children who can understand some words. Gather together a number of things around the house - like a bowl, cup, spoon, some fruit, a toy. Check to make sure the child knows the names of these things. Then sit about one metre away from the child, with your back to him so that he cannot see your lips moving as you talk. Ask him in a normal voice to give you the objects, one after another. Can he hear you ask for the cup, the bowl, the spoon? This is one way of finding out if children are hearing, or if they are lipreading in order to understand what is being said to them.

Remember: Never rely on just one test. Try again on another day in order to make sure. Maybe the child was tired. If a child is not hearing well, he should be taken to a health worker for a thorough check-up.

How well do babies hear? Children can help to find out how well the babies in the family can hear:

- They can play games with their baby brothers and sisters. For example, they can make a rattle from seeds or small stones. They can creep up quietly behind the baby and shake the rattle gently or make a quiet sound (but one that **they** can hear easily). They should not stand right behind the baby but at an angle of about 45°. Does the baby turn its head and look towards the sound?
- They can call out the baby's name from different places in the room. If the baby does not seem surprised, or does not turn his head towards the noise, he is probably not hearing well. He may need to be taken to the health worker to have his hearing properly checked.

Talk to the mother. Does the mother feel that her baby does not always hear what is happening or when she calls his name?

Looking after baby's ears. Older children can regularly check the ears of smaller brothers and sisters to see that there is no pus or dirt or small objects in them. If they see anything wrong, they should tell an older person who should take the child to a health worker for help.

Children Can Help

Older children can be very helpful to younger ones who are having difficulty hearing. They can help them **to hear**; they can help them **to speak**, and **to communicate** in other ways with family and friends.

Very few people are completely deaf. There is almost always some hearing left, and it should be used. It is often difficult to know how much a deaf child, especially a baby, is able to hear. So it is important to give him plenty of practice in listening to different sounds, and to people speaking to him.

Hearing games for children to play. Children may think of games to play with babies such as:

- singing songs to babies and teaching them to young children;
- telling stories and changing the voice to sound like different people in the story; some may be soft, others loud, others angry.

Older children can help a young baby start to listen for sounds. Sit the baby on your knees and sing into the ear, play music, speak loudly and clearly. Do this several times each day. Don't give up if at first the baby does not seem to notice the sound. Keep on trying. Repeat the sounds which the child reacts to.

Older children can play games with the young child, to encourage him to try and speak. Take some familiar objects - only two to begin with. Hold one up and say its name. Put it in the child's hand and then say the name twice gently in his ear. Encourage the deaf child to say the word if he is able. Praise any attempt he makes to speak, even if it is not clear. Let him try again. Do not force him to speak. If he can, he will do it in his own time.

Communicating with Others. Sometimes the deaf child is angry and seems naughty (he may cry and scream) because he does not understand others, or they do not understand him. Always be patient. This is particularly important for children with almost no hearing.

Brothers and sisters often understand the deaf child better than his parents, and can help him communicate with those around him, by talking, signing and lipreading.

Talking. Older children can help others to remember the rules for talking with children who have difficulty hearing:

- Put the child at the front of the class.
- Talk to the deaf child as much as possible.
- Use a good, clear voice.
- When talking to a deaf child, stand or sit so that he can see your face and lips so that he can lipread.
- Always show pleasure when a deaf child uses his voice, and praise any attempt at speech, even if it is not correct.
- Use signs when necessary, but do not stop talking to the child at the same time.
- Use short, simple sentences.
- Change the word, if he does not understand.

Using signs. Encourage other children in the family to make up signs to represent the words he needs. Everyone in the family can learn them. When using signs, always speak at the same time so that the child can learn to lipread the words.

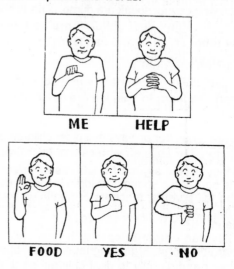

Make up a sign language

Lipreading. Some deaf people lipread very well. Others find it very difficult. Some words are easier to lipread than others. All deaf children should be given the chance to lipread. Make sure that they can see your face and lips when you are speaking to them. This allows them to see the expression on your face and the shape the lips are forming.

Here are some games older children can play with others who have difficulty hearing. Do not spend more than ten minutes with a game, as the child will get tired.

- Point to yourself and say your name. Point to the child and say his name. Do this many times during the day. Ask another helper to say·the names with you, while pointing to the right person. Let the child join in.

- Give the child different objects to give to other people, saying, 'Give the cup to Robert!' Similarly you can ask the deaf child to throw a ball to different children whose names are called out by an older child.

Make Toys and Play Games

Older children can make toys for deaf children and teach them the names of the toys. They can make a book of pictures pasted on cloth so that the deaf child can begin to learn the names and say them.

It is very important that older children think of games that deaf children can play with them. Never leave a deaf child out of play activities. Take turns in talking and singing songs to a deaf child. **Remember, he can only learn by watching and copying what we do. If he is left alone, he cannot learn.** You must go on and on helping him, until he learns.

Find Out and Discuss

Ask the children to find out if anyone is having hearing problems at home, in the community, in the school. How old are they? How did they become deaf? How do they communicate with others? What things can they do well?

The children can discuss ways of protecting their ears and their hearing. They can learn to watch for the warning signs, like ears that are sore and infected. They can learn to prevent young children pushing sticks and other dangerous things like seeds and stones in their ears. Like our eyes and our teeth, our ears are very precious.

HELPING CHILDREN WHO CANNOT SEE WELL

A child who does not see well can understand what is happening around him if others take the time to explain to him.

THIS CHILD MAY APPEAR STUPID BUT HE CANNOT SEE WELL

Recognising the Signs
The child:
- bumps into things and falls easily.
- has difficulty in reading far or close objects.
- has difficulty writing in straight lines.
- has difficulty threading needles.
- holds books very close to his face when reading and sometimes has tears.
- may complain of headaches or itchy eyes.
- fails to catch balls when playing.
- wears clothes inside out.
- arranges items incorrectly.
- brings the wrong objects when asked to bring something.

How can you teach children to understand children who cannot see well?

Blindfold the children
- partially
- completely
- only one eye

and ask them to read from the board or explain a poster on the wall. Then ask them to feel objects, smell, taste and listen to conversations.

Let them talk about their experiences after they have removed the blindfold. What did it feel like? Could they rely on their other senses? What could they not do or did they find it difficult to do when they could not see well? How could they help someone who did not see well? What did they want to happen when they were blindfolded?

Checking children's eyesight. Older children can help to make an eye chart.

Each child can make an 'E' shape of the right measurement and glue it onto the chart. It is very important to give each 'E' the correct shape. It should be black on a light background and each 'leg' of the 'E' should be the same size and the same size as the spaces between the 'legs'. The teacher can make a stencil of the right size. The children can then make another 'E' out of cardboard or other stiff material. First let the children test each other. Hang the chart where the light is good. Make a line on the ground, six metres from the chart. The child being tested stands behind this line with the large cardboard 'E'.

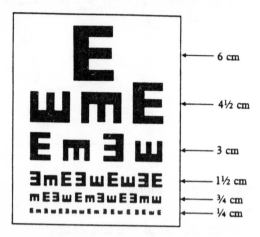

Each eye is tested separately while the other eye is carefully covered. Another child points to the shapes on the chart. The child should point to the larger letters first and then to smaller and smaller letters. The child being tested must hold up his 'E' in the same direction as the one being pointed to by his friend.

When the children know how to give the test, help them think of ways to give the test to young children especially those who will soon be going to school. At school, the children in higher grades can test the sight of those in the lower grades.

How can we help someone who does not see well?

- Let children sit in front of the class.
- Refer any child who does not seem to see well to a health worker.

- If necessary and possible, get the child glasses.
- A child who sees well can read with the child who does not see well and they can work together.
- Encourage children who do not see well to use their other senses, i.e. hearing, smell, taste, touch.

FOLLOW-UP

Find out if the children understand what it feels like not to see well or not to hear properly. Ask them to say what it feels like either in a story, a play or a poem.

Can they remember the signs which tell us that a child may be having difficulty seeing or hearing? What can they do if they see these signs?

Ask one child to tell the others what he would do if he found a baby at home who did not see or hear well.

Ask the children if they know anyone in their families or communities who cannot see or hear well. Are they doing anything to help? What are they doing? Do they think that these people are stupid or do they understand that it is more difficult for them to understand what is happening?

Have any of them been able to help a younger child who is deaf? Let them tell a story about what they have done, and discuss it with the others.

USING THIS SHEET

Teachers and youth leaders may be the first to notice that a child in the classroom is not seeing or hearing properly. They can encourage children to identify other children who may have difficulty hearing and include them in their activities. They can pass on some of the ideas suggested here to children through group activities at school or in club meetings. Mathematics teachers can help in making the 'E' shapes.

Headmaster and teachers can do a great deal to encourage parents to send such children to school and to teach other children to find ways of helping them and including them in their activities.

Health and community workers, parents, scout and guide leaders have a special responsibility for those who are deaf or have difficulty seeing. They should encourage such children to go to school and other children to include them in their activities.

Children can tell teachers, parents and other relatives about friends who have weak hearing or eyesight. All children can learn to understand and help children who do not see and hear well and behave towards them as they would to any other child. They can make sure that they include them in their games and make them feel part of the group.

CARING FOR CHILDREN WITH DIARRHOEA

THE IDEA

Diarrhoea is dangerous because it can both kill and cause malnutrition. It can be prevented by **keeping clean, using clean water** and by **eating properly.** Children who get diarrhoea may die because they become **dehydrated,** that is, their bodies lose too much water. The liquid they lose must be put back in their bodies. A **Special Drink** can be made by children to help replace the lost water when a child has diarrhoea and prevent dehydration.

What is Diarrhoea?

Diarrhoea means frequent, watery stools. Often children with diarrhoea also vomit and have severe pains in the abdomen or tummy. The stools may smell strongly and also pass noisily. Diarrhoea is caused by swallowing germs which can live in dirty food and water and human or animal stools. The body tries to get rid of the bad germs from the body through the diarrhoea.

Diarrhoea is Dangerous

Children who have diarrhoea lose a lot of water, especially if they are vomiting and have a fever. Children may die of diarrhoea, usually because they lose too much water and salts from their bodies and nobody helps them to drink. This loss of water and salts is called **dehydration.** The family should understand that the water lost in diarrhoea needs to be quickly replaced.

What to Do When a Child Has Diarrhoea

Act immediately! Do not wait for signs of severe dehydration.

We can prevent serious dehydration occurring by doing the following:

* Give the child plenty to drink to replace the water that is lost, as soon as the diarrhoea starts;
* Give the child enough food to keep him/her strong.

What Are the Signs of Dehydration?

The child is thirsty, or may appear irritable, restless or half-asleep. The mouth and tongue become dry and there are few tears when the child cries. Eyes appear sunken and when the skin is pinched, it returns to normal slowly.

These signs only appear if the child becomes **very dehydrated** from diarrhoea. **A child with these signs is in great danger.**

Take the child to a health worker if any of these danger signs of dehydration begin or if the diarrhoea lasts more than two days. Keep giving the child liquids (the Special Drink is best) while going to the health centre.

Where and how these activities have been used

Diarrhoea and dehydration are still widespread causes of infant and child mortality and this information which can save lives is therefore of crucial importance. It not only saves lives but helps the children and the community realise how much **children** can do to promote health.

Programmes all over the world use the activities in different ways. This activity sheet and the Child-to-Child reader, *A Simple Cure,* are used very widely.

Often before we can act, we need to **find out:**

- how local communities treat diarrhoea in children, e.g. do they continue to breastfeed?
- what rehydration drinks are locally available (e.g. rice water and tea) and which can be used?
- what local medical advice is given?

When these are known it is easier for children to take action. For this reason many programmes encourage **surveys** by children to find out not only how serious the problem is but also how messages can best be spread.

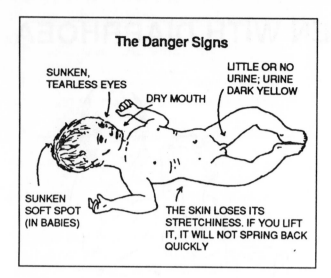

The Danger Signs

SUNKEN, TEARLESS EYES

LITTLE OR NO URINE; URINE DARK YELLOW

DRY MOUTH

SUNKEN SOFT SPOT (IN BABIES)

THE SKIN LOSES ITS STRETCHINESS. IF YOU LIFT IT, IT WILL NOT SPRING BACK QUICKLY

How Can Diarrhoea Be Prevented?

Diarrhoea can be prevented by:

- keeping ourselves and our surroundings clean;
- eating properly, so the child grows well;
- using clean water.

Keeping Clean (*see* also Activity Sheet 3.3)

> **BY KEEPING CLEAN, WE CAN PREVENT DIARRHOEA**

Dirt, rubbish, stools and urine contain germs which can cause diarrhoea. These germs can be carried by flies as well as on dirty hands. Keep these germs away from food and drinking water.

Wash your hands:

- after using the latrine;
- after cleaning children who have urinated or defaecated;
- before cooking or eating;
- before feeding children.

Remember to wash the children's hands too. The children can discuss why this is necessary.

Use a latrine. If there is none, make sure that the whole family passes stools far from the house and far from any water. Stools passed near the house should be taken away and buried.

Remember! Small children's stools are more dangerous than adults' stools.

Healthy Food (see also Activity Sheet 2.1)

Breastmilk is the best food for babies and helps to prevent infections, including diarrhoea. Breastfeed babies for as long as possible. Dirty feeding bottles cause diarrhoea.

When they are about four to six months old, all babies should begin to take other foods, as well as breastmilk. Soft mashed foods, like porridge and fruits, given frequently are best.

The food we eat should be fresh and prepared in a clean place, using clean pots and utensils. Cooked food should be eaten while hot. If it needs reheating, it should be well heated before it is eaten.

Keep flies away from food and always wash your hands carefully before handling and eating food. Wash food in clean water before cooking or eating it.

Clean Water (see also Activity Sheet 3.4)

Make sure water for drinking is clean. Take it from the cleanest possible source. Keep it in a clean, covered container, and use this water for drinking and cooking only.

Keep the source of water clean. Keep animals away. People should not spit, throw rubbish or wash themselves or their clothes near the place where people get their drinking water. Never urinate or defaecate in or near water.

Treating Diarrhoea

1. Plenty of Fluids

The most important thing is to be sure that the child drinks as much liquid as he loses, from the time the diarrhoea starts. Rehydration is putting back into the child's body the water that has been lost because of the diarrhoea and vomiting.

Giving lots of liquid to a child with diarrhoea may at first increase the amount of diarrhoea. This is all right. Most of the fluid will still be absorbed and the body is trying to get rid of the germs in the diarrhoea. A child with diarrhoea needs one cup/ glass of liquid (small glass for a small child) each time he/she passes a loose stool.

CHILD
ONE GLASS EACH STOOL

ADULT
TWO GLASSES EACH STOOL

2. Continue Feeding

Sometimes mothers stop giving food to a child who has diarrhoea. This is a mistake. The sick child needs food so that he has enough strength to fight the illness. Breastmilk is the safest and best food for babies. Encourage older children to take their usual food, several times each day. Be patient. Sick children need to be encouraged to eat. (*See* Activity Sheets 6.2, **Caring for Children Who Are Sick** and 2.1, **Feeding Young Children: Healthy Food**.)

3. Medicines

Medicines are not important for most cases of children with diarrhoea and in all cases are less important than fluids and food. NEVER give medicine without the advice of a health worker. Anything that puts water back into the child helps to fight dehydration, e.g.:

- many of the herbal teas and soups that mothers give to children;
- mother's breastmilk which gives the child both food and water. It is important to continue breastfeeding a baby with diarrhoea. (Milk in a bottle is never as good as breastmilk.);
- rice water (the water in which rice has been boiled) or any other liquid in which food has been cooked, with a little salt, is an excellent liquid for preventing dehydration;
- any other liquid drink, e.g. coconut water, lime or lemon water, diluted fruit juice, weak tea or soups.

The Special Drink

The best liquid is a **Special Drink**, called **Oral Rehydration Solution**. This drink can be made from packets of oral rehydration salts, available from health centres and sometimes shops. However, children can easily make the Special Drink themselves using salt, sugar and clean water and so help to treat diarrhoea in younger children and babies.

Making the Special Drink

The **Special Drink** is very easy to make. For one glass at a time:

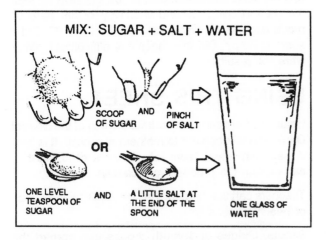

MIX: SUGAR + SALT + WATER

A SCOOP OF SUGAR   AND   A PINCH OF SALT

OR

ONE LEVEL TEASPOON OF SUGAR   AND   A LITTLE SALT AT THE END OF THE SPOON

ONE GLASS OF WATER

For larger quantities, mix FIVE to EIGHT level teaspoonfuls of sugar, plus ONE level teaspoonful of salt with ONE LITRE of clean water. (A teaspoon is a small spoon that holds not more than 5 ml of water.) In your community, it may be easier to make smaller quantities than a litre at a time. The children can consult their teacher/health worker to see what quantity is normally used locally.

If it is too salty, then throw it away, and make the drink again, using less salt. Make just enough for 24 hours. Next day, throw away any that is left over and make some more if necessary.

Ways of measuring the Special Drink may be a bit different from place to place. The children can find out from the health worker how mothers are taught to make the Special Drink. How do they measure the water, sugar and salt?

How to Give the Special Drink

The **Special Drink** must be given as soon as the diarrhoea starts, that is, as soon as the stools are watery. Give a little at a time in sips from the glass or from a spoon. Even if the child does not want it, or spits, gently insist, and persuade him to drink it all, a little at a time. Even if a child vomits, wait ten minutes, then try again. The amount he vomits will be less than you have given him. Let the child rest after every five sips if he wants to. This may take some time, day and night, and older children can help their mother by taking turns during the night.

How Much?

The drink should be given each time a stool is passed. A child under two should have half a glass each time. An older child requires a full glass each time. An adult needs two glasses each time. Continue giving the **Special Drink** as long as the stools are even a bit watery. Do not stop until both urine and stools are normal. This may take 1 or 2 days or even longer.

ACTIVITIES

Children can collect information about diarrhoea and how common and dangerous it is. How many times have their younger brothers and sisters had diarrhoea in the last year (or during the last rainy season, or since some big festival)? They can find out at what ages it is most common by counting how many times children of different ages had diarrhoea.

They can see how often breastfed babies and bottlefed babies get diarrhoea. Which get diarrhoea the most? Why?

How many children in the community have died of diarrhoea? This information can be used later to help decide if different health activities have made a difference to children's health.

Children Can Experiment

1. Carry out an experiment with two cut flowers or plants. Put one in a container of water and leave the other without water. Ask the children why the plant without water has died. Water is necessary for life, and plants - and people - cannot live without it.

2. The children can bring a small, hollow gourd to school. (If no gourd is available, an old ball, plastic bottle or anything similar will do.) Draw a mouth and some eyes on the gourd (see illustration).

Make a hole in the top of the gourd, and a small hole with a plug in the bottom. Fill it with water and cover the opening at the top with a small, thin, damp cloth. Then pull the plug out and let the children notice how the cloth sags into the hole. Discuss how this compares with the head of a baby with diarrhoea.

3. Mark a line on the hollow gourd (or whatever was used). Water should never fall below this line, or else the gourd will be too empty. For a person, this means dehydration and death. As long as just as much water is put back as that which is lost, the water level will not go down (so the child will not get dehydrated). A child with diarrhoea needs one glass of liquid each time he passes a loose stool.

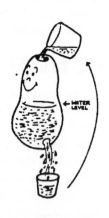

Children Can Learn to Make the Special Drink

The children can prepare the Special Drink, and then drink some of it to check that it is no saltier than tears.

Children Can Work in the Community

The children can demonstrate their 'diarrhoea dolls'. They can make up plays and puppet dramas about diarrhoea and how to care for a child with diarrhoea. They can also invent songs and stories, and make posters showing how to prepare the Special Drink. They can discuss where to show them to help others learn how to make and use the Special Drink.

FOLLOW-UP

Discuss with the children how much they have learned.
- Do they think they have been able to help the community?
- Have other people in the community learned some of the same information?
- Have many of the children used what they know in the home and the community?
- Do fewer babies and children suffer and die from diarrhoea as a result of this activity?

Counts can be made each month, after six months and after a year to see, for example:

- how many children - or their mothers - have made the Special Drink for those with diarrhoea;
- how many cases of diarrhoea there have been in the children's families;
- whether any children in the community have died of diarrhoea.

Is there a difference between babies who are bottlefed and those who are breastfed?

Ask children who have used the Special Drink for another child with diarrhoea to tell the story to their friends, explaining how and when they (or their parents) made and used it. How long did they give it? Did it seem to help? Did they have any difficulties? What were the results?

USING THIS SHEET

Health workers can demonstrate the use of the Special Drink, and talk about it to mothers at clinics. It is best if they themselves have rehydrated a child, so they can explain the process very clearly.

Teachers can teach about the Special Drink in science or health lessons.

Scouts, Guides and youth groups can spread the knowledge about preventing dehydration, and, if it does occur, how to treat it quickly.

Children can make the Special Drink and help feed it to sick brothers and sisters.

This sheet should be read together with Sheets No 3.3, **Children's Stools and Hygiene** and 3.4, **Clean, Safe Water.**

CARING FOR CHILDREN WHO ARE SICK

THE IDEA

When some young children are ill, they need someone with them most of the time, to comfort them, to care for them, to wash them, to give them food and drinks, and, as they get better, to play with them and to keep them occupied and happy. Mother does all this best. Older children can help. They can also do some of the household work to give their mother more time to be with the sick child.

There are a number of ways an older child can help a younger brother or sister who is ill:

- by sitting with the sick child and keeping him company;
- by comforting and caring for him;
- by keeping the sick child clean;
- by playing with him;

and by knowing what to do for particular symptoms, such as fever, difficult breathing, vomiting and diarrhoea.

Companionship

Young children who are sick need someone with them, if possible, all the time, to provide reassurance and to help every time they need anything.

Comfort

A sick child is unhappy, sometimes because he is in pain, or because he is frightened, often without really knowing why. A caring brother or sister will be able to find out what the sick child needs and comfort him by touch and word. You can do things for him which he may not be able to do for himself, to help him through his illness - make him comfortable in bed, keep him warm, or cool, protect him from bright light, keep off flies or just keep quiet so he can sleep.

Drinks

A sick child needs to drink a lot, about two pints of liquid a day. This can be cold water, milk, weak tea, fruit juice or soup. If there is diarrhoea, the Special Drink is best (*see* Sheet No 6.1, **Caring for Children**

Where and how these activities have been used

This activity is particularly concerned with older children helping younger ones - and **all** older children have a right and duty to know the main contents of this sheet. But it is also important to know how sick children are looked after in the community. In some communities adults may have ideas about treating sick children which are quite different from those in this sheet.

Ask the following questions (the answers are in the sheet):

- If a child has a high fever, do you (i) cover her up with blankets, or (ii) try to keep her cool?
- If a sick child wants to eat, do you (i) keep her drinking liquids only until the fever has passed, or (ii) encourage her to eat soft foods?

with Diarrhoea). Small drinks offered often may be the best way to persuade a child to drink the amount he needs.

Food

Although sick children usually do not want to eat, they need food just as much as when they are well. Encourage them to eat by offering them things they like, and can easily swallow. It will be easier if you give them small amounts more often. Soft foods like mashed bananas, rice or porridge, which do not need to be chewed, are best. Patient, regular spoon-feeding will give the sick child strength through the illness.

Cleanliness

Sick children are more comfortable if you wash them regularly with soap and water, or just wipe them with a damp cloth, and put clean clothes on. Every time they vomit or have diarrhoea they need to be thoroughly cleaned and comforted.

Play

As sick children begin to recover, they need to be kept interested and happy. An older brother or sister can read or tell stories, sing songs and play games with them.

Particular Symptoms

Fever

A child with fever needs to be kept cool by being uncovered, fanned and wiped with a damp cloth. As he cools down, he needs to be lightly covered again.

Difficult breathing

Young children often get ill with colds and coughs which get better after a few days. If the breathing becomes difficult, noisy or quick, this is a sign of a more serious illness, and you must get help without delay from a doctor or health worker.

Vomiting

Children often vomit when they are ill. Sometimes coughing makes them vomit. When they vomit, clean them, and change their clothes if necessary. Then give a small drink. If a child goes on vomiting, put him to lie on his side to reduce the risk of his choking on the vomit. A child who vomits again and again should be taken to a health worker.

Asking for help

Whenever you are looking after a sick child, you must be sure to get help if the illness seems to get worse. Watch especially for fever, vomiting, bad diarrhoea, quick breathing or increasing drowsiness. Find out where to go for help.

Diarrhoea

Any child who is ill may have some diarrhoea with loose stools. This needs no special diet, only the regular food and drinks already described. More serious diarrhoea with frequent watery stools must have immediate treatment with the Special Drink of sugar and salt in water (*see* Sheet No 6.1, **Caring for Children with Diarrhoea**), and the child should be taken to a doctor or health worker.

Give the drink a little at a time, and make sure that the sick child drinks one glass of Special Drink for each stool he passes. Keep on giving the Special Drink until the stools are normal. This may take more than one day.

MIX: SUGAR + SALT + WATER

A SCOOP OF SUGAR AND A PINCH OF SALT

OR

ONE LEVEL TEASPOON OF SUGAR AND A LITTLE SALT AT THE END OF THE SPOON

ONE GLASS OF WATER

ACTIVITIES

Children can discuss

Ask children how it feels to be sick: When were you ill? How did you feel? What did others do for you? What did you want most of all when you were sick? What made you feel good when you were sick?

Children can experiment and observe

One of the children can run around until she is hot. Then she can be wrapped up tightly in a cloth or blanket for some time, including the back of her head. Ask the child how she feels now. Then uncover her so that the body heat can escape.

> **It is not good for a child with a fever to be wrapped up tightly in too many blankets or clothes**

Food can be mashed and passed down a tube of bamboo or through a narrow-necked bottle. Let the children see how soft food goes down easily, whereas hard and lumpy food sticks.

> **A child who is sick can swallow soft food without working hard to chew it, and the soft food goes down more readily**

Let them discuss the illnesses of younger brothers and sisters. Who looked after the sick child? Were the older children able to help in any way? What do you think they **could** have done to care for the younger child? Is the mother happy to have help from the older children?

If the children have already discussed the signs or symptoms of illness (*see* **Looking After Our Eyes** (3.2), **Caring for Children with Diarrhoea** (6.1), **Polio** (6.5), **Coughs, Colds, Pneumonia** (6.7)), they can ask each other questions to see how much they remember. They can discuss the various symptoms, and tell how they can help a young child who has those symptoms to feel more comfortable.

Children can practise

A child who is hot from running can be wiped with a damp cloth, to show how it cools the hot body. Children can be shown the correct way to wash a sick child, perhaps by the health worker. They can be encouraged to practise on a doll, or even each other.

Children can show how they would prepare food for a child who is ill, and how they would give it to the child. Would they just leave it beside the child in a bowl? How often would they offer food to a sick child? Let one child play the part of the sick child, and be given drinks and soft food on a spoon.

If the children have already learned how to make the Special Drink which must be given to children with diarrhoea (Sheet No 6.1, **Caring for Children with Diarrhoea**), they can talk about how to do it, and make some in class.

Children can find out

Find out who takes care of sick people in the community, and find out how they do it. What are the most important things they do for the sick person?

Children can make cartoons
Children can make strip cartoons, or posters, or cards to show the different stages of an illness and the care that must be given at each stage.

Children can make a play or tell a story
A group of children can make up a play to show how to care for a child who is ill. One child can pretend to be sick. Other children can act and mime how they can care for him and comfort him: wash his clothes; help him eat; give him many drinks; bathe his head and hands and mouth and so on. They can play the part of all the different people in the family, and show what they do when a little child is ill.

Or children can tell a story to show the others what they did when one of the younger children was ill at home.

FOLLOW-UP

Find out how many of the children have cared for a sick child at home. What did they do? What could they have done better?

Perhaps they could keep diaries or medical cards to record how they helped. Did any of them stay up in the night to help mother give liquids to a child with diarrhoea or vomiting, or high fever?

Ask the children questions to see how much they remember about the importance of:
- proper food and drink;
- comfort and care;
- cleanliness.

USING THIS SHEET

There are many ways in which **older children** can help and comfort younger ones who are ill. This will help the sick child to get better more quickly. It will also help the mother who will have many extra jobs to do when a child is sick.

Teachers in school can teach older children the ways they can help by using these ideas in health lessons, perhaps using short plays or mime, or telling stories. **Health workers** can use these ideas with groups of children in the community, in a queue at the health clinic, in youth groups, or in schools. **Youth leaders, and Guide and Scout leaders** can adapt these activities and perhaps award a badge or certificate for proficiency in child care.

This sheet should be used together with **Children's Stools and Hygiene** (Sheet 3.3) and **Clean, Safe Water** (Sheet 3.4).

WORMS

THE IDEA

A parasite is something which gets its food from our body. Worms are parasites. They get into our body in many ways. They can make us very ill, stop children from growing well and even kill them. Worms can be prevented by simple hygiene and sanitation practices and can be cured with medicines.

Treat all the family for worms

Worms and Parasites

Millions of people have worms and other parasites in their bodies. They get into our bodies in different ways. There are many different kinds of worms, some large, some so small that we cannot see them. Sometimes the ones we cannot see are worse than the bigger ones. Children get even more worms than adults.

How Do They Make Us Ill?

Some people think worms in the body are not dangerous. This is wrong. Worms are very dangerous because they live off us, by taking the food or sucking the blood inside us. They make us weak because they eat our food. Children with worms can be bad-tempered and tired, and do not do well at school. Worms stop children from growing properly. They make it easier for other diseases to attack children. Children with worms do not get better from other illnesses quickly. Sometimes worms even kill children.

How Do We Get Worms?

Worms can multiply very rapidly: one worm can lay thousands of tiny eggs which we cannot see. When a worm is inside the body it lays thousands of eggs which pass out of the body. They can pass out through leg ulcers, in the urine or in the stools.

If the stools are left where we walk and sit and eat, the eggs in the stools get onto things we touch: furniture, water, soil, dust, etc. Flies can move from the stools and carry the eggs onto our plates and cups, or onto the food we eat.

We swallow these eggs without knowing, and they grow into worms inside us. Then they travel through the different parts of our body until they find a good place to grow, usually in our intestines where they have easy access to our food.

Some Common Harmful Worms

There are many different kinds of worms and parasites. These are some of the most common ones:

Threadworm. These are very common especially in young children. They are tiny white worms like bits of thread. Threadworm can be seen on a child's anus especially at night, because that is the time when the female comes out to lay her sticky eggs which are too tiny to see but make the child's anus very itchy. This makes the small child scratch and collect eggs under his nails. Then he leaves the eggs on whatever he touches, e.g. his own mouth, food, the bedding and his clothes. In this way, he can swallow more eggs, and the whole family can easily get threadworm.

Children with threadworm are tired because they sleep badly, and uncomfortable because they itch. They may be bad-tempered and not very strong.

Where and how these activities have been used

These activities are closely linked with Section 3 (Personal and Community Hygiene) and like these they are often best passed on by example. Health committees in schools and health-conscious families at home can set such examples.

Many general rules of hygiene not only prevent the spread of worms but also the spread of many other diseases and this makes children aware of the effect their actions can have on other people, their families and the community as a whole.

Characters in comic strips or radio plays such as Dirty Dorji in the **Bhutanese** Child-to-Child programme provide good and amusing examples of how not to behave.

Some children in **Oaxaca, Mexico,** did a project on worms. They did a play showing how dirty hands and food make it easy for worms to spread. They also used a balloon filled with water and spaghetti to help them imagine worms in the intestine.

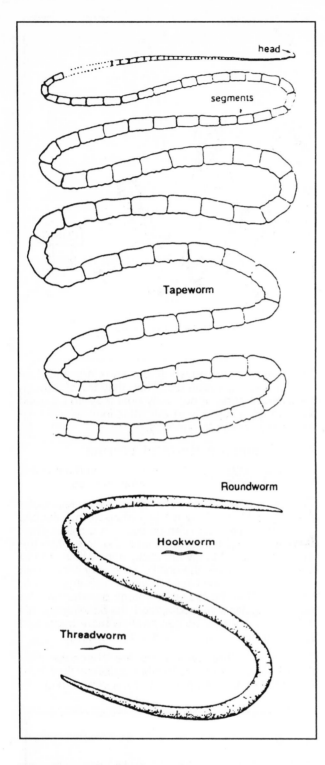

head

segments

Tapeworm

Roundworm

Hookworm

Threadworm

What can we do?

To prevent threadworm:
- wash hands and bottoms;
- keep clothes and bedclothes clean;
- cut fingernails short;
- dispose of children's stools away from living and play places.

To cure threadworm:
Threadworm can be easily cured if the whole family takes worm medicine.

Roundworm. These worms are pink and long, with pointed ends. They can easily be seen in the stools and sometimes children cough and spit them out. But most of them swim about in the intestines and

live there for a long time, laying thousands of eggs. These invisible eggs have hard shells. When the eggs come out of the body in the stools, their hard shell allows them to live in the ground for a long time, especially in damp, shady places. These eggs get into water, flies carry them on their legs, they can be found on fruit and vegetables that are not washed well, and even on our hands. When we swallow them we cannot see them.

Children with roundworm have stomach pains and do not feel hungry. Sometimes they are thin but have a big abdomen and they become weak and thinner. Too many roundworms can block the intestines by multiplying and forming a big ball. Sometimes roundworm gets into other parts of the body and can cause death.

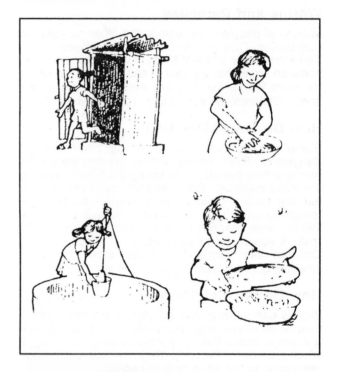

What can we do?

To prevent roundworm, we can:
- wash our hands;
- get rid of stools safely;
- use the latrine;
- kill flies;
- use clean water;
- observe the rules of good hygiene.

To cure roundworm, the whole family takes medicine.

Hookworm. Hookworm is very dangerous because it cannot be seen or felt when it goes into the body through our skin (feet, hands, bottoms). Once the worms are in our body, they hook onto the intestine and suck blood. Their millions of eggs pass out in the stools. Then they hatch into larvae (young worms) which get into bare feet when we walk on them, or into children's bare bottoms when they sit on the ground.

Hookworms suck children's blood. Children get anaemia (too thin blood), they become weak, tired, ill and can even die. They get other illnesses more easily and do not get well quickly. Sometimes they cannot learn and think well at school and they do badly in their studies. If someone has anaemia, their skin, gums, fingernails and the insides of their eyelids become pale and they are weak and tired.

THIS GIRL IS TIRED AND WEAK. SHE HAS HOOKWORM

SHE PASSES STOOL IN THE FIELD. THE HOOKWORM EGGS ARE IN THE STOOL.

A BOY WALKS ON THE STOOL. THE LARVAE GET INTO HIS BARE FEET.

THE BOY NOW HAS HOOKWORM. HE FEELS TIRED AND WEAK BECAUSE THE HOOKWORMS ARE SUCKING HIS BLOOD.

REMEMBER: ALL INTESTINAL WORMS ARE SPREAD BY BAD SANITATION AND POOR HYGIENE.

What can we do?

To prevent hookworm, we can:
- wear shoes;
- dispose of stools cleanly and always use a latrine;
- make a clean place for small children to play and crawl.

To cure hookworm: If we think children have hookworm they must go to the clinic. Ordinary worm medicine is not enough. A doctor or health worker can give other medicine, which is more effective.

Tapeworm. There are many kinds of long, flat tapeworms. The largest come from beef or pork that is not well cooked. Tapeworms have a head and a body which is made up of many short pieces (or segments).

As the tapeworm grows, its end segments become heavy with eggs and break off. These pieces pass out of the body in the stools where they can be seen. When cows and pigs eat, they swallow some of these eggs which then get into their flesh. Then people eat this meat and the tapeworm eggs with it.

Tapeworm can make us tired and weak, and can be very dangerous, especially for young children.

What can we do?

To prevent tapeworm:
- Always cook meat thoroughly before eating it to kill any tapeworms.
- Always use a latrine.

To cure tapeworm: Special medicines can cure tapeworms.

> REMEMBER: *The Health Centre can give simple treatment for worms. It is important to get this so that children and others can get well and stop worms from spreading to others.*

Community action can help to prevent worms from spreading if everyone cooperates by observing the rules of good hygiene and especially:

- building and using latrines;
- getting rid of little children's stools safely and quickly, away from places where we sit and eat;
- keeping the places where people live and eat clean and free from flies, stools and other dirt;
- washing hands before eating and after using the latrine;
- keeping food and water safe from flies and dirt;
- cooking food well, and storing it safely.

> REMEMBER: *Every person in the community must help. If ONE person does not follow the rules, they can SPREAD WORMS to HUNDREDS of other people.*

ACTIVITIES

What we learn about worms is no use if we only observe the rules of hygiene at school and forget them at home. If we use the latrine at school and do not help our younger brothers and sisters to use it at home we cannot get rid of worms.

Finding Out

Worms. Who in the group has worms? How can you tell if a small child has worms? (Scratching anus, sleeping badly, restless, tired, bad-tempered, pale, stomach ache, not hungry, presence of worms in the stools.) Do people at home have them? Have you seen worms? Where? Do you know people who have worms you can't see? Do your younger brothers and sisters get more than you? Why?

Latrines. Where are there latrines? At home? How many at school? How many for teachers? How many for children? Do you know any public ones? Who looks after them? Make a guide or map to the latrines you know. Which of them have a cover and are kept clean?

Water. Where do people get their drinking water? Is the source of drinking water clean? Where can they wash their hands before they eat and after they have been to the latrine?

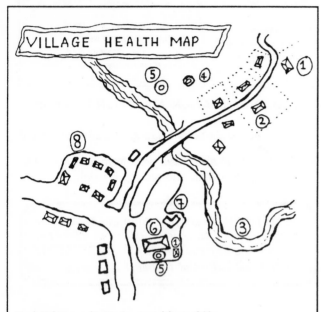

1. **Latrines — keep clean and free of flies**
2. **My house — clear any children's stools from around the house**
3. **Stream — clear snails**
4. **Well — fence off and keep clean**
5. **Washstand — wash hands before eating and after using the latrine**
6. **School — use latrines and washstand**
7. **Kitchen — kill flies, cook meat well, wash fruits and vegetables before eating**
8. **Market — keep clean**

Discuss

How can children get rid of worms?

Draw a worm cycle, for a tapeworm, a roundworm or a hookworm. Write a story called 'My Life as a Fly' or 'My Life as a Worm'. Write songs about worms and flies.

Draw and discuss a health map which shows dangerous places where worms are spread. Show how flies spread germs and worms. Watch the flies and see where they go. Then draw a plan of their journey on the map.

In maths, work out how many eggs one female roundworm can produce in three months if she lays 200,000 eggs every day.

Taking Action

Begin by observing the rules of hygiene (Activity Sheet 3.3, **Children's Stools and Hygiene**). Keep clean, and use a latrine. Keep all water supplies clean and safe (Activity Sheet 3.4, **Clean, Safe Water**). Protect cooked food from flies, and wash raw fruit and vegetables before eating.

Start at school. How can you keep it clean, and make it free of worms? You can kill flies, improve and cover latrines, provide water for washing hands, keep the compound clear of dirt.

Make sure the family at home understands about worms. Teach younger children to use latrines (Activity Sheet 3.3, **Children's Stools and Hygiene**), make latrine covers, keep a water-saving tin to wash hands (with soap if possible) after using the latrine. Learn to make this tin. Make fly swats, and keep flies away from food and latrines.

Keep a clean, safe place where small babies can play (Activity Sheet 1.5, **A Place to Play**).

Make posters and picture stories about:
• taking children to the clinic for treatment;
• keeping the places we sit, walk and eat clean and free from stools and flies;
• how worms get into our bodies;
• the different kinds of worms.

Hang these posters up at school, at the market, at home.

Give puppet shows, mimes, songs, dances, at home and on open days at school.

Report to teachers, parents, health workers when there are flies, worms, dirt, or problems with latrines.

FOLLOW-UP

How many children can remember the main idea three months later? How many have been able to use the information, at school, at home? What did they do?

Are there more latrines, latrine covers, children wearing shoes? Who has gone to the health centre for worm treatment?

Have the older children helped the younger ones by getting rid of stools, showing them how to use the latrine, talking about worms with their parents? How else did they help?

Did anything else happen at home or in the community after the children started passing the message?

USING THIS SHEET

Health workers can help mothers and older children at the clinic where children are taken for treatment. Youth workers can use youth groups to make surveys and carry out the activities for preventing and treating worms in children.

Teachers can work to make sure that latrines are built at school, and help to spread the knowledge about worms in their daily teaching, at open days, using these activities with children and their families.

Children can do all these things. They can tell people at home and children who do not go to school about them. They can tell older people when they think they or their younger brothers or sisters have worms.

This sheet can be used together with **Children's Stools and Hygiene** and **Clean, Safe Water** (Sheets 3.3 and 3.4).

IMMUNISATION

THE IDEA

Every year, five million children die and five million are disabled from diseases which could have been prevented by immunisation against the germs which cause them. Children can understand how immunisation works, which diseases can be prevented by immunisation, and the correct immunisation programme for themselves, their friends and their families.

People say, **"Our children are not sick, so why should we take them to the clinic?"**

The answer is, **"Because we want to have them immunised to protect them against some serious diseases which they may get later."**

Immunisation means making the body strong and well-prepared to fight particular diseases.

Each year, in every village and community, some babies and young children die from diseases like measles and tetanus. Others are disabled for life by diseases like polio. **This can be avoided by immunisation.**

We can look at the diseases which can be prevented by immunisation, and then we can look at how immunisation works.

Diseases That Can Be Prevented by Immunisation

Measles. Pradeep has had a high fever for six days, with red eyes, a runny nose, noisy breathing and a cough, and a rash all over. He has measles and is very ill. If he gets better, he will be weak for a long time and may catch other diseases.

Diphtheria. Rosa breathed in some diphtheria germs which settled in her throat and made it sore. Her neck swelled. Her breathing became noisy and difficult. Then her breathing stopped and she died.

Tuberculosis (TB). Musa's uncle had a cough for a long time and there was blood in his spit. He coughed up the TB germs which Musa and his baby sister breathed. The germs settled in Musa's lungs. He began to cough, lost weight, and became weak. His baby sister died.

ALL OF THESE COULD HAVE BEEN PREVENTED BY IMMUNISATION!

Where and how these activities have been used

Children have been used to spread immunisation messages all round the world - often in association with UNICEF. In **Togo**, for instance, a mass campaign was planned in which children, "les élèves protecteurs", were central.

While it is valuable to have children passing on songs and slogans devised by adults, it is even more effective when children themselves create and interpret messages. An excellent example of this is the play, *Diseases Defeated,* which was originally made by children and their teacher at the City Primary School in **Kampala, Uganda**, and has been taken up round Africa, televised world-wide and turned into a story book read by thousands of children.

This play, which has been translated into many languages, tells the story of a "committee of deadly diseases" who meet to discuss their great difficulties because Child-to-Child is preventing them from killing children in the way they used to do.

Tetanus. Joseph cut his foot in his field. Tetanus got in with the dirt. A week later all his muscles became tight so he could hardly breathe. They took him to hospital, but we do not know if they can save him.

When Vimia had her baby, they cut the cord with a dirty knife, and germs got in. A week later the baby became stiff and stopped sucking; he later had convulsions and died.

THIS COULD HAVE BEEN PREVENTED BY IMMUNISATION

Whooping Cough. Four-year-old Amin caught whooping cough from his friends and gave it to his sister Fatima and baby Myriam. They have all been coughing, vomiting, losing weight and becoming weak. The baby goes blue with the cough and may die.

THIS COULD HAVE BEEN PREVENTED BY IMMUNISATION

Polio. Odongo, Opio and Akello caught polio when there was an epidemic some years ago. They and a lot of other children were ill with it. They were left paralysed and will always be disabled.

THIS COULD HAVE BEEN PREVENTED BY IMMUNISATION

In some countries, immunisation is given against other diseases too, such as meningitis, yellow fever and cholera. Find out from a health worker if your country does, and if so, teach about these as well.

How Does Immunisation Work?

Immunisation builds protection in the body against the germs which cause these diseases. How does it do this?

When we are ill, it is because a tiny germ that can only be seen under a microscope has entered the body. The body protects and defends itself by making special 'soldiers' for killing those particular germs. These soldiers, which are specially armed to fight a certain kind of germ, are called antibodies.

Sometimes, when a disease enters the body:

- the body **has not made enough** soldiers or antibodies in advance, or
- the antibodies **are made too late** to prevent or fight the disease.

If the disease is very serious, or if the child is very weak - perhaps he has been ill before, or is malnourished - there is a risk that he will die before the body can make enough antibodies to fight the disease.

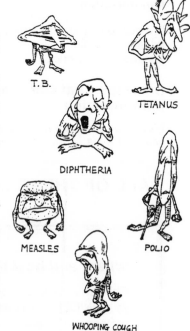

T.B.

TETANUS

DIPHTHERIA

MEASLES

POLIO

WHOOPING COUGH

Immunisation is a way of encouraging the body to make enough of the right kind of antibodies in advance of the disease. Then, when the disease comes, the body is ready to fight it. For diphtheria, tetanus, whooping cough and polio, immunisation must be given at least three times before enough antibodies are produced and protection is complete. For these diseases, it is very important for children to be taken back for their second and third injections at the right times. For some diseases like polio and tetanus, the antibodies made in the body by the immunisation will not last for an entire lifetime, and so we need a second immunisation five or ten years after the first, to remind our body to make more antibodies.

When a child is immunised, the immunisation will sometimes make a small swelling, or make the child feel unwell. This is the body's way of learning to fight the disease and nothing to worry about..

The Immunisation Programme

Your country has an immunisation programme against these diseases. Make sure that all families with children know about this programme. Immunisation should be given by qualified health workers who are part of this programme. If possible, talk to your health worker to learn about this programme.

What is the right time for immunisation? Programmes change with new and local knowledge. Know your own country's programme.

Immunisation Programme§

Before birth (to be given to the mother)	Tetanus	
As soon as possible after birth	BCG (against TB)	first
	Polio	first
Age 6 weeks	DPT*	first
	Polio	second
Age 10 weeks	DPT	second
	Polio	third
Age 14 weeks	DPT	third
	Polio	fourth
As soon as possible after 9 months	Measles	
Age 5 years	BCG	second

§ Recommended by the World Health Organisation (1985)
* One injection against Diphtheria, Whooping Cough and Tetanus

---

Remember: Immunisation still helps to prevent disease even if the spaces between the immunisations are longer than they should be. Also remember that even some immunisation is better than none.

IN ORDER TO STAY HEALTHY, WE MUST ALL BE IMMUNISED

ACTIVITIES

Children can find out about the immunisation programme in their community. Where is immunisation given? Are there certain days and hours for immunisation? What sort of injections are being given? (Teachers, youth workers and health workers can help children to find out this important information.)

Children can find out who needs to be immunised. Children can find out what diseases members of their family have had and discuss them in class. Which illnesses have they had? How did it make them feel?

In school, identify any children in the class and in the children's families who have not been immunised. Get children to check with their mothers and report back. If growth charts or other records are used, show the children where immunisation comes on the growth chart. Remind them of the dates for immunisation. Children must keep immunisation cards safe, and always have them when they go to the health centre.

If any young child in the class or group, or any child in their families, has not been immunised, check with health workers to see how it can be done.

Children can keep records. Children and their teachers can support the clinic by keeping records for all the families of the children in the class, or even if possible for all the families in the village.

Children can help in the family. Older children can make a birthday card to take home for a new baby in the family or neighbourhood. They can hang it on the wall as a reminder. The class can help to design the card, so that it shows the right times for the local immunisation programme.

Keep reminding the mother and father to look at the baby's clinic card and the birthday card, to remind them when immunisations are due.

When the time comes, help the family to take the baby to the clinic.

During the day after immunisation, help to look after babies and comfort them if they feel unwell and cry.

Children can help in the community.

They can pass the message. Children can make birthday cards for babies, make posters, and make up songs and dances.

Children can make up plays and puppet and mime shows, such as one about a family where the children are immunised and another where they are not. Or about what happens when someone in the family who is not immunised gets one of the diseases which can be prevented.

Another play might show the unpleasant and crafty Germs who wait around for those who have not been immunised. They include Measles Germ (with red spots), Polio Germ (who limps), Whooping Cough Germ and TB Germ (who cough). Some children can take the part of the Germs; others can be the antibodies.

YOUR IMMUNISATION CARD	
HAPPY BIRTHDAY (WRITE THE BABY'S NAME HERE)	TICK OR COLOUR THE SPACE FOR EACH IMMUNISATION GIVEN
WE HOPE YOU HAVE ALREADY HAD YOUR FIRST TB + POLIO VACCINE	
AT SIX WEEKS OLD YOU NEED DPT + POLIO	
AT 2½ MONTHS OLD YOU NEED DPT + POLIO	
AT 3-4 MONTHS OLD YOU NEED DPT + POLIO	
BEFORE YOU ARE 1 YEAR OLD YOU NEED MEASLES	
WHEN YOU ARE 5 YEARS OLD YOU WILL NEED BCG AGAIN	

They can help in immunisation campaigns. Children can help others to know about immunisation programmes and to prepare, with adults, for the visit of the immunisation team or health worker in the community. They can show their posters and plays, and make sure that everyone in the community knows about the immunisation programme.

FOLLOW UP

Children can discuss among themselves to make sure that they all remember about the immunisation message. Have they understood it properly? Have all the children in the class been properly immunised? What about their brothers and sisters? Their parents?

Children can count how many people disabled by polio there are in their age group; how many there are among people who are ten years older; twenty years older. Is there a difference? Why?

Children can try and ask their grandparents what happened before immunisation.

USING THIS SHEET

Teachers, including religious teachers, **youth group leaders** and **community development workers** could introduce these ideas to groups of children, if possible with help from **health workers**. It is important for children really to understand about immunisation if they are to pass on the message and help their families and communities. **It is important for teachers and youth leaders to give the message regularly and not just once.**

This sheet should be used together with Sheet No 6.2 **Caring for Children Who Are Sick.**

POLIO

THE IDEA

Polio is caused by a virus which can leave a child weak and disabled. It is spread through stools or coughing and sneezing. It can leave limbs paralysed and cause muscles to shorten or contract so that joints cannot be straightened or, in some cases, cannot be bent. Arms and legs that are paralysed and backs that are twisted and weak can never be cured, but the healthy muscles can be taught to make up for the damaged ones.

Children can help to build up muscles damaged by polio. They can spread the message that **polio can be prevented by immunisation**.

The physical disability need not affect the child's overall physical, mental and social development and other children can be friendly and help provide opportunities for her to lead an active life and take part in their activities, including play, work and study.

What is polio?

Polio is a disease which can sometimes injure the muscles of the body. When children get polio, they may have a fever and signs of a bad cold or 'flu for some days. While they have fever, they need to rest very quietly. Sometimes the fever is very slight and it is almost impossible to know that the child is suffering from an attack of polio. Not all fever leads to polio **BUT** if children have fever and then become weak in the arms, legs or back, they must be taken to the doctor or health worker

In some cases, the child just seems to have a cold and there are no permanent effects but in severe cases, children who have had polio may permanently lose the strength in some of their muscles. One or more limbs - arms and legs - may be paralysed, and the spine or backbone may become twisted. The bones and muscles of the damaged limb become thinner than the other limb and do not grow as fast. The unaffected limbs may become stronger to compensate.

Preventing Polio

Polio can be prevented. The most important thing that children can do is to make sure that everyone they know has been protected from polio by immunisation (*see* Sheet 6.4, **Immunisation**). Immunisation is a way of encouraging the body to make enough soldiers (we call them antibodies) to fight a disease when it attacks the body.

Children are immunised by an injection or by swallowing a few drops of a liquid vaccine. Both methods work very well, but must be given by trained health workers who know how to look after the vaccine, and make sure that it is strong enough. The vaccine often has to travel thousands of miles before it is given to the children, and this may take some months. The vaccine must be kept cold all the time or it will not work properly.

Children must have three doses of the vaccine and come back later for an extra dose or 'booster'. Older children can make sure that younger ones receive all

---

Where and how these activities have been used

Usually restricted to special programmes on disability or linked with immunisation campaigns. In certain countries and areas where polio is very widespread, e.g. India, this sheet becomes a special priority. The Child-to-Child story book, I Can Do It Too, supplements this sheet. The book, Disabled Village Children, by David Werner, contains much more information on this topic.

Very important in the teaching of health workers and in encouraging children to help and play with children who are disabled as a result of polio. The information about exercises and preventing contractures is very useful. Crutches and other aids for the disabled can be made in school or college handiwork periods. Stories and dramas about the "cold chain" are very valuable.

four doses. This is important, for if the booster is missed, the child will not be properly protected against polio. However, if the child has diarrhoea, a fever or a cold, he should be asked to return for his vaccine when he is well as it will be more effective then.

Children should **never** be given unnecessary injections, especially if they have a fever or diarrhoea, as the local irritation caused can turn a mild, undiagnosed case of polio into paralysis.

Helping a child who is paralysed

Children can help other children who have been disabled by polio, especially by telling their friends that there is nothing wrong with the child with polio, except weak muscles. Their minds and feelings are not affected. The child who has had polio will still be able to do many things that the other children can do. There are many things they can do together. They can play and work together just like any children do.

It is also very important to discover ways of getting the child to school. He may be just as intelligent as any other child and needs to be stimulated like them.

Limbs that are paralysed by polio will never become strong again BUT other muscles in the paralysed limb can be taught to work better and to do at least part of the job that the paralysed muscles can no longer do. Older children can help those who have had polio to do exercises after they have been shown how to do them by a trained health worker. Exercises of the right kind can help to prevent the child's body becoming deformed or crooked.

Most of all, children can help disabled children by including them in their activities. All children learn and grow through play. They learn faster if they are part of a group and if exercises are made into games. Play games with the child with polio, read and talk together. Be friends!

ACTIVITIES

Preventing Polio from Spreading

Everyone Must Be Immunised

* Check to make sure that each child has been correctly immunised against polio, including the 'booster' doses. The children can make a chart for the wall with the names of all the children who live near them and find out if they have been vaccinated. When they have been vaccinated, they can put a tick beside the name. The aim is to have a tick beside every name. If the children are not sure, they can ask their mothers to look on their health clinic card.

* Any child who has not been immunised should be encouraged to do so as soon possible. What about brothers and sisters - have they been immunised? Have they had their 'booster' dose?
* Find out from health workers when the immunisation can be done and encourage mothers and fathers to make sure that all the children in the family have been immunised properly, including the booster.
* The children can carry out a campaign in the community with placards informing everyone of the necessity of polio vaccine and the times when they can be vaccinated.
* The children can do a play for the community with the polio monster who is defeated by the vaccine as part of the campaign.
* Keep reminding those who have not been immunised, and work towards having a mark against everyone's name.

Older children can help younger ones who may be frightened of having the immunisation. They can:

* explain that polio vaccine is usually given in the form of drops and therefore does not hurt;
* go to the clinic with the younger ones, and comfort them if they feel frightened;
* play games with them while they wait at the clinic;
* make sure that the younger children go back to the clinic for two more doses and the booster dose when this is necessary. This is very important because the protection will be less if any doses are missed.

Working with Health Workers

Older children can help health workers make sure that the vaccine is kept cold and works properly by cooperating with them when they come to immunise children. They can:

* watch that the electricity is working;
* make sure that the health worker is told at once if the electricity stops, as this may make all the vaccines in a refrigerator useless (after how long?);
* make sure that the vaccine is safe in a cold box, if there is no electricity, and that all cold boxes are kept in a cool place.

Give drops to baby   Prevent this   Mark on chart

Children can work together before the arrival of the health worker by making posters and plays, songs and dances which tell about the immunisation programme and encourage all families to make sure that all children are protected.

Helping the Disabled Child

Contractures. These occur when some muscles become shorter causing the limb to become deformed. The joint is not able to move as well as before. In some cases it is difficult to straighten the joint and in other cases to bend it. Most contractures can be prevented through exercises and other measures. It is far easier to **prevent** contractures than **correct** them. Correction can take a long time and be uncomfortable or even painful but this may be necessary before a child can walk or look after himself. Older children can help prevent or correct contractures by putting the child with polio in a good position and doing certain exercise with him. Some pictures showing positions and exercises from *Disabled Village Children* by David Werner are shown on the following page. If you require more information on this subject, we suggest you consult this excellent book.

Exercises. Doctors or trained health workers can teach older children to work at home with children whose bodies have been damaged by polio. When a child has polio, he needs rest and good food at first but then he should be examined by a health worker to see what exercises are suitable and how much strength the child can regain and how.

Older children can help paralysed children to do exercises to regain their strength. It is always easier to do exercises if they are made into a game, and it is more fun for the disabled child if they can do the exercises with the help of other children. This makes them get stronger faster. It is also a great help to the parents who may sometimes be tired.

Equipment. The doctor or health worker may decide that the disabled child has enough muscle power to learn to walk. The child must therefore practise walking regularly. Older children can build rails outside the house to help the child take exercise and to begin using the different muscles in his legs.

Older children can also make a simple crutch or cut a stick to help the disabled child to walk. They can hang a rope over the bed, so that he can pull himself up, if he is not strong enough to sit up by himself.

Being Friends. Children can remember to include children who are disabled in their own play and work as much as possible. If a disabled brother or sister is small and cannot walk, the older children can find a way of carrying him with them, of taking him to school, and including him in their games.

If the disabled children are bigger, the older children can make a trolley, or perhaps the local carpenter can make a wheel-chair with bicycle wheels. The older children can help to move the chair or trolley around.

FOLLOW-UP

After one or two months, quiz the children to see if they remember the important points about polio: what are the symptoms? why is it dangerous? How can we prevent it? How can we help those who have been disabled by it?

During the year, keep checking to make sure that every child in the class or group has been immunised against polio and had the booster doses. Does the wall chart have every child's name on it?

Have the children been able to identify and help a child who has been disabled by polio? If so, what have they done to help? Have they helped with exercises? with equipment? by being friends? What problems have they overcome? Have they been able to help the child over a long period of time, so that their help has made a difference to the child as well as the child's family.

USING THIS SHEET

Teachers can explain how immunisation protects the body, as part of the health or science lesson.

Health workers can advise parents and show how to make simple aids.

Children can make health cards and remind others of immunisation dates, especially for the booster dose. They can help polio victims to do exercises, and make equipment for them to use.

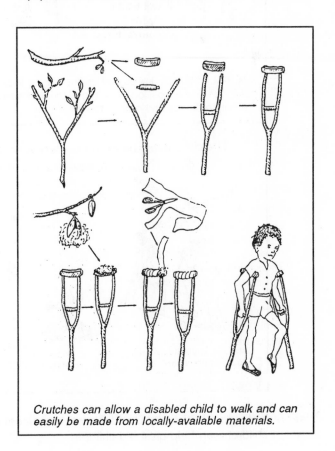

Crutches can allow a disabled child to walk and can easily be made from locally-available materials.

If a child is likely to develop contractures or has begun to develop them, try to position her to stretch the affected joints. Look for ways to do this during day-to-day activities: lying, sitting, being carried, playing, studying, bathing and moving about. Contractures can develop quickly so early positioning is very important.

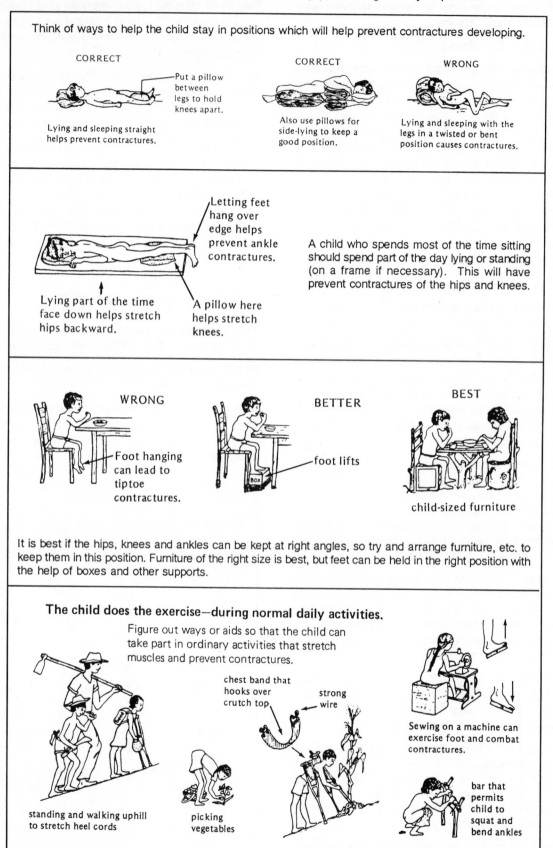

Think of ways to help the child stay in positions which will help prevent contractures developing.

CORRECT

Put a pillow between legs to hold knees apart.

Lying and sleeping straight helps prevent contractures.

CORRECT

Also use pillows for side-lying to keep a good position.

WRONG

Lying and sleeping with the legs in a twisted or bent position causes contractures.

Letting feet hang over edge helps prevent ankle contractures.

Lying part of the time face down helps stretch hips backward.

A pillow here helps stretch knees.

A child who spends most of the time sitting should spend part of the day lying or standing (on a frame if necessary). This will have prevent contractures of the hips and knees.

WRONG

Foot hanging can lead to tiptoe contractures.

BETTER

foot lifts

BEST

child-sized furniture

It is best if the hips, knees and ankles can be kept at right angles, so try and arrange furniture, etc. to keep them in this position. Furniture of the right size is best, but feet can be held in the right position with the help of boxes and other supports.

The child does the exercise—during normal daily activities.

Figure out ways or aids so that the child can take part in ordinary activities that stretch muscles and prevent contractures.

standing and walking uphill to stretch heel cords

picking vegetables

chest band that hooks over crutch top

strong wire

Sewing on a machine can exercise foot and combat contractures.

bar that permits child to squat and bend ankles

Disabled Village Children by David Werner and Sheet No. 5.1, **Disabled Children** suggest many other ways in which children can help disabled children.

SMOKING - THINK FOR YOURSELF

THE IDEA

Children between the ages of 10 and 14 are often under a lot of pressure to start smoking. They notice others smoking, and advertising companies make smoking seem very attractive. To help them decide whether or not to smoke, children need to know much more about the effects of smoking on their bodies, their health, their activities and their family life.

A Smoker's Story

Joseph, aged twelve, lived with his family in a village. One day, his fifteen-year-old brother came back from town, and offered him a cigarette from a new pack. Joseph puffed away. At first, he felt sick, but he did not want his brother to think he was a baby. He finished his first cigarette. Soon he was smoking one cigarette a day. Then two, then five and then ten a day, until he became addicted to cigarettes. He felt sick if he did not have one.

One morning, Joseph woke up with a bad cough which did not get better. So he went to the health clinic. There he saw the health worker. She told him that his cough was caused by his smoking. She knew this because his breath smelled and his teeth were stained yellow. She told him that when he had a wife, she would not like him to smell. She also said that he would have bad teeth if he continued to smoke. He thought to himself, 'I must try to give up smoking.'

Joseph had always been a keen footballer, but after a few months of smoking he noticed that he could not run about the pitch as quickly as he used to without getting out of breath. He was very upset when he was not chosen to play for his team in the big match. As he was no longer in the football team, Joseph met his friends outside the bicycle shop, where they chatted and smoked. Joseph and his friends saw the cigarette advertisements on the side of the shops showing famous sportsmen and women. Unfortunately, there was no one to tell them that advertisements are not always honest. Several more friends joined the group outside the shop.

For a few months, Joseph was satisfied. But he missed the football team and began to visit the sports ground where the team was practising. He longed to play again but he knew that if he wanted his body to be fit enough, he must give up smoking and start training again. He talked to several of his friends outside the shop, and three of them agreed to try to give up smoking. Although it was not easy, two of them, including Joseph, succeeded. Once he had stopped smoking, Joseph began training again and after a while was fit enough to rejoin the team.

Where and how these activities have been used

Increasingly used in **Asian**, **African** and **Latin American** countries, especially in town schools, but still often not considered the priority it deserves to be. In Europe, however, it is often seen as one of the first and most profitable Child-to-Child activities which can be undertaken because of the increasing evidence of the close relationship between smoking and ill-health. However, stressing more immediate consequences like "not smelling very nice" is often more effective than considering long-term risks like lung cancer or cardiovascular disease.

Analysing media adverts (*see* Child-to-Child story book, *Deadly Habits*) has proved very successful, e.g. in **Zambia**. Links with mathematics (costs of cigarettes versus cost of food) has also been successful in **Uganda**.

It is very important to help children not to start smoking as stopping can be very difficult and to this end drama and role-playing centring round learning to say "no" is frequently used. The context can then be widened to include drugs, alcohol, sex, etc. It is also important to stress the harm done to others who do not smoke themselves but are near people who do.

Children need to understand that:

- **Smoking causes disease and poor health.** Those who don't smoke are usually healthier and fitter than those who smoke.
- **Smoking is expensive** and uses money that could be used for food, clothes and other things.
- **Smoking is addictive**: once you start, it's hard to stop.

Children who see that non-smokers are often fitter, healthier and cleaner than smokers can think for themselves about whether or not to smoke.

A Threat to Fitness and Health

Smoking injures people's bodies in many different ways.

It causes disease

Lung/throat/mouth/bladder cancer. Cancer occurs when body cells grow out of control into a lump called a tumour. A cancer is very serious because it prevents the part of the body where it is growing from working properly. It can spread to other parts of the body and cause death. You cannot catch cancer from other people. Cancer is more likely to happen to a smoker than a non-smoker.

Bronchitis. Smoking injures people's lungs, so that they:
- get more coughs and colds;
- are short of breath after exercise;
- cough every day, especially when waking up;
- bring up thick, sticky mucous when coughing;
- feel generally unwell.

Heart disease. Smoking makes the heart work harder. It increases the heart rate, because there is less oxygen in the blood when people smoke. That means that children who play sport but smoke do not do as well as if they did not smoke. And when they get older they are more likely to suffer from heart disease.

Smoking is very harmful to babies. If a mother smokes, the chemicals in the cigarette can injure her unborn baby. Babies can be born smaller and weaker, or even die if the mother smokes. Babies and young children can get chest troubles - coughs and wheezes - if their parents smoke.

Smoke from cigarettes hurts even those who don't smoke. It causes eye and throat irritation, coughing and even cancer. This is because non-smokers breathe in the smoke as if they smoked the cigarette themselves. Some

people may be so affected by tobacco smoke, especially those with chest trouble, that they find it difficult to breathe.

Cigarettes and matches are dangerous because they cause fires when they are thrown away or dropped carelessly. At home people's lives may be in danger, and in the fields and forests, animals, birds, people and precious crops may be endangered or even destroyed by fires caused by careless smokers. Where else can cigarettes cause fire? (Football stadiums, markets, cinemas, stations, and even in cars, lorries and buses.)

Cigarettes are Poisonous

What actually causes the injuries to smokers' bodies and those around them? Cigarettes give out harmful chemicals:

- *Tar*, a sticky mixture of irritating chemicals and cancer-causing substances collects in the lungs.
- *Nicotine*, a poisonous drug, makes the heart beat faster, and also affects blood vessels and nerves. It is very addictive.
- *Carbon monoxide and other poisonous gases* take the place of oxygen in the blood, which the body needs to stay healthy.

A Costly Habit

- Money is wasted on cigarettes when it could be used to buy more useful things for the family.
- Land which should be used for growing food is used for growing tobacco for cigarettes or for chewing.
- Smokers are ill more often than those who do not smoke, so they are absent from work, and need more medical attention.
- Governments have to spend money trying to stop people from smoking, while cigarette companies spend a lot of money trying to get people to smoke.

Why Do People Smoke?

Why Begin?

Different people smoke for different reasons. For example:

- Sometimes they smoke because they see other people who are important to them (e.g. mother, father, brother, sister or friends) smoking and they want to try it.
- Sometimes they smoke because advertisements on the radio, television or at the cinema, in the newspapers, magazines and on posters encourage them to buy cigarettes. Also, cigarette companies like to sponsor sports and social events. Advertisements often make smokers seem attractive and exciting, young and happy, rich and successful.

But this is misleading. Smokers are likely to have poorer health and to be less fit. Because they spend more money on cigarettes, they have less to spend on looking good.

Why Carry On?

Once they start smoking, people become addicted to the tobacco. Smoking becomes a habit because it is easy to do, a part of everyday life. They find it difficult to stop and may even feel quite ill if they do. They may have:

- poor sleep;
- bad dreams;
- difficulty in thinking and concentrating;
- depression and anxiety;
- craving for cigarettes.

But this is only temporary. Friends and family can help a person who is trying to stop smoking. Before too long they will feel better and be healthier.

Remember: It is easy to start smoking, but it is difficult to stop. The body gets hungry for cigarettes.

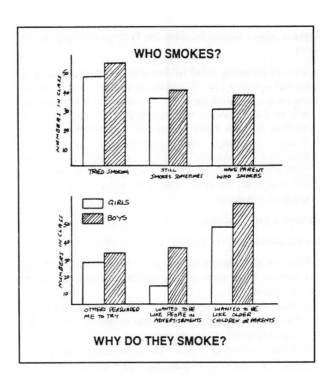

WHO SMOKES?

WHY DO THEY SMOKE?

> ## SOMETHING TO THINK ABOUT
>
> In some countries people are getting wise about their health. They are smoking less and less. This means less money for the tobacco companies. So these companies would like to encourage people in *other* countries to smoke more.
>
> There is evidence that more men, women and even children in developing countries are beginning to smoke. The cigarettes they smoke are often even more harmful because they have more tar and nicotine in them.
>
> **Don't let the cigarette companies tell you what to do. Make up your own mind.**
> **Think for yourself!**

ACTIVITIES

Children can find out.

- *Advertising.* Carry out a survey of billboards, or collect advertisements from newspapers, cinemas and magazines, or on the radio.
  - How often are cigarettes advertised?
  - What do the advertisements stress?
  - How do they make you feel?
  - What do the advertisements **NOT** tell you?
- *Smoking and the family.* Find out how many children in the group have parents, brothers or sisters who smoke.

Talk about how smoking affects the family.

What is it like to live with a smoker?

Can the children illustrate these or other effects on posters, and perhaps take them home to put up on the wall?

Does the fact that someone in the family smokes make it more likely that the child will begin to smoke?

- *People who smoke.* Carry out a survey of people who smoke including the children themselves, as well as people outside the group:
  - what age did they start?
  - why did they start to smoke?
  - why do they smoke now?
  - is it easy or hard for people to stop smoking?
  - have they tried to stop?
  - what effects have they noticed on their health?
  - would they encourage young people to smoke?

Include non-smokers as well, and find out why and when they decided not to smoke, or to give up smoking.

Invite someone who has given up smoking to come and talk to the group.

DON'T SMOKE!
IT SHORTENS YOUR LIFE

DON'T SMOKE!
IT MAKES YOU COUGH AND WHEEZE

DON'T SMOKE!
IT DAMAGES TASTE & SMELL

DON'T SMOKE!
IT CAUSES CANCER & HEART DISEASE

Make a report and/or illustrate the findings with a chart or table.

- *Cost of smoking.* Find out the cost of one cigarette or a packet of cigarettes. Work out the cost of the number of cigarettes smoked each day, each week, each month, and for a whole year. Work out how much rice or flour or meal could have been bought with this money.
- *Poison in cigarettes.* Demonstrate the harmful substances contained in a cigarette. An adult smoker can take a white cloth and blow tobacco smoke through it. A brown stain will appear on the cloth. This is tar which collects in the lungs of smokers.

Children can discuss

- How people decide whether or not to smoke.

- Find out and discuss what children think about smoking:
  - Where, why, when did you decide to smoke or not to smoke?
  - What disadvantages do you think there are in smoking?
  - Do parents and friends help you to decide whether or not to smoke? What do they say?
  - Is there anything you can do to help someone decide not to smoke? Or to stop smoking? What?

- Why do you think people smoke? Ask people who smoke and others who do not smoke. Compare and discuss their answers. Make a list of all the reasons suggested. Does the list give you ideas about:
  - How to help people who are trying to stop smoking?
  - How to encourage people to stop smoking?
  - How to reduce pressure on others to start smoking?

- Organise a debate. Possible topics include:
  - Smoking should be forbidden in all public places, including buses and trains.
  - Government should double the price of cigarettes.

- Pretend you are different people in the community; for example:
  - a parent
  - a doctor
  - a government minister
  - a teacher
  - an advertising company executive
  - a farmer
  - a teenager

  and discuss what action you would take about:
  - smoking generally
  - smoking and pregnancy
  - increasing taxes on cigarettes
  - banning smoking in public places
  - decreasing the amount of land where tobacco is grown
  - controlling cigarette advertising
  - more and more children starting to smoke
  - informing others about the dangers of smoking
  - the danger caused by cigarette smoke to non-smokers.

Children can pass the message

- Especially to other classes or groups of children. They can make use of:
  - reports for other children and for the family
  - pictures/posters for public display or to take home
  - creative writing, like a story or poem
  - talks from smokers, advertisers, marketers, for example
  - plays
  - music/songs.

- Children can display posters or sing songs in places where others will see and hear the message: in schools, health centres, around the village and market and at home.
- Have a story and poetry competition.
- Make plays, and act them out for the group. For example:

  Three little pigs live in a house made of bamboo. A hungry wolf who smokes, wants to eat them. So he tries to blow the house down. But the wolf can't take a big breath and can't blow the house down. His coughing can be heard all around the village.

  Act out the story of Joseph at the beginning of this activity sheet. Make it longer and show how he was able to help other smoking friends and his own family.

  Five children arrange to meet at their favourite meeting place. One of them produces some cigarettes and offers them to the others. One of them says, 'No thank you. I don't smoke'. The others ask, 'Why not?' What does he say? The others try to persuade him. How does he answer them? Make up the play as you go along, discussing and arguing.

FOLLOW-UP

Can the children tell why smoking is dangerous?

Have any of the children in the group stopped smoking? What about brothers and sisters, mothers and fathers, their friends?

Have the figures on the bar chart, showing the number of smokers in the group and their parents, changed - for better or for worse?

Have children found any specially good way of encouraging people to give up smoking, or of helping those who are trying to stop?

USING THIS SHEET

Teachers can include many of these activities in health, maths, science and physical education lessons. Teachers themselves might set a good example for children by not smoking in or near the school, if at all.

Youth and community leaders can also set a good example for children. They can also help children in groups to carry out public information campaigns in the community, and help them to locate the best places to pass the message.

Children themselves have an important role to play in putting pressure on others to stop smoking, or even better, not to begin smoking.

COUGHS, COLDS, PNEUMONIA (A.R.I.)

THE IDEA

Everyone gets coughs and colds. Most coughs and colds get better without special medicine. But sometimes colds turn to pneumonia. Four million children die of pneumonia every year. The clearest sign of pneumonia that everyone can learn to recognise is QUICK BREATHING. Pneumonia needs immediate treatment with special medicine given only by a doctor or health worker. Breastfeeding, good food, a smoke-free home and immunisation against whooping cough and measles can help prevent pneumonia.

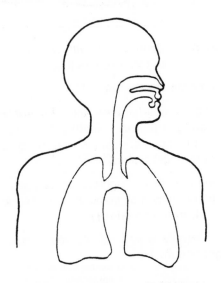

The Respiratory Tract

The respiratory tract is that part of the body into which the air we breathe enters. The air reaches the nose and throat, and goes through the windpipe to the lungs.

Infections are illnesses caused by germs (viruses and bacteria). Acute infections happen suddenly and last a short time.

What is A.R.I.?

Coughs, colds and pneumonia are all Acute Respiratory Infections (A.R.I.).

Everyone Gets Coughs and Colds

Throughout the world people get coughs and colds. Young children get more than older children, between three and eight colds every year. In colds, the infection is only in the nose and throat. The signs and symptoms of a cold are:

- a runny nose;
- a blocked nose;
- a cough;
- sometimes a sore throat;
- sometimes children feel ill and tired and do not want to eat.

Where and how these activities have been used

Although this is a new Child-to-Child activity (1988) it is quickly becoming widely used because of the recognition of Pneumonia as one of the greatest (sometimes **the** greatest) killer of young children. The story book, *Not Just a Cold,* is used in English and Urdu and is being translated into many other languages.

The activity of recognising fast breathing and estimating the rate (50 breaths a minute) makes a useful link with mathematics and is fun to do. Many programmes now use a pendulum made from a string and stone to help count breaths (see sheet). Again it is important that the children know when a child needs to see a health worker.

Warning: Before passing on the messages in this sheet check - do health posts in the communities have antibiotics to treat babies?

Coughs and colds are caused by viruses. They are made worse by smoke. Tobacco smoke and cooking smoke make a cold more likely to turn to pneumonia.

Most Coughs and Colds Do Not Need Special Medicine

Special antibiotic medicine does not help to cure colds. Babies and children will usually get better in a few days. We can help them if we:

- keep them comfortable - keep them warm if they are cold, or cool if they are hot;
- give them plenty of soothing drinks;
- encourage them to eat, by giving small quantities of food often;
- clean their noses (especially babies before feeds);
- keep the air round the child clean and smoke-free.

Pneumonia

Pneumonia can:

- start on its own; • follow from a cold;
- follow from measles or whooping cough.

All children can get pneumonia but babies under one year are more likely to get it than older children.

In developing countries pneumonia is usually caused by bacteria. *Therefore, special **antibiotic** medicine can help save lives.*

Recognising Pneumonia

The clearest and surest sign of pneumonia is **quick breathing**. A healthy baby, lying still and not crying, takes about 30 breaths a minute. But a baby with pneumonia, lying quietly, takes more than 50, sometimes 70 or 80, breaths a minute. *Quick breathing, more than 50 breaths a minute, could mean pneumonia.*

How to Count Breaths

We all breathe quickly sometimes, especially when we run, cry or move about a lot. This quick breathing is not pneumonia.

We must not count a child's breaths when he has been restless, crying or struggling. Count the breaths of a child who is sleeping or resting quietly. Watch the child's chest without disturbing it.

Count the number of breathing movements for one minute. Fifty breaths or more can mean pneumonia.

Mothers usually know when their babies are breathing too fast even without a watch. If you have no watch look carefully and decide whether the breathing is too quick.

What to Do

If you are sure the breathing is too quick (50 or more) or if you think it may be, the child must be seen immediately by a doctor or health worker. Special antibiotic medicine can cure pneumonia if started early

and given by a doctor or health worker. Their instructions must be followed carefully and correctly.

Can Pneumonia Be Prevented?

Children who are well-fed (*see* Activity Sheet No 2.1, **Feeding Young Children - Healthy Food**) are less likely to get pneumonia. Babies who are breastfed are less likely to get pneumonia.

Measles and whooping cough can cause pneumonia. Both can be prevented by immunisation (*see* Activity Sheet No 6.4, **Immunisation**).

Children in homes where people smoke are more likely to get pneumonia.

ACTIVITIES

Finding Out

The children can interview each other and find out:

- How many of them were ill in the last six months?
- How many had coughs and/or colds?
- What were the symptoms? What did they feel like?
- Did the colds get better soon? Or did they get worse and lead to fever? How many children developed fever? How many did not?

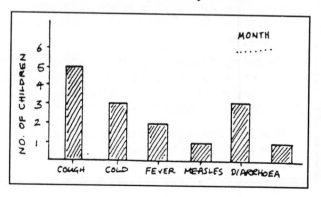

- What did they do to make themselves better?
- What helped to make them better?

Share the information and write a survey report. Make charts showing the information and display it.

Extend the survey to the children's families, to other families in the area. This time, also find out:

- how many people (if any) had pneumonia;
- for how long?
- did it get better?
- what helped?

Compare this information with that on coughs and colds. Did the children notice anything interesting about their information, for example:

- Who had most colds in the community - babies or old people?
- Who had pneumonia? During which months?
- Was the medicine made at home or did it come from the doctor or health worker?
- Was there anything else that they noticed?

If a child or an adult remembers having pneumonia, they can talk to the children about it. (How did it start? How did they feel? What did they do to get better?)

Learning the Signs

(1) The children can test each other to make sure that they know the signs or symptoms of pneumonia.

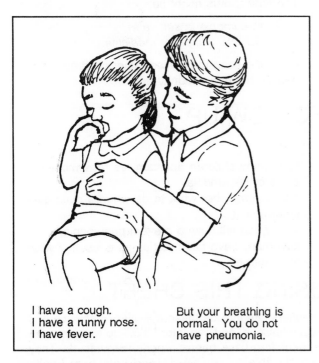

| I have a cough. I have a runny nose. I have fever. | But your breathing is normal. You do not have pneumonia. |

They can ask each other questions:

Question: I am lying quietly. I have a runny nose. I am breathing very quickly, about 50 breaths a minute. Do I have pneumonia?

Answer: You could have. You should see a health worker as soon as soon as possible.

Question: I have a runny nose. I have a cough. I have fever. Do I have pneumonia?

Answer: No! Your breathing is normal so you do not have pneumonia.

(2) If the children have a watch or clock, they can learn to recognise the quick breathing (50 breaths each minute) which is a sign of pneumonia. Working in pairs, start by counting each other's breaths for one minute. Write down the number of breaths. Then one child does one of the activities in List A below, the other an activity from List B. Let them count each other's breaths after each activity, then change over and continue. Each time write down the result.

If they do not have a watch, a third child can act as timekeeper, counting up to 100 at a steady speed, or walking up and down at the same pace. Children can compare the rate of breathing for different activities even if they cannot measure accurately.

A	B
Sitting quietly	Running on the spot very fast
Reading	Skipping 30 times
Standing still	Jumping as high as possible
Humming	30 times
Writing	Digging
Counting	Lifting something heavy

By comparing different rates of breathing, children will soon begin to understand what is normal, what is a little fast, and what is very fast (the danger sign).

(3) The children can make three pendulums from string which does not stretch and stones. With the stones attached, the strings should be two metres, one metre and 35 centimetres long. They can then swing them to see how fast they go from side to side. They should notice that the shortest pendulum takes the least time to swing from side to side and that the longest pendulum takes the most time to swing from side to side. In fact the longest pendulum swings from

one side to the other and returns to its original position in the same length of time as a normal adult takes to breath in and out again. A normal baby breathes in and out again in the same time as the middle pendulum takes to swing from one side to the other and return to its original position. If the baby is breathing at the same rate as the short pendulum, it is breathing very fast and should see a health worker straight away.

Preventing Pneumonia

Children can find out how many children in the school or community:

- have been immunised;
- need immunisation;
- need to complete the immunisation process.

Children can make cards to remind parents about immunisation (*see* Sheet No 6.4, **Immunisation**).

Children can make posters which show how pneumonia can be prevented. They can help each other or their families can help. If families help, they may also learn. Display the posters in class, the children's homes, public places.

They can discuss what foods will help prevent pneumonia. Can they make up a menu for the week which contains such food? Is it expensive to get the right kind of food?

They can keep a list of all they eat at home and see if the right food is included and how frequently (*see* the sheets on Feeding Young Children). They can help their parents to plan the meals well.

They can draw a plan of their houses. With the help of their parents, can they identify the smokiest areas? (Cooking area? Fire corner?) Can they identify the least smoky area? (Near the door? a window? in a cross-current?) How can they make sure that babies are kept away from smoke?

How can they clear the house of smoke quickly?

Passing the Message

Children can:

- display their posters showing the signs of pneumonia and colds at parent days, at home, or in public places like the market and clinic;
- teach their families the signs of pneumonia;
- find two other people in the neighbourhood to whom they can teach the signs;
- make up a story or play about someone who knew the signs of pneumonia and helped to save a life;
- make up a play using the following characters:
  - the patient (a child with a cold which becomes pneumonia);
  - an anxious family;
  - someone who knows the signs;
  - a health worker.

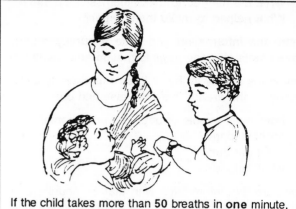

If the child takes more than **50** breaths in **one** minute, take him to the health centre **immediately**.

- make a puppet show to tell the story of someone who had pneumonia, and share it with other children and families. The play should ask the following questions:
  - What started it (cough, cold, no immunisation, measles)?
  - What were the signs?
  - What did the patient feel?
  - How was the pneumonia cured?
  - How could it have been prevented?
- make up a song with the chorus:

  Do not worry, do not fret,
  This is not pneumonia yet.

The final chorus might be:

  Pneumonia is setting in.
  Ask the doctor for medicine.

- teach the song to families, other children, other people in the community.

FOLLOW-UP

Find out:

- how many children and families remember the signs of pneumonia;
- if they remember what to do when a child gets pneumonia;
- if they can tell how to prevent pneumonia;
- how many have taken action as a result of what they learned.

USING THIS SHEET

Teachers can include these activities in science and health lessons, and can later follow-up to make sure that children have been properly immunised. They may be able to get advice and help from health workers and community leaders, so that the children really know the signs of pneumonia, what treatment is best, and the importance of immunisation.

Children can help by passing the message to friends and families. They can carry out projects with the help of adults which will help to reduce the danger of pneumonia to their families and the community.

MALARIA

THE IDEA

Malaria is a killer disease. One million children die of it every year. The disease leaves many others weak and unable to work or study properly. Malaria is spread by Anopheles mosquitoes and affects people in many countries. It is even coming back to countries from which it has been driven out. There are important government programmes to control malaria and we all need to work together to support these and prevent malaria from spreading.

Children can also help by preventing mosquitoes from breeding and biting people, and by knowing what to do when someone has malaria.

A Story

Joseph had a sister called Flora. She was ten months old. One day she had a very high fever and was shivering. She was very ill. Joseph and his mother took Flora to see the nurse. The nurse said Flora had malaria. She had been bitten by mosquitoes.

Joseph did not understand. He had been bitten but he had not caught malaria. The nurse said that only some mosquitoes gave children malaria.

The nurse gave Flora's mother medicine and told her exactly how much to give and when. The medicine was bitter so it was not easy to get Flora to take it. But the nurse said it was very important that Flora should finish all the medicine.

So Joseph and his mother gave Flora the medicine. They kept her cool. They gave her drinks. Flora was better. She did not like the medicine but Joseph and his mother remembered what the nurse had said and so they gave Flora the medicine for two more days. Now Flora is well again, but she always sleeps under a net to stop the mosquitoes biting her at night.

Malaria: Some Important Facts

What causes us to become ill? The germ which causes malaria is called Plasmodium and it is carried by the female Anopheles mosquito. Other mosquitoes do not carry malaria, but they are a nuisance and may carry other diseases.

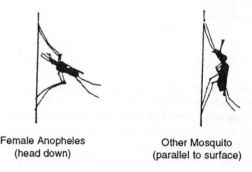

Female Anopheles
(head down)

Other Mosquito
(parallel to surface)

Anopheles mosquitoes can pick up the Plasmodium germs by biting people who have malaria. The germs develop inside the mosquitoes which can then pass them on to another person.

Where and how these activities have been used

In countries where Malaria is common, this sheet is always a priority, but use will vary widely depending on the local situation **which always needs to be checked with the health worker.** For example, it is useful to know:

- What kind of malaria is present? How serious is the problem?
- What are the prevention programmes in the area? How can children help?
- How much protection do people have and how much can they afford (e.g. nets, window netting, sprays)?

Although older children may take some responsibility for younger ones, e.g. protecting them at night, most action here is taken by children working together. It is important for children with adults to work out realistic things to do and, if possible, ways in which they can see results, e.g. less mosquitoes, less malaria.

When the female Anopheles mosquito bites a person, the malaria germ enters the person's blood. It travels to the liver and then back into the blood. This takes about 12 days. Then the person begins to feel unwell and gets fever, often with sweating, shivering, headache and diarrhoea. This fever passes but keeps coming back and may get worse unless it is treated with the correct medicine. It is very dangerous for young children.

Health workers can test for malaria. They take some blood from the sick person, spread it on a glass slide, and look at it through a microscope. If there are Plasmodium germs in the blood, the health worker will be able to see them.

The more bites you have, the more chance there is that one of them will be by a female Anopheles mosquito which is carrying the Plasmodium germ.

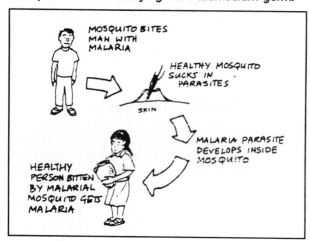

The Life of the Anopheles Mosquito

Female Anopheles mosquitoes lay their eggs in still water, such as puddles, ditches and ponds. After the rainy season, there are many more mosquito breeding places and therefore more malaria. Other mosquitoes breed in places like latrines, cesspits and even water pots. The Anopheles mosquitoes don't usually breed in these places.

Mosquito eggs are small and black and float on the water. They hatch into larvae which grow quickly. The larvae of the Anopheles mosquito float parallel to the surface of the water. The larvae of other mosquitoes hang at an angle from the surface of the water.

After another day or two the pupa becomes a mosquito which is ready to fly away.

The adult Anopheles mosquito hides in cool dark places during the day. The female bites during the night and sucks up blood to mature her eggs.

How We Can Prevent Malaria

To prevent malaria we must stop Anopheles mosquitoes from biting people.

Keeping Mosquitoes Away. If possible, the windows, doors and other openings in a house should be screened, so that mosquitoes can't get into the house. The best way to prevent mosquitoes from biting at night is by sleeping under nets.

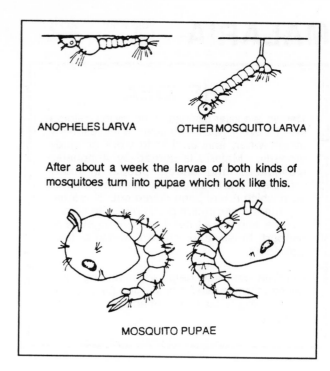

After about a week the larvae of both kinds of mosquitoes turn into pupae which look like this.

MOSQUITO PUPAE

These nets must be:
* put over the bed before dark;
* tucked in well after you get into bed; and
* kept in good repair by sewing up any holes or tears.

Remember:
* Mosquitoes can bite through the net if you sleep close to it.
* Mosquitoes go on biting until it is light. Stay under the net until it gets light.

In some countries nets are now being treated with a chemical called **permethrin**. This helps to keep the mosquitoes away and can kill them.

In the evening, at night and until the first light of day, as long as the mosquitoes are active, we can wear clothes which cover the arms and legs to protect them from mosquito bites. In places where there are no nets or screens, a blanket or thick cloth can help protect the body.

Mosquitoes can also be driven away by putting a repellent on skin or clothes (especially around the ankles), by using mosquito coils or even smoke from grass or leaves.

Killing Mosquitoes. We can also kill mosquitoes when they get into the house. Regular government spraying programmes are very helpful and everyone should cooperate with these. When the walls of the house are sprayed, the insecticide should be allowed to remain on the walls. Mosquitoes resting on the walls will then die.

Preventing Mosquitoes from Breeding. We can also try to stop Anopheles mosquitoes from breeding by:
* filling up puddles of still water around the house with earth and stones;
* putting small fish which eat larvae into ditches and ponds;
* putting oil on the surface of small ponds to stop the larvae from breathing.

Other mosquitoes can be prevented from breeding by carefully covering water pots and containers with cloth or by putting oil or special chemicals into latrines.

If a Child Has Malaria

A child with malaria needs to be treated or the disease may get worse and the child could even die.

The usual medicine for treating malaria is called chloroquine. (The medicine may have different names like Malariaquin, Nivaquine or Resoquin.) There are other medicines which may be available and which may work better than chloroquine in some places.

It is important to take the full recommended course of the medicine to make sure that all the Plasmodium germs are killed. Since the medicine tastes bitter, children sometimes want to stop taking it once they begin to feel better, but before they have finished the course. They must be helped to take the full course.

NORMAL DOSES OF CHLOROQUINE TO TREAT MALARIA*

AGES	FIRST DAY		SECOND DAY	THIRD DAY
	FIRST DOSE	ABOUT 6 HOURS LATER		
LESS THAN 1 YEAR OLD	$\frac{1}{2}$	$\frac{1}{2}$	$\frac{1}{4}$	$\frac{1}{4}$
1-3 YEARS OLD	1	$\frac{3}{4}$	$\frac{1}{2}$	$\frac{1}{2}$
4-6 YEARS OLD	2	1	$\frac{1}{2}$	$\frac{1}{2}$
7-11 YEARS OLD	2	1	1	1
SMALL 12-15 YEARS OLD	3	$1\frac{1}{2}$	1	1
LARGE 12-15 YEARS OLD AND ADULTS	4	2	2	2

* Recommended number of tablets containing 300mg chloroquine base

A child with fever caused by malaria needs to be kept cool but not cold. Sponge the child's body with cool water.

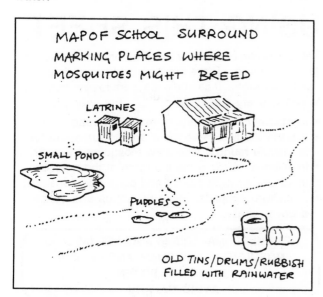

MAP OF SCHOOL SURROUND MARKING PLACES WHERE MOSQUITOES MIGHT BREED

LATRINES
SMALL PONDS
PUDDLES
OLD TINS/DRUMS/RUBBISH FILLED WITH RAINWATER

Sometimes the child will be shivering. But putting too many clothes or blankets on a child with a high fever or at the shivering stage of an attack of malaria is dangerous. Medicines like paracetamol can reduce the temperature.

When children sweat, they lose liquid. They should be given plenty to drink. As soon as they can eat again, they should be given food to build up their strength (see Sheet No 6.2, **Caring for Children Who Are Sick**).

ACTIVITIES

Finding Out

Where is Malaria Common?
Some government programmes have managed to control malaria in some places, but in others malaria is spreading. Find out where malaria is most common:

* in the world;
* in your country;
* in your district.

Ask teachers, health workers or local malaria control officers. Is it spreading or is it getting less? Are fewer people getting ill, or more? Why? Draw maps to show where people are getting sick because of malaria.

At school, find out from other children in the group:
* how many children or others in their family have had malaria in the last year;
* how often did they have it;
* in which months did they fall ill.

Use this information to keep records, or make simple graphs to show:
* the months of the year in which people get malaria (mostly in the rainy season);
* the months in the year when it rained and there were many puddles;
* the ages of those with malaria;
* who went for treatment.

Children can plan and keep such records throughout the school year.

Discuss how such information could be useful to children, their families and the health workers.

Where Do Mosquitoes Breed?
In the rainy season, make a map of the area of the school, and mark on it all the places where mosquitoes might breed. Then check all those places, to see if there are larvae in them. Are they Anopheles larvae? How do you know? Can you get rid of the water in which the mosquitoes are breeding? How?

What Do People Know About Malaria?
Using the information in this activity sheet, write down the important facts about malaria. With the help of their teachers children can then make up a simple questionnaire to find out what families believe about malaria, and what they do about it. What can children do once they have collected this information?

Observing the Mosquitoes

In the Environment. Find out where mosquitoes are most plentiful. Which kind of mosquitoes are they? Where are larvae found? What kind of larvae are they?

In the Classroom. Collect larvae. Put them in a covered jar or other container with water, grass and some mud in it. Observe them. You should put a little bread or flour on the water for them to feed on.

Children can draw and write about what they see.

Preventing Malaria

Children can help prevent malaria in many different ways:

- Make sure that nets are properly used. It is most important to cover sleeping places of very young children. Older children can make sure that younger ones stay under the nets until first light and that nets are well tucked in.
- Check for holes and tears in nets regularly and sew them up.
- Kill mosquitoes in the house.
- When the spray teams come, help carry food and other things out of the house.
- Destroy breeding places. Fill puddles with earth and stones. Put oil on shallow ponds (old engine oil from cars and lorries works well).
- Make and fit covers for water pots and containers. This helps to prevent other mosquitoes from breeding there.

Teachers, children, parents and health workers need to work together to prevent malaria. Find out what others are doing.

Helping Children Who Are Sick

When young children get malaria they need help quickly, or they may die. Older children can watch for the signs of malaria and tell adults when the young ones need treatment.

Children with malaria feel very ill. Older children can help to comfort them, keep them cool, and give them drinks (*see* Sheet No 6.2, **Caring for Children Who Are Sick**).

It is very important that children take the right course of medicine at the right time. (Children's doses vary according to the age and size of the child.) After the first dose they may feel better, but all the germs are not yet killed. Older children must help others to understand how important it is to finish the medicine.

Passing the Message

Children can help spread the important messages about preventing and treating malaria to parents and other adults, as well as to other children. They can do this in many ways.

Make up a play or dance. The children can mime the Plasmodium germs and the medicine. The medicine (like policemen) comes in several times. The first time the medicine catches most of the malaria germs but some germs hide. It takes three more times before all the germs are caught.

Children can act, mime or dance:

- the life cycle of a mosquito;
- careless and careful families and villages (some can act the part of clever mosquitoes);
- germs and medicine;
... and many more topics.

Make posters. Posters by the children can show:

- how malaria is spread;
- how it can be controlled (particularly in 'danger periods' like after it rains);
- that pregnant women need to visit the health clinic;
- why children need to take the full dose of medicine.

Be sure to put the posters where they can be seen by many people.

Write stories. Children can write and illustrate stories like 'Joseph and Flora' and share them with others. Some titles might be:

- Mrs Mosquito and her Friends;
- The Day the Spray Team Came to Our Village;
- Careless Moses (who didn't take the full course of medicine).

Sing Songs. Children can make up 'Prevent Malaria' songs and teach them to families, friends and to other children.

FOLLOW-UP

Children can test themselves and others on the facts about malaria.

They can keep records and help the school to do so. Look at the charts after some months. Have cases of malaria increased or fallen? Are some months worse than others? Why? Are more people using nets and protecting their neighbourhood? What have the children done to help at home? at school? in the neighbourhood? Let them describe their experiences.

Children can and must continue to be aware of the dangers from mosquitoes and continue to take action such as filling puddles. This is especially important after the rains.

USING THIS SHEET

This sheet can be used by **health workers** and **youth group leaders**. There are also many ways it can be used in **schools**. It can help teachers to plan activities in nearly every subject in school. For example:

- in maths, make graphs of malaria spread;
- in social studies, make maps and do surveys (where is malaria found? where do mosquitoes breed?);
- in science, observe the life cycle of the mosquito;
- in language, write stories and plays about malaria;
- in cultural subjects, make up songs and dances, draw pictures.

> REMEMBER: MALARIA IS A KILLER DISEASE
> MOSQUITOES ARE QUICK AND CLEVER
> DON'T GET BITTEN
> AVOID MALARIA

MEDICINES - WHEN AND HOW THEY CAN HELP US

THE IDEA

Everyone has taken medicine at some time. Medicines help us in many ways. But often medicines are not necessary and we can get well without them. One problem is that people often expect the health worker to prescribe lots of medicines and to give them injections when they are sick. In many cases it is enough to get plenty of rest, plenty to drink and good food to eat to help the body fight off the disease and get better.

When we take medicine we must be careful where we get it from and how we take it. If children learn the correct facts about medicines and how to use them safely they can help to improve the health practices of their family.

How are medicines used?

1. *Medicines which prevent diseases.* Some medicines and vaccines protect us from certain diseases. Babies must be immunised against six dangerous diseases.

2. *Medicines which cure diseases.* Some medicines cure certain diseases. There are different medicines for different diseases. Diseases must be treated as soon as possible before they become too serious. When a child is very ill (e.g. very high fever; breathing very quickly; vomiting; blood in his stools or severe diarrhoea), he should be taken at once to a trained health worker who will know which medicine to give. Some medicines cure in a short time, others take a very long time (e.g. the medicine for tuberculosis takes at least six months to cure.)

3. *Medicines which help us feel better but do not cure.* Many diseases or health problems, such as colds, flu, or most cases of diarrhoea cannot be cured by medicines. They must be cured by the body itself.

A Story

Sara's baby had a bad cold. She took him to the health worker and asked for an injection. The health worker told Sara that the baby did not need an injection and that he would get better with rest, good food and lots to drink. But Sara did not believe her. She went to a man in the market who gave the baby an injection and asked for a lot of money. Four days later Sara's baby had a high fever and a hot, red sore where he had been injected, because the man had used a dirty needle. Sara was very worried and went again to the health centre. She now believed the health worker's advice.

Medicines may be given in different ways:

- in tablets (or capsules)
- in liquid or drops
- in ointment
- by injection

Where and how these activities have been used

Many medicines have undesirable side-effects so it is important to take them only when we really **need** them, when they are really **useful** and above all **to follow the instructions carefully.**

This is a new sheet and only just coming into use. The topic, though considered very important by WHO, is usually left out of school health education syllabuses. It is a very worthwhile and valuable one. Apart from its medical importance it is particularly important as a social studies topic. We should investigate:

- Why people buy medicines;
- How sellers (including advertisers) sell them;
- How we can begin to find the difference between what we really need, and what we do not.

Few skills are more important for citizens to learn.

Sometimes we take Paracetamol or other medicines when we have a fever or headache or stomach ache. This helps the pain to go, but does not cure the disease which causes the pain. After a few hours the pain will come back. It will not go away until our body has cured the disease.

4. *Medicines which control diseases*:
There are some diseases which cannot be cured but can be kept under control by taking medicine regularly. For example, a person with Asthma, Diabetes or some kinds of heart disease needs to take medicine regularly to keep as well as possible. Some people need to take medicine all their lives.

When looking after sick people, give them:

- plenty of clean water and other drinks;
- good food. Young children should eat a small amount many times a day;
- the right amount of medicine at the right time.

Home remedies and traditional cures

Many home remedies have great value, some have less. Some may even be dangerous or harmful. Home remedies, like modern medicine, must be used carefully.

Home remedies that help
For many diseases home remedies work as well as or even better than modern medicines. They are often cheaper and in some cases safer. For example, teas made from herbs and plants can help for coughs, colds and indigestion. Older people may know which plants are useful for certain complaints in their area. Children can make sure that a person with diarrhoea drinks plenty of liquids (*see* Activity Sheet 6.1. on **Diarrhoea**.)

Home remedies that harm
Good home cures must not be confused with unhygienic practices which may harm people. For instance, animal dung may contain dangerous germs and must never be applied to a wound or to the umbilicus of a newborn baby.

We should only use home remedies if we are sure that they are safe and we know how to use them. If someone is seriously ill and has a high fever, it is safer to treat their disease with modern medicines on the advice of a health worker.

Misunderstandings about medicines

Many people believe that if they are ill they must take some medicine. We should realise that our bodies will recover from most diseases whether we take medicines or not. When people go to the health worker, they expect to be given some medicine and are disappointed if they get none. *Medicines are expensive and cost money which could be used for buying good food.* It is also dangerous to over-use medicines when they are not necessary.

Many people believe that it is better to take medicine by injection rather than by mouth. Most medicines work just as well, or better, when taken by mouth. Injections should only be given for particular diseases and for immunisation. *Receiving an injection from an untrained person can be very dangerous.* If needles are not cleaned and sterilised (by being boiled in water), they can spread diseases, including AIDS.

It is dangerous to take the wrong medicine or too much medicine. It is wrong to believe that a larger dose of medicine will make a person get well quicker. It could even kill. It is also wrong to take too little and not to finish all the medicine.

The people who make medicines and beauty products often try to make us buy them through attractive, misleading advertisements, e.g. an advertisement for a vitamin tonic might say, "This tonic will make you strong and clever." We know which foods have the vitamins and minerals we need to eat to grow well and strong (see Activity Sheet 2.1 on **Healthy Food.**). Therefore it is much more sensible to spend money to buy these foods than to buy an expensive bottle of tonic which may be useless.

Where do we get our medicines?

We must be careful where we get our medicines. Sometimes medicines are kept too long or left in the heat, in the sunlight or damp places. In these cases they may become useless and sometimes could be dangerous. The label on the medicines should have a date. If that date has passed, the medicine may be bad.

The dangers of medicines for young children

Young children often swallow medicines thinking they are sweets or nice drinks. Some common medicines can easily kill young children if they take too much. We must prevent this by keeping medicines out of young children's reach.

Children need different treatment from adults. They get different illnesses and need different doses (amounts) of medicines.

AS-126

Some common medicines like Aspirin can harm babies. Babies and pregnant women should only take medicines on the advice of a health worker.

Safe use of medicines

Children can help themselves and their families to use medicines safely and correctly. Here are some simple rules:

- Only use a medicine when it is needed. Often rest, good food and lots to drink are enough to help a person get better.
- Listen carefully to instructions from the health staff or read the label. Help others to understand these instructions.
- Make sure that all medicine containers have instruction labels.
- Take the medicine if possible with food at the right times and in the right amounts.
- Always finish the full course of medicine even if you feel better.
- Don't share medicines with anyone else.
- Keep all medicine in a cool place out of the reach of young children.
- Only adults and responsible older children should give medicines to children. Young children should never give medicines to other children.

ACTIVITIES

Finding out

The children can find out :
- What are the most common local diseases?
- What medicines or cures are given for them?
- Where can people get these medicines or cures?
- Do people spend a lot of money on them?
- Are these medicines necessary?
- Do some people make their own cures?
- What kind of cures? Are they helpful or harmful?
- When people are sick, who helps and advises them?
- Do people expect to be given medicines or injections when they go to the health worker?
- What medicines are kept at home? Are they stored out of the reach of small children?
- How much is a bottle of "tonic" (medicine which is supposed to make us strong)? Compare the price of one bottle of tonic with an orange, a kilo of green vegetables, or other local nutritious foods. Which is the best use of money?

The children can visit the health centre to find out more about the use of medicines.

Discussing

- The health worker can discuss with the children about the different kinds of medicines, when they are necessary and when they are not and how we can use them safely.

- The health worker can bring some empty medicine bottles with instructions written on the labels and the children can practise reading and understanding the instructions.
- Children can discuss together with teachers, parents and health workers how they can promote the safe use of medicines and decide on action which they can take to help their families and neighbours.

Taking action

Older children can help in many different ways:
- Help the parents when a small child does not like taking medicine by amusing the small child, telling her stories, persuading her, singing to her, rewarding her when she takes it.

- Think of ways to give tablets to young children. One way is to mix the tablets with a little sweet liquid. In preparing this follow these steps:

  1. *Wash your hands.*
  2. *Follow the health worker's instructions and take the right amount of tablet.*
  3. *Put the tablet in a cup and crush it into powder with a spoon.*
  4. *Mix the powdered tablet with a little clean water (no more than 2 spoonfuls), milk, sugar, porridge or other food to make it easier for the child to take.*
  5. *Give the mixture to the child with the spoon or from the cup. It may be necessary to hold down the child's hands.*
  6. *If the child spits out the mixture, give one more dose perhaps trying a different method.*

The children can discuss this idea with their parents and help them next time a small child needs to take tablets.

- Help feed sick children in small quantities frequently and keep them clean. Remember: Always wash your hands after looking after a sick person.

- Check that a sick child has taken the medicine regularly by making a chart and ticking off the times when the child has taken the medicine and making sure the child finishes the course.
- Make drinks like herbal teas and the Special Drink (ORS) and give it slowly and frequently to children when they have diarrhoea.

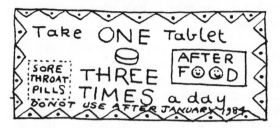

- Make a label with instructions for taking medicine. Include: the dose; how to take it; when to take it; how often to take it; for how many days.
- Read medicine labels for people who cannot read and remind them to take their medicine.

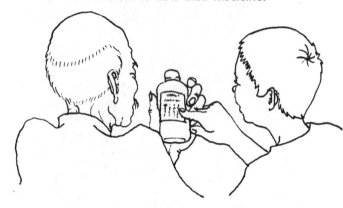

Passing on the Message

The children can help to spread these messages to their family and community in many ways:

- **Make up a play or a puppet show.** For example, acting the story of a false doctor who comes to the village with bottles full of different coloured water.

He makes a long speech which the people believe. They buy his medicines and he goes away with a lot of money. No one gets better. He comes back next year, but this time the people chase him away.

- **Draw posters** to show the rules about safe use of medicines, e.g.
  - sick people need good food and plenty to drink;
  - medicines should be kept out of the reach of young children.

Make up songs with these health messages and teach them to their friends.

Write stories like the one about Sara and her baby. Other stories could be about:
  - How the family learned that Grandmother's herbal drink and Grandfather's oranges were the best treatment for little Abdullah's cold.
  - How Mimi helped her brother take his medicine safely.
  - How foolish Arthur took all his medicine at once and nearly died.

- **Find an advertisement** for some kind of medicine and discuss it with their friends. What does it say? What does the picture tell us? Should we believe it? Why or why not?
- **Organise a school open day** with safe use of medicines as the theme. This could include drama and puppet shows, stories and poster exhibitions.

FOLLOW-UP

- Children can **make up quizzes** to test each other on the facts about safe use of medicine.
- They can **keep records** about the diseases in their families and the treatment which was given. How many times have they taken medicine? Who advised this? Have they helped anyone to take medicine correctly? Have they treated cases of coughs, colds and diarrhoea with medicine or with plenty of liquids and good food? What happened? How many injections have been given other than for immunisation? The children can keep these records over a few months and compare their findings.
- They can find out whether people still expect always to be given medicine or injections when they go to the health worker.

USING THIS SHEET

There are many ways in which **older children** can help their families use medicines safely. **Health workers** can help older children understand these messages and plan together how they can pass on these messages at the clinic and at community meetings. **Teachers** can do the activities with children in different lessons at school and in the community. **Youth group leaders**, including **Scout and Guide leaders**, can involve children and young people. They can develop an achievement badge for which children need to demonstrate how they have helped others to use medicines safely and wisely.

This sheet can be used with **Caring for Children with Diarrhoea** (Sheet 6.1), **Caring for Children who are Sick** (Sheet 6.2) and **Coughs, Colds and Pneumonia** (Sheet 6.7).

AIDS

THE IDEA

Every country has AIDS. In some countries the number of cases recognised so far are very few. In others the disease is wide-spread and many people are dying. In all countries everybody, including children and young people, must learn the facts about AIDS. Children everywhere in the next ten years of their lives will be in danger of catching the AIDS virus. In countries where many young adults are infected, the future of the society depends on their children's knowledge, attitudes and practice.

This sheet gives explicit facts about how the AIDS virus is caught and how it can be prevented. It also looks at people's attitudes and practices concerning AIDS. It aims to develop in children, their teachers and their families an openness to discuss these sensitive issues, a confidence to take decisions for themselves, and a sense of caring for people with AIDS.

WHAT DOES 'AIDS' MEAN?

A **Acquired**
means 'to get'.
AIDS is acquired (or got) from other people who have the AIDS virus.

I **Immune**
means 'protected'.
The body is normally immune (or protected) against many diseases.

D **Deficiency**
means 'a lack of'.
With AIDS, the body has a deficiency (or lack) of immunity against many diseases.

S **Syndrome**
means 'a group of different signs of a disease'.
When people have AIDS they have a syndrome or many different signs of disease.

WHAT IS AIDS?

AIDS is a disease which attacks the body's protective system. The body is unable to protect itself properly from other diseases such as diarrhoea, TB, coughs and sores in the mouth. With AIDS, these diseases make people very sick and they may even die.

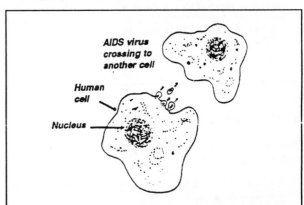

Here the AIDS virus, which is much smaller than a human cell, is leaving one cell before entering and infecting another cell. (Drawing from a microscope picture.)

AIDS may take 2-10 years to develop but the infected person can pass on the virus even if they show no signs of disease. AIDS is caused by a virus (Human Immuno-deficiency Virus [HIV] which we call 'the AIDS virus' in this sheet).

Where and how these activities have been used

Although this sheet is new, many activities in it have been developed from programmes such as those in **Britain, USA, Zambia** and **Uganda**. Many AIDS programmes concentrate on adolescent children and still need to do so. **The activities in this sheet are designed for children of primary school age.** Those who know the facts about the spread of AIDS world-wide all agree that the sooner children are armed with the knowledge of how to avoid AIDS the easier it will be to prevent its spread.

The approach will vary greatly according to the religious and social beliefs in a country. Before working with this sheet, teachers, health workers and community leaders need to discuss what messages are likely to be acceptable at different ages and in different local communities.

Remember: (a) that knowing facts about AIDS is not enough. Role play and drama are vital. Childrenare vulnerable; they must gain the confidence to say "no";

(b) this sheet is about caring for people with AIDS as well as preventing it. We must learn to accept and help those who are infected rather than rejecting them.

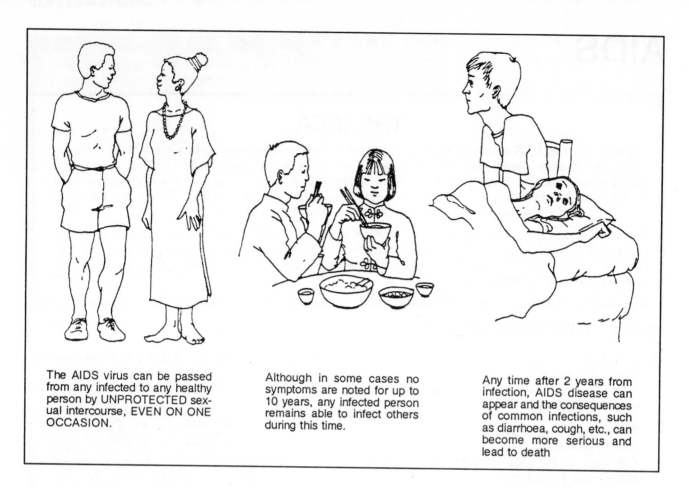

The AIDS virus can be passed from any infected to any healthy person by UNPROTECTED sexual intercourse, EVEN ON ONE OCCASION.

Although in some cases no symptoms are noted for up to 10 years, any infected person remains able to infect others during this time.

Any time after 2 years from infection, AIDS disease can appear and the consequences of common infections, such as diarrhoea, cough, etc., can become more serious and lead to death

HOW IS AIDS SPREAD?

There are two main ways of getting AIDS. The AIDS virus is transmitted:

- By sexual intercourse (vaginal or anal) with any infected person;

- Blood-to-blood, if someone receives blood containing the AIDS virus from another person:

  - by sharing needles or using unsterilised needles (for injections);
  - by transfusion in a hospital or clinic where the blood has not been properly tested;
  - by using unsterilised instruments that cut the skin (for circumcision, scarification, tattooing, ear-piercing, etc);

However, unborn babies **can** also get the AIDS virus from their mother's blood during pregnancy.

AIDS IS NOT SPREAD BY

- Shaking hands
- Touching
- Breathing
- Kissing
- Mosquitoes and bed bugs
- Caring for those with AIDS
- Cutlery and cooking utensils
- Bedding and clothing
- Toilets and latrines

> MOTHERS WITH AIDS SHOULD CONTINUE BREASTFEEDING. BREASTMILK IS STILL THE BEST FOOD FOR BABIES.

PREVENTING THE SPREAD OF THE AIDS VIRUS

The AIDS virus must be prevented from passing between one person and another. It is impossible to tell by looking at someone whether they carry the AIDS virus. Therefore it is very important to protect oneself against catching the virus.

HOW CAN THE AIDS VIRUS BE PREVENTED FROM SPREADING BY SEX?

- By staying with one faithful sexual partner. The more partners people have, the greater the risk for both of catching the AIDS virus.

- By having safe sex. Kissing, cuddling, touching are safe sex. Penetration by the penis is not.

- By using a condom always. Condoms, if used properly, will do much to protect people from AIDS and other sexually transmitted diseases.

- By drinking less alcohol. Alcohol causes people to lose their judgement about safe sex. Drugs such as marijuana, hashish, cocaine, heroin, etc. can do the same thing.

- By seeking early treatment for sores or unusual discharge from the penis or vagina. People with these sores or discharge are more likely to catch and spread the AIDS virus.

HOW CAN THE AIDS VIRUS BE PREVENTED FROM SPREADING BY BLOOD?

- By ensuring that needles, syringes and cutting instruments are thoroughly washed after use and sterilised by heat or chemicals. In national immunisation programmes, health workers have been specially trained in giving injections safely.

- By asking for medicines which can be given by mouth instead of by injection.

- By avoiding contact with other people's blood. When giving first aid, it is important to cover cuts and sores and wash hands well afterwards.

- By reducing the number of blood transfusions. Because blood can carry many diseases, doctors now choose to give fewer blood transfusions.

WHAT CHILDREN CAN DO

AIDS worldwide is a new problem and requires changes in behaviour everywhere. Governments can make some changes but families, communities and schools play an important part.

PEOPLE HAVE LIVED IN THE SAME HOUSE AS SOMEONE WITH THE AIDS VIRUS FOR MORE THAN 10 YEARS WITHOUT GETTING AIDS

School children are the future community and must learn to be responsible for others as well as themselves. Guided by school teachers, health workers and community leaders, children can learn how to protect their family, their partners and themselves against AIDS. Children and young people can make decisions about their own behaviour and thereby offer safer patterns of sexual behaviour for the community. For example, in Zambia there are over 600 'Anti-AIDS Clubs' organised by students in schools throughout the country. The main aim of these clubs is to give information on how AIDS is spread and how to avoid it.

Here is part of a letter from a club member to the 'Anti-AIDS Project' in Lusaka which initiated the clubs:

I received the things you sent and I was very, very glad. I've signed on the membership card and I've kept the promises which I must promise to follow as a member of the Anti-AIDS club. I've got questions for you to help me .....

CARING FOR PEOPLE WITH AIDS

We all care for each other, in our families and communities. Sick people, small children, old people and orphans need our care. When a person has AIDS, they may feel lonely and frightened. We need to show that we care for them.

People with AIDS need food, support, medical care, physical help and particularly family and friends who will accept them and listen to them. They can be encouraged to live an active life wherever they are. We can help them to lead a healthier life by encouraging them to eat well, smoke less and drink less alcohol.

We cannot catch the AIDS virus by caring for someone who is sick with AIDS. We must remember:

- to protect the person with AIDS from infections;
- to protect ourselves and others from the AIDS virus.

We do this by following the usual hygiene principles:

- Covering open wounds on our hands;
- Washing hands before and after caring for the sick person;
- Washing hands before handling food;
- Keeping the sick person and surroundings clean.

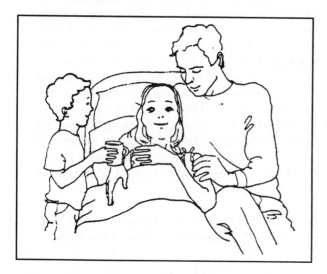

ACTIVITIES FOR SCHOOL AND YOUTH GROUPS

All teachers, not just the health education teacher, have a responsibility to include teaching on AIDS in their lessons. There are also many opportunities for teaching about AIDS on other occasions where children and young people gather together - in clubs, religious meetings, youth and scout/guide groups. The adults leading these sessions can choose the appropriate activities. (In the following examples the word 'teacher' can apply to all adults working with children.)

WHEN AND WHERE TO DISCUSS ABOUT AIDS

- In health clubs or special anti-AIDS clubs, in which the children learn about how AIDS is spread and make a commitment to protect themselves and teach others how to prevent AIDS.

- Sometimes it is easier to talk about these sensitive issues in single sex groups. The groups of girls or boys can discuss issues about AIDS, share their concerns openly, and support each other to have confidence in the decisions they need to make. It is easier if the adult involved is also of the same sex.

GETTING THE FACTS RIGHT

Children can:

- Play a 'true/false' game. The teacher writes down true or false statements about AIDS on separate pieces of paper, e.g.: 'You can catch the AIDS virus from mosquitoes' (false); 'You can't catch the AIDS virus by shaking hands' (true). On the floor mark three areas - 'TRUE', 'FALSE' and 'DON'T KNOW'. Each child takes one statement, puts it on one of the three areas and explains the reason for their choice. Anyone else can challenge the decision.

- Write quiz questions about AIDS and discuss the answers in pairs.

FINDING OUT ACTIVITIES

Children can:

- Where possible, find out from newspapers or government health departments the number of AIDS cases in the country. Work out the percentage of the total population this figure represents.

- Visit a local health centre. Health workers can talk about why they give injections and demonstrate how needles and syringes are sterilised.

DISCUSSION AND ROLE PLAY ABOUT AVOIDING AIDS

Children can:

- Imagine how AIDS might affect their lives. They can shut their eyes and imagine their lives in two

years' time. The teacher can ask questions like: 'Who will you be living with?'; 'Who will your friends be?'; 'How will you show your love and friendship?'; 'Might you try drugs, alcohol or smoking?'; 'How might AIDS enter your lives or the lives of your families and friends?' The children can then imagine their lives in 10 years' time and answer the same questions. Finally they can imagine that they are parents and have children aged 13. What advice would they give them?

- Make a role play about different married couples and how they treat each other. Which are the happiest marriages?

- Discuss situations when it is sometimes difficult to say 'No' and list the reasons. In pairs, children can role play different situations, imagine how people might try to persuade them to do something and how they could say, 'No' in a way which is polite but firm, e.g. when asked:
  - to have a cigarette;
  - to go somewhere with a stranger;
  - to go out for the evening.

- Find out what guidance their religious books give on sexual practices.

DISCUSSION AND ROLE PLAY ABOUT ATTITUDES TO PEOPLE WHO HAVE AIDS

Children can:

- Collect newspaper cuttings concerning AIDS and discuss the attitudes the articles suggest.

- Write poems expressing their feelings about AIDS and its effect upon their own or other people's lives.

CHILDREN IN ROLE-PLAYING GAMES

- Use pictures, e.g. of someone caring for a friend with AIDS, to help them to imagine how they would feel in the role of one person in the picture. They can ask questions about what events led to the scene shown and what might happen in the future.

- Create short plays, for example about caring at home for a person with AIDS. They can first act the play themselves, then each make a simple puppet for their character and perform the play with puppets to the rest of the school or the community.

- Collect and discuss stories from religious books of people caring for the sick.

- Fill in the details of a story, for example about an imaginary school pupil thought to have AIDS. The children divide into groups representing, in this example, the pupil, other pupils, teachers and parents. Each group separately considers: 'What do I feel?', 'What are the main effects on me?', and 'What do I want to happen?'. After 15 minutes the groups reassemble and share their discussions.

- Listen to the following stories:

> 'A young woman returns to her village from a neighbouring city. As she walks across the square people shout at her "AIDS! AIDS!" Her stepfather insists that she gets an AIDS test before she lives in the family home. The test is positive.'

> 'A group of politicians see a video showing a person dying of AIDS and make a policy that everyone should be tested and those carrying the virus should be locked up.'

> 'The colleagues of a woman whose husband has AIDS refuse to work with her. She is sacked.'

Then try to answer these questions:

- What do you think about these situations?
- Why do people react in these ways?
- Will these reactions help to control the spread of AIDS?
- What would you do if you were any of the characters in these stories?

PASSING ON THE MESSAGE

Children can:

- make up and perform songs, plays and puppet shows about AIDS;

- design and make posters to display in class and on open days;

- join in the promotion of sports for better health of people with AIDS.

FOLLOW-UP

Teachers can:

- ask children different questions to find out if they know:
  - what spreads AIDS;
  - what does not spread AIDS.

- ask children to write stories:
  - about people catching the AIDS virus;
  - about caring for people with AIDS.

  Then look at the stories. What do they tell us about children's **knowledge** and about their **attitudes**?

- ask children to find out how many local schools or youth groups have clubs and activities which look at AIDS. What do they do? Have the children joined them?

- find out if children have:
  - taken part in anti-AIDS campaigns;
  - helped anyone with AIDS;
  - warned other children about the risks of AIDS.

MAKING OUR OWN ACTIVITY SHEETS

Who Makes Activity Sheets and Why?

Activity Sheets often need to be locally produced to reflect local priorities and to suit the need of local groups who use them.

The contents of Activity Sheets, therefore, need to be written in a language which these users can easily understand. Activity Sheets should never contain complicated medical language which frightens and confuses users.

Activity Sheets are often made by a small group of people, each of whom has a particular contribution to making the sheet work well, e.g.

- a doctor or health worker who understands the medical priorities;

- a teacher or youth worker who understands how to communicate with children;

- a local community member who knows about the children or the area and what is acceptable and not acceptable;

- a writer or story teller who knows how to make the sheet interesting and fun.

> **REMEMBER**
> People who have contributed to making Activity Sheets become very much more committed to using the sheets as a result.

Guidelines for Making an Activity Sheet

What is an Activity Sheet?

An Activity Sheet offers general suggestions for a 'Child-involved' approach to one topic or theme. It is NOT a set of teaching notes.

It is often designed to be used not only by teachers but also by organisers of non-formal education such as health clubs and scouts, though in certain cases it can be produced to fit the needs of just one group.

Some criteria for choosing the content of a Sheet

- The topic must be a real priority for the people who are using it.

- The content must be absolutely medically correct and reflect up-to-date medical thinking.

- The topic and activities must be within the capability of children.

- The activities must be interesting for children and fun for them to do.

What does the Sheet usually contain?

1. A summary of the main content.
2. The main concepts.
3. Activities. (Remember to include 'finding out' activities; activities for the class; activities in families and activities in the community.)
4. A section on evaluation (called 'follow-up').
5. A section on 'how to use this Sheet'.

(**Note:** You may wish your Sheet to have a different order or different sections.)

How to go about your task

1. Select the topic or topics you wish to cover. (Our experience is that no more than four persons can usefully work on a Sheet.)
2. Study other Sheets.
3. Brainstorm on the 'content' section. Then write it.
4. Brainstorm on the 'activity' section, then write it.
5. Write the evaluation (follow-up) section.
6. Lastly write the 'idea'.
7. Decide what illustrations you want and do roughs of them.
8. Get a medical consultant to read through the text and look at the roughs of the illustrations.
9. Get a language expert to read through the text.
10. Type up (or get typed). Paste in roughs.
11. Final read through by panel.

> **REMEMBER**
> WRITING AN ACTIVITY SHEET IS A VERY TRICKY JOB. EVERY WORD MUST COUNT.

CHILD-TO-CHILD

APPROACHES TO LEARNING AND TEACHING

by
Audrey Aarons

TAKING ACTION
FOR HEALTH
EDUCATION
WITH THE
CHILD-TO-CHILD
APPROACH

For:
leaders
trainers
teachers
writers

ABOUT THIS SECTION

Who is it for?

- It is for teachers and health workers who want to improve or initiate health education activities using Child-to-Child. It will help them to relate children's learning to the health needs of the community.

- It is for trainers of teachers and health workers who want to develop training programmes and learning materials for health education that include a Child-to-Child approach. It will help them select content and activities that encourage children to take action for better health in their communities.

How will they use it?

- **Individual** teachers and health workers can use it to plan learning activities for the children they know, the school they work in and the community they are from.

- **Groups** of teachers and health workers in a school or from a cluster of schools who meet together to share ideas and resources can use it to plan units of work for health education.

- **Trainers** of teachers and health workers can use it in workshop situations to plan inservice training and write materials for health education.

How is this Section organized?

- Part I discusses the importance of health education for children. It discusses the role it has in linking their learning with good habits, and with home and neighbourhood activities. It shows how to help children acquire skills that lead to making better decisions about their health.

- Parts II and III show some examples of practical activities for learning about health that have been tried by teachers. The activities are analysed so that they can be used by teachers and others to help them develop their own programmes. Some guidelines are given to help plan better health education programmes using a Child-to-Child approach.

The above parts will be useful in workshop situations.

- Parts IV and V list a variety of methods and materials that use a Child-to-Child approach and how to use them in health programmes. Teachers can try these ideas and adapt them. They can add their own ideas to share with others.

GETTING STARTED WITH CHILD-TO-CHILD.............

- Read the Activity Sheets in Section 2. Choose a topic that suits your environment. Try one idea from it. Discuss the result with your colleagues. Try another and think of ways to add or change it. Try to develop your own ideas further.

- Organize a workshop. See Sectin 5 for some ideas on how to do this. Together discuss and plan how to incorporate ideas in your programmes. Parts 1 and 2 of this Section may also help you.

- Ask others to help you to try ideas for activities - community leaders, health workers, teachers. Try activities that suit your programmes. Discuss them with your colleagues.

1. THINKING ABOUT HEALTH EDUCATION PROGRAMMES FOR CHILDREN

Here are some questions to think about and to discuss with others, particularly in workshop situations. The discussion will help to focus on the need for better health education, the needs of communities and ways to introduce a Child-to-Child approach to health education.

1.1. What is health education?

Health education is about learning to consider choices and to make decisions for our wellbeing as an individual and as members of a community. Our actions are based on the information we have and the practice we have in making decisions. These are affected by our values and attitudes. We make decisions as individuals about our health and wellbeing. These decisions may as often depend on community or political actions. They should be made in consensus with others such as parents, religious leaders, health workers, teachers.

Health and wellbeing are important aspects of our lives and learning how to be healthy is an important part of education. And children need to be healthy in order to learn.

1.2. What is a Child-to-Child approach to health education?

The Child-to-Child approach helps children to learn about health in active and meaningful ways. It helps them to find out information and to take action for the better health of themselves and others.

Child-to-Child approach:

- Is linked to **important** messages in health.
- Is concerned with activities which children **can do** either themselves or with a little help from adults.
- Emphasises activities which **interest** children and which they **enjoy**.

Child-to-Child messages

Child-to-Child activities can be grouped into six main "families":

- Child Growth and Development
- Nutrition
- Personal and Community Hygiene
- Safety
- Recognizing and Helping Children with Disabilities
- Prevention and Cure of Disease.

1.3. Why have health education in school programmes?

For many children who attend primary school or other alternative types of school programmes it is the only opportunity they have for formal education. These schools are usually in the neighbourhood. Outside school the children are active members of their families with responsibilities for child care, collection of water and food preparation.

We need to develop education programmes that contribute skills and knowledge to build on these experiences. The children can learn to apply their knowledge to their own health and wellbeing and they can learn to share this knowledge with others. They are an important link between school and community in the development of better health for all. Child-to-Child approaches help to do these things.

1.4. What are the aims of school health education programmes?

Health education programmes for schools can have different components. They can aim to provide:

- a healthy school environment that has clean drinking water, facilities for rubbish disposal, adequate shelter in and out of the classroom and safe and pleasant grounds.

- a centre for health services for children that includes basic medical and dental services for monitoring growth and development of the children, immunization services and school food programmes.

- a health education programme that helps children to develop skills and understanding so that they can learn to be responsible for their own health and contribute to the health and wellbeing of others at school, at home and in the neighbourhood.

- extra-curricular health activities through health clubs, Red Cross and Crescent groups, scout

organizations or 'little doctors' that help to link school activities to community programmes and life outside the school.

1.5. What are the aims of out-of-school health education programmes?

Children are involved in out-of-school programmes of many kinds. Some are extra-curricular to school programmes like health clubs, Junior Red Cross, or scouts. Some are part of special programmes for out-of-school children like literacy classes, trade schools or programmes for child-minders. Some are part of a nutrition, agricultural or mother-and-child programme.

All of these aim to improve the health of the community but many have a special focus like first aid (Junior Red Cross), health of mothers and babies (MCH), nutrition and agriculture (special programmes for girls), a healthy environment (scouts).

These programmes can help children to care for themselves and to care for others. They can learn to take action and to pass on information that helps others to be healthy.

1.6. What is the focus of teaching and learning in a Child-to-Child approach?

To help children develop skills for health we need activities and programmes that do some of these things:

- Focus teaching and learning on the health concerns of the children and their families, the health concerns of the school and its environment, the community and its environment. These can be identified by discussion with teachers and children, with health workers, parents and community leaders.

  e.g. – the local policeman may identify causes of traffic accidents.
  – the children can identify which children have been sick and what disease they had.
  – health workers may have a nutrition programme underway.

- Use the children's own experiences as the starting point wherever possible. It gives a sense of purpose and meaning to what is learnt. It relates their learning to their own environment.

  e.g. –Where is the best place to collect clean water? Why?

- Help the children to find out information for themselves through investigation, experiments, discussion between themselves and others at home and in the neighbourhood. It helps them to understand why and how events occur. It helps them to understand how to establish principles to apply to new situations.

  e.g. –Water some plants and not others. What happens? Why?

- Help the children to make decisions and to take action. This relates learning to the application of knowledge. It helps children to develop a sense of responsibility and take action for themselves, for others and for the neighbourhood environment.

e.g. – Make a safe place to play, establish safety rules, make salt and sugar drink for diarrhoea.

1.7. What do we know about schools and communities and out-of-school groups?

Health workers, teachers and children live and work in different environments. To plan learning activities that are realistic we need to have a picture in our mind of the kind of classroom and the kind of community in which they are working.

- **COMMUNITIES**

In what kinds of communities are the health programmes located? Some may be small agricultural villages in rural areas that have few facilities. Some may be fishing villages near a river, on a lake or by the sea. Some may be small towns or large crowded cities.

Their location will determine the facilities and the resources available to teachers and the children.

What are the health priorities of these different communities? It may be that health workers, parents and teachers perceive their health needs in different ways. It may be that national health priorities and local health needs are perceived differently.

These perceptions of priorities will affect the choice of content for health programmes.

What community development activities are already being undertaken? It may be that different communities are already working to develop agriculture, nutrition, mother and child care or water and sanitation facilities. There are a number of people in the community with skills and knowledge that contribute to the wellbeing of all.

These people and their activities provide an opportunity to learn from others and to share health programmes and materials with them. Contact them and work together.

• SCHOOLS

What facilities and resources do teachers have? Some schools will have good buildings and some equipment. Others will be very crowded or operate on a shift system. Teachers' experiences and their confidence in trying new ideas will vary.

Planning learning activities has to be realistic and take into account the resources of teachers and schools. What can be achieved in each school will vary accordingly. Let them decide what is best for them.

What health related activities are being carried out already in schools by teachers and health workers? Some schools may have regular visits from health workers. In some schools children may be members of Red Crescent or a health society. In other schools teachers may have incorporated health themes into other subjects of the curriculum.

It is useful to identify these health activities and learn from the teachers, health workers and children. These ideas can be shared with other schools and the activities developed further.

• OUT-OF-SCHOOL GROUPS

What is the main age group and how often do they meet together? Some out-of-school programmes meet for a short time each day four or five times a week. Others meet only once a week or even monthly. Some programmes are for mothers and children together, others for young primary school age children and others for adolescents. The kind of activity that leaders and teachers undertake will depend on how much time is available at each meeting. It will also depend on whether the programmes are linked to literacy, nutrition or other community programmes.

What kind of short-term activities as well as longer series of activities will suit the interest level and time available? Link with other health workers and teachers to share ideas.

2. PLANNING HEALTH EDUCATION PROGRAMMES

This Chapter looks at ways to establish health education programmes for children that include a Child-to-Child approach. It will be useful in a workshop situation where groups of teachers and health workers meet together to share ideas and to plan longer term programmes for schools or out-of-school programmes. It lists some planning decisions: Who will be responsible for programme development? and what materials will they produce? what health topics are best suited to children? and how will they learn it? Following this (in Part 3) are examples of learning activities and materials that are appropriate to children. These will guide groups producing programmes and learning materials for health education.

How will leaders introduce Child-to-Child activities in out-of-school health programmes?

- through **extra-curricular activities** where children meet at the school after hours. These can link health activities at school to home and neighbourhood.

- through **special education programmes** for out-of-school groups of girls, adolescents, women which may focus on special health needs.

- through **social and community** organizations like Junior Red Cross, scouts, Junior Jaycees, youth clubs which may want to link with community development activities.

- through **health and community development programmes** like immunization campaigns, water and sanitation projects, clean-up week.

How will leaders develop health activities?

- through discussion with community leaders to identify a short-term action programme.

- through a sequence of skills like first aid that can be linked to a badge scheme in scouts or youth organizations.

- by working with leaders and teachers of out-of-school programmes to decide the priorities of health topics and the kind of links that can be made with literacy and other skills.

What needs to be considered?

Who is the leader? What resources are available - time, materials, people? What community programmes exist? What priorities exist? Who else should be consulted? How long can a project be?

How will teachers introduce health activities in the classroom?

- as **subject teaching** with a place in the time-table each week and with a syllabus that gives a sequence of topics and activities for each level in the school; or,

- as an **extra-curricular** activity organized through a health society or Red Crescent group which has a loosely arranged series of meetings and activities; or,

- as **health across the curriculum** where health topics are used as examples in other subjects like science, social studies, maths, language and religion.

How will schools develop a health programme?

- through discussion and planning at staff meetings and parents' meetings.

- in collaboration with health teams who visit the school to offer services to the children and community such as first aid, immunization, dental, maternal and child care.

- by working with parents and school management groups to establish a school health policy to improve the health environment of the school.

How will ideas be shared?

The ideas about school and community health programmes that are developed can be replicated for others through the writing of health materials. In this way the experience gained by individual leaders, health workers and teachers can be built on. Their ideas can be adapted and their experiences shared with wider groups of leaders, teachers and others to help them conduct similar programmes of health education.

2.1. Selecting planning groups

The first planning decisions are to decide what kind of health programmes are needed and who will develop these programmes and produce learning materials. To be relevant the programmes need to be based on experience and be the contribution of those who know communities, classrooms and children well. These will be teachers, health workers, community leaders, parents and the children themselves.

Health workers can contribute from their experience of health practice and identify local health priorities. Community leaders can contribute information about current health projects and health needs as perceived by adults. Teachers understand how children learn and know about the classroom context. Trainers of health workers and teachers have skills related to teaching and learning and the preparation of materials.

Select the members of the working group from among these people and any other people with an interest in health. Decide how they will work together. Who will work with teachers and children in schools and out-of-school to try ideas and review them? What printed materials are to be produced and how will they be distributed and explained to others? If this is through inservice training or workshops and meetings, who will conduct them? Who will follow up with visits? How will leaders and teachers report back and share experiences?

2.2. Selecting an approach

Deciding the manner in which you want the children to learn (the approach) is as important as selecting what you teach (the content).

Three approaches to health education are illustrated in this manual. They are:

- **an action-oriented** approach which for the children means using knowledge, practising skills and taking action towards the wellbeing of themselves and others. This might be in the classroom, outside of school, in the neighbourhood or at home.

- **a community-oriented** approach which emphasises the social aspects as well as the physical aspects of health education. This links school learning with the needs of children as members of groups at school, at home and in the neighbourhood.

- **Child-to-Child** which emphasises learning to take action for the health of others, particularly other children, and to pass on health messages at home and in the community. Thus it includes both an action-oriented and community-oriented approach.

These approaches overlap and may be present to different degrees in one programme. This will depend on the topic, the age and the stage of the children and resourcefulness of the leaders, teachers and the community.

2.3. Selecting the content

Decisions about what to include in programmes and materials will depend on the place, the time available, the age group and the leaders. Is it a series of activities linked over a month of weekly meetings? Is it for a year's work or a month's work? Is it to be the whole school health curriculum? The answer to these questions will determine the scope of the programme.

(i) To select a broad range of topics the planning group might begin by doing these things:

- **List** health priorities as set by health workers, community leaders, teachers.

- **Find out:** What community health programmes already exist? What aspects should be included in school programmes? Which schools and youth groups already have programmes of health activities? What activities can we include? If it is a school programme, what topics, concepts, learning skills are covered already in the curriculum? How can these be linked to health?

- **Decide:** Which topics to select, for which group of children? Which skills and concepts? Will all schools and youth groups do the same things or will there be some options for different environments?

- **Check:** Is there a balance in the choice of topics and themes - physical, social, mental aspects of wellbeing? Is the selection appropriate to children, teachers and the community? Are they topics on which children can take some action for themselves, for others?

(ii) To select content specific to individual topics and themes, the group might do these things next:

- **Identify** the topic or theme.

- **Decide** why this is important and what they expect children to learn.

- **List** learning activities related to this topic. What do they need to know? What can they find out? What can they do to help themselves, others, the environment for better health?

- **Check** with community feelings about these activities.

- **Select** from the learning activities those that are appropriate to the level of the children, the scope of the topic, the realities of the context, the sensitivities of the community.

- **Decide** in which order the activities take place.

- **Explain** to others who should be involved.

If it is a school programme:

- **Examine** the total curriculum for links to other subjects and match activities to skills, concepts, topics.

If it is an out-of-school programme:

- **Match** it with other health and community projects.

- **Decide** what will be done at school or meeting, at home, in the neighbourhood.

- **Plan** how to find out how well it worked and develop the ideas further.

2.4. Selecting activities

The kind of activity you plan for children to learn from will be based on the content and the approach you have chosen. Here are some questions to consider when selecting learning activities for children.

- What activity can the children do in the meeting, in the classroom, at school? How will it help them learn about the topic?

- What activity can children do at home or in the neighbourhood either as a group or individually?

- Does the activity start with what the children know already? Does it use their experiences?

- Does the activity help them collect information, discuss it, interpret it, plan to take action for better health?

- Does the activity help them to communicate with others and enlist their support?

- Is the activity appropriate for the age of the children, the time available, the school context, the resources that are available, the feelings of the community?

SUMMARY:

These important steps summarize the main ideas of a Child-to-Child approach to planning health education for children.

In planning a sequence of learning activities about health try to include these steps:

- **recognizing and identifying a situation,** a need or a health problem.

- **learning more about it,** finding out what people do and think about it. This includes **interpreting and analyzing** the information to see how many? why? where? when? and **understanding** the sequence of events, cause and effect, the principles that apply.

- **discussing and deciding on action** to prevent or cure the problem, to care for self and others, to pass on information.

- **taking action** together as a group or as an individual.

- **checking** to see how well the ideas worked, what else needs to be done or needs to be changed to do it better.

- **developing** the ideas and understanding further to link them with other knowledge and actions.

Remember:

- try to plan for children to learn **about** something and **how to do** something.

- plan activities for the children that can be done in the meeting, the classroom, at school, at home, in the neighbourhood.

To illustrate a programme of activities some examples are given in Part 3.

3. HEALTH EDUCATION PROGRAMMES IN ACTION

In this Chapter there are examples of how a teacher, a youth leader and a trainer used a Child-to-Child approach to health education. The programme of activities in the three examples are developed using the steps set out in Part 2 - Selecting content and Selecting activities. It might help you to start a programme of activities for yourself using a similar sequence of steps. It would be interesting to do this with a group of leaders or teachers and health workers and to compare the ways in which your programmes are different from each other. You will each want to select ideas appropriate to your own locality and situation.

Programmes of health education in primary schools are usually organized in one of three ways. As a separate **subject** in the curriculum or as an **extra-curricular** activity or integrated with other subjects **across the curriculum**. Decisions about this are often made at central level. Whichever way is chosen teachers will need the support of health workers and others to prepare programmes and to implement the ideas in their schools.

3.1. A School Programme

Here is an example from one school which has implemented health education programmes through the curriculum. This example shows how the teacher planned the programme. This can serve as a reference for those who want to develop their own school health programmes using a Child-to-Child approach.

Because this is a health programme in the school curriculum the teacher must think about the knowledge and skills children need to learn. Teachers also need to think about the approaches and activities that link with other learning going on in the classroom.

For example, in this teacher's programme she has included activities of different kinds:

> some discussion;
> some investigation by the children;
> some recording and analysis of their survey through classifying;
> some writing, acting and talking.

The teacher has included classroom activity and some things to be done outside and at home.

She has tried to involve others in the community who may have special knowledge or skills - like the health worker and policeman. And she has tried to link the activities to other skills children are learning in different subjects.

Teachers remember:

In managing children's learning activities in health it is a good idea to:

- discuss your plans with other staff members

- check your information with health workers and community leaders

- let parents know why children are gathering this information

- think about the timing of activities: how long they will take and when will they be done?

- prepare children carefully if they are going into the community: politeness and sensitivity are important.

This is a Grade 4 teacher's plan for a unit of work.

Unit: ACCIDENTS

Questions	Ideas for teaching and learning
Why is this unit important?	• Many children are injured or die because of accidents. • Accidents need not happen. • Children can learn to prevent accidents.
What do I need to do to help me to teach this well?	• Find out about accidents in the community: the main causes and kinds of injuries. • Consult with health workers, police and local leaders to ask what children can do to help prevent accidents.

What will children find out about?	• Children find out about accidents. They can find answers to these questions:
	  – Who has had an accident? Who has been hurt?
	  – How did it happen? Where did it happen?
	  – Who came to help? What did you do then?
	  – What happened to the injured person after they were treated?
	  – How can accidents be prevented?

How will the information be collected and organized?	• Through **discussion** in class and by asking questions. Through mime and acting what happened.
	• Through planning and conducting a survey at school, at home and in the community. Find out:
	  a) Who has had an accident at school? Where did the accident occur? Which class was the child in?
	  (b) Who has had an accident at home? Where did it occur? why?
	  (c) Who has had an accident in the neighbourhood? where? why?

How will we use the information?	• Analyze the information so that children find answers to these questions:
	  – Where did most accidents happen?
	  – What kinds of accidents happened most?
	  – Which age groups have most accidents?
	
	• The children can make charts and graphs to show the result of their search.
	
	• We can discuss the results and think about what to do to help others and to prevent accidents.
	
	• We can invite the community leader and discuss our findings.

What action can we take? – to prevent accidents – to give help and first aid – to pass on information	• We can learn safety rules and make the school a safe place to play. • We can learn simple first aid and where to get help. Ask the health worker to help with this. • We can make a play about accidents - a stupid careless person and a wise helping friend and perform it in the community centre.
How well did the activities work?	• Are there fewer accidents at school? • Is the school a safer place to play? • Do little children still walk home with older children who know the road rules?
What can we do next to build on these ideas?	• Make toys and a play area for the small children at school. • Learn first aid appropriate to minor accidents at school.

These are some of the activities the children did, after the discussions:

1 They made a picture story book about someone they know who had an accident.

This links with language activities.

2 They made graphs and tables to share the results of their survey.

Who had an accident?	Where?	What happened?	The injury
Gani	at school	fell over a big stone	hurt his knee
Bela	in the house	cut herself with a big knife	her finger was cut and had some stitches

This links with maths and social studies activities.

The accidents happened here :

at school	/ / / /
on the road	┼┼┼ / /
in the field	/ /
in the kitchen	┼┼┼ ┼┼┼ /

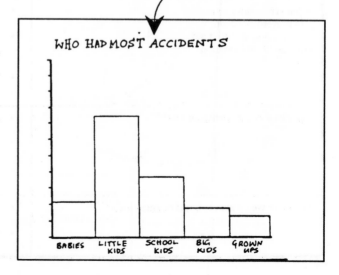

WHO HAD MOST ACCIDENTS

BABIES LITTLE KIDS SCHOOL KIDS BIG KIDS GROWN UPS

3 They learnt first aid and practised it at school

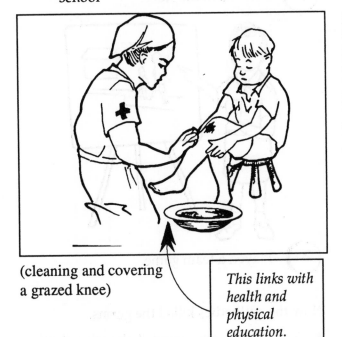

(cleaning and covering a grazed knee)

This links with health and physical education.

4 They made a safe place to play for small children at school.

This links with community service

Children and young adults participate in community organizations of many kinds. These may be organizations like scouts, junior Red Crescent, youth brigades.

These organizations usually meet regularly but only for 2-3 hours each week or each month.

Sometimes the organization has a special focus like first aid or community service.

Some of the characteristics of groups like these will have implications for the way in which activities are undertaken.

Perhaps:

- they only meet together for a short period of time. So, activities have to be planned to fit the short time available.

- they may have few materials to make things like posters, books or record cards.

- they are voluntary so activities for participants should be enjoyable as well as useful.

- the participants will be of different ages and with different experiences - some of them may not have much schooling. Activities need to be matched to their interests and their special skills.

This is a plan of activities undertaken by one youth organization - the scout group. The activities were carried out over one month of regular weekly meetings. It was linked to a community immunization campaign that the health workers organized.

The health worker, the community leader and the scout leader discussed the plans together.

- the health worker offered to give special information to the scouts

- the community leader offered support and to find ways to inform others about what the scouts were doing.

IMMUNIZATION CAMPAIGN

- the Scout Group did this over 4 meetings in one month.

1st meeting   **FIND OUT**

- Talk about immunization. What is it? Why is it necessary? How often? Who has it?

- The health worker comes to the meeting, tells a story using the flannel board about two families, one which makes good decisions, the other which does not.

- Play a game in teams - antibodies versus germs.

Between meetings, the scouts count young children in the neighbourhood needing immunization.

2nd meeting   **PLAN HOW TO HELP**

- Discuss what you found out. How many children need some extra immunization? How many need all the series?

Talk about importance of completing the whole series.

- Make up a song about immunization — 1 for measles, 2 for BCG, 3 for DPT, 4 for polio.

- Make record cards for families to remind them when the next shot is due.

Between meetings - pass messages to families about clinic times for immunization.

3rd meeting   **PASSING ON IDEAS**

- Plan a play to perform in the community about one family who did not want to have immunization, the other who did.

Rehearse the parts.

- Plan the discussion to follow on from the performance. Who made good decisions? Why? What would happen if......? What would you do?

Between meetings, perform the play at the community centre. Ask the health worker to help with the discussion after it.

4th meeting   **HELPING OTHERS AT THE CLINIC**

- Scouts help bring young children to the clinic.
- Scouts help complete record cards at clinic.
- Scouts help amuse waiting children.

These are the activities the scouts did:

1 Listened to the story.

2 Played a team game.

How the antibodies killed the germs.

- Two teams - one "germs", the other "antibodies".

- In the field draw two lines in the middle. Germs try to cross to other side from A to B. If antibodies catch them they have been "immunized" and join the antibodies' team in the middle of the two lines.

3

Counted children in the neighbourhood

under 2	┼┼┼ ///
over 2 and under 5	┼┼┼ ┼┼┼ /
over 8	┼┼┼ ///

4 Made a record card for each family.

Record Card
Name .... Birth ....

MEASLES   I
BCG   II
DPT   III
POLIO   IIII

5 Made posters with the immunization times and displayed them in appropriate places.

Immunisation times

6 Performed a play for the community to show the importance of immunization,

7 Accompanied some children to the health centre for their immunizations.

3.3. A Literacy Programme for Girls Who Do Not Go to School

This is an example of part of a health education programme that is linked to functional literacy. The group of girls who do not go to school meet regularly with a teacher-leader for six months of the year. The programme includes literacy, family health, agriculture and child care.

The teacher-leaders of the classes are older girls from the community who have been to school. These girls meet with a trainer once a week to plan their activities and programmes.

There are many other programmes like this one. For example, special classes for boys who help with agricultural activities in the morning; special classes for children in refugee camps and classes for older children who left school early.

These types of programmes usually:

- meet regularly during the week for a longer time

- have some materials for reading and writing

- are planned to link reading with knowledge to improve daily life.

Here we can see how the **trainer** helped the literacy teachers to plan some activities for the week. The trainer used a Child-to-Child activity sheet as a starting point.

What the **literacy class teacher** did.

- She used ideas from the planning meeting with the trainer and did these things during the week. The girls in the class practised what they learnt at home and with young children who came to class with them.

USING A Child-to-Child ACTIVITY SHEET to help get ideas for a programme.

- out-of-school girls' literacy class

What the trainer did to help the literacy class teachers.

MAKING A CHOICE

Which one? CARING FOR CHILDREN WITH DIARRHOEA

Why? Because diarrhoea is a common problem in our community. Older girls can prevent and treat it.

GETTING INFORMATION

- Read the Activity Sheet.

- Find out about the local situation. Ask the health worker about local beliefs; local cures; the fluids she is recommending.

- Try the experiments yourself to see how they work.

DECIDING WHAT TO TEACH THE LITERACY TEACHERS

- Decide which **information** the teacher-leaders need to know:

  – what is diarrhoea?
  – why is it dangerous?
  – how can it be prevented?
  – how can we treat it?

(Refer to Activity Sheet and Health Workers' information)

- Decide which activities the leaders might do with the girls.

  – learn recipes for making soups
  – learn how to make special drink
  – do the experiments about fluid loss
  – keeping records.

PLAN WITH THE LEADERS

- Do the activities (above) together to see how they work

- Make links with reading - a recipe, the special drink

- Make links with writing - write instructions for special drink, make a record card

- List the teaching points

- List the discussion questions.

THINK ABOUT FOLLOW UP

- How well did it work?

- What can we do next?

M-16

Activity 1.
LEARNING ABOUT THE DISEASE

- Talk about it. Ask these questions. Discuss:

  - What is diarrhoea? What names does it have in the village?

  - What happens to babies who have diarrhoea for a long time?

  - Why is diarrhoea dangerous?

  - Which babies get diarrhoea most often - those who are bottle-fed or those who are breastfed?

  - What do you do if someone has diarrhoea?

  - How can we prevent it?

CHILDREN WITH DIARRHOEA					
AGE	0-1	2	3	4	5
BOTTLE FED	IIII	II	I	I	
BREAST FED	I	III			
DEATH	I		I		

- Make a record card. Find out who had diarrhoea last week. Keep the record for one month. Talk about the results each day.

Activity 2.
LEARNING MORE ABOUT IT

- Teacher read Child-to-Child storybook, "A SIMPLE CURE". Let them act the story. Talk about it. Let them borrow the book to take home to read.

Activity 3.
TAKING ACTION

- Making special drink with sugar and salt.

- Writing instructions on a piece of card to take home to pin on the wall in the kitchen.

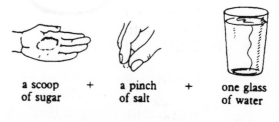

a scoop of sugar + a pinch of salt + one glass of water

DON'T USE TOO MUCH SALT

Activity 4.
UNDERSTANDING REASONS FOR FLUID LOSS

- Do the experiment (see Activity Sheet No.6.1) and discuss. How much fluid is lost? How much can we replace? What happens if plants don't have rain or water? What happens if we don't have water?

- Make models to take home to tell aunties and grandmothers.

Activity 5.
TAKING ACTION

- Making a nutritious soup. Preparing food for sick babies. Use local recipes.

4. LEARNING ABOUT HEALTH: A CHOICE OF METHODS

In teaching about health there are a number of ways to introduce ideas to children that encourage them to participate in learning. Some of these methods need additional materials but many do not. Some are more appropriate in a school setting but most can be tried with any group whether in school or out-of-school.

In this Chapter, there are ideas of how to teach using:

– chalk and talk, writing stories, experiments and demonstrations;

– storytelling, dramatization, working in communities, campaigns, working in groups.

At the end is a chart showing the various methods suggested in the Child-to-Child Activity Sheets.

4.1. Chalk and talk

For many teachers the most familiar setting is a formal classroom with a chalkboard and the children's exercise and textbooks. The chalkboard can be used by the children as well as the teachers as part of health education activity. Use it to do these things:

- **make lists** that the children or teacher can add to. For example, when talking about foods available in the market, list them, classify them according to season, by food value.

- **draw pictures** in a sequence. Discuss the cause and effect of actions. For example, drinking dirty water collected from the river. What happened? why? how can we change the story?

- **make action lists** for a clean up campaign in the neighbourhood. Who will do it? when? who with? who do we inform?

- **write instructions** how to make the salt and sugar drink. Children practise following the instructions and make the drink.

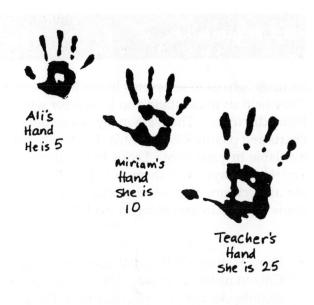

Ali's Hand He is 5

Miriam's Hand She is 10

Teacher's Hand She is 25

- **measure** children's and teacher's hand, height, arm span. Talk about growth.

- **draw a graph or chart** to summarize information collected by the children. For example, how many accidents have happened? to whom? where?

Most of these activities involve **discussion** based on the teacher asking questions and the children giving answers.

Try having the children in groups so that they can discuss the information amongst themselves.

Write some questions on the board. Let each group discuss a different one.

Each group can present their findings as an oral report, summarized on the chalkboard or prepared as a poster for display.

At the end of the discussion, remember to come to some conclusion. What can we do about it for ourselves? What can we do to help someone else? Who should we **tell about** it?

4.2. Picture talks

Pictures help us to see events in our imagination. They help us understand and remember what is being discussed. There are many health posters, charts and picture kits available. Find out what is available in your area. Learn to use them in a variety of ways. Use them to tell health stories about decisions that were made. Use them to **show how to** do something or explain.

- Draw pictures on the chalkboard or on paper. Cut out pictures for flannel boards, flip charts, chainbooks 'comic' style, story rolls. Choose a health theme. Ask questions like: what is happening now? before? next? why?

- Children can use their own pictures and stories about health ideas as a way of sharing information with others.

- Use a **flannel board** to build up a story about some health decisions that were made. Children or teacher can tell the story. They can also act the story. Complete the story. Discuss and give different viewpoints on problem solving or action taken in the story.

- In **making** pictures or cutouts for flannel boards, think about the size of the pictures. Is everyone able to see it easily? Is it clear and are the proportions right? Can the pictures be used in many ways at different times? Store them and carry them carefully.

- When **using** the flannel board or a sequence of pictures, discuss each one as you show it - who is it? What are they doing? Why? What do you think will happen next? How would you feel? What else could they do?

4.3. Story telling

In most societies there is a rich tradition of story telling. Encourage children to collect these stories and tell them at school. Invite story tellers to the school. Find stories about customs, about origins of food and disease, about other health related ideas.

- tell stories in class, at school assemblies, whilst waiting at health centres. Tell stories to children who are sick, in hospital. Make up stories about children and others who solved health problems, who didn't get immunized, who were saved by the sugar and salt drink.

- story telling groups. Encourage children to tell stories to small children. Organize groups at school, at home for story telling.

- use pictures to tell stories.

  Make a series of pictures on separate cards or sheets of paper. Tell a story about an accident. Mix the order of the pictures and get children to say which happened first, next, last.

  Or, put the pictures in sequence but leave one out. What happened in the one that is missing? Name the people in the story. Act it.

  Or, use comic style pictures and block out the speech in the balloons. Ask children to make up the speech. Let them act the story.

Talk about the decisions made. Change the events. Change the ending.

• make up songs, riddles and poems about personal hygiene habits, cleaning teeth, washing hands, keeping flies away. Teach other children. Use them in plays and puppet shows to pass on information.

If you are reading the story from a book, let the children see the pictures. Stop occasionally to ask - what do you think will happen next? why did they do that? how did she feel? was that a good idea - why?

Read it slowly and dramatically. Discuss the events at the end. Think about the actions - what would you do?

• If the children are listening to a story, encourage them to think about the people in the story and what they did.

Discuss with the children each event in the story. What happened first? How did they feel about it? What do you think about it? What did they do then? Why? What was the result? Was it a good decision? How would you feel? Can we change the story? How? What would happen then?

Think about the story. What action can we take - act it? mime it? make a storybook or a picture series? a puppet show? who will be the audience?

Are there some decisions we should take for ourselves? for others?

4.4. Dramatization

As well as telling stories that have health ideas and messages, children can act stories with masks, or by dressing up, by using puppets or by mime.

These can be based on stories they have heard or read or that they themselves make up. They can present them to other groups in the community to teach about a health issue in a lively and interesting way.

• dramatize stories and events told in the stories. Dress up and act them for others. Put on these plays for others at the school, at home. Discuss different endings and different actions that could have been taken by the people in the play.

• use **role play** to imagine how it felt in a situation like being blind, lame or the mother whose child is saved from a bad accident. What is the sequence in the action in the story?

• children can make puppets to use in class, at school assemblies or in the community. They can act health stories to entertain as well as to share information.

Discussion after the puppet play can focus on different endings, alternative behaviour of the characters. This leads to thinking about the options that are available and how to make decisions.

• draw a face on a paper bag that has the bottom folded over to demonstrate how to clean teeth.

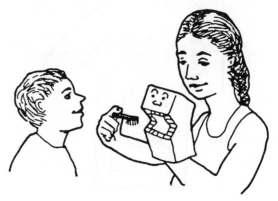

- use finger puppets on each hand to tell a story to a sick child.

DRAW ON FINGER NAIL

OR

WRAP PAPER AROUND FINGER

OR

USE A MATCH BOX

- use cardboard stick puppets to explain how to give fluid to children who are sick with diarrhoea.

Plan

- tell the story several times

- talk about the characters - what are they like?

- will you use masks? dress up? use puppets?

- how will it end?

- who will take part? where will you perform it? who for?

- what are the health messages?

- how will you follow up with discussion? a recipe? some hints? a decision? a discussion?

- who will lead it?

Role play:

- getting inside another....how does it feel? how can we help? what can we do? who do we tell?

Remember:

For puppet plays as with dramatisation you need to plan the story events carefully to give the health message you want. Planning the discussion afterwards is also important. Think about who will lead this discussion so that the audience can decide their own actions.

4.5. Reading and writing

Learning to read and collect information are important life skills. Learning how to use the information to lead healthy lives is part of health education and an important part of passing on health messages to others.

(i) Reading health stories

- Collect **story books** that have health themes. These might be stories about social issues, agricultural decisions, environmental issues as well as about physical health. For example, adventure stories about dirty water, about a child hero who is crippled. Children can read and discuss, read and act, read and tell, read and draw, read aloud to others.

- Collect **newspapers, magazines, posters and pamphlets** that have health information on them. Let the children read them, use them to get information for their project work. Use these for class reading exercises.

(ii) Children can write health stories and health messages

- **write stories** to read to others, to make into books for smaller children, to give to a sick child. The stories can be adventurous or humorous about health events and decisions.

- **write letters** explaining about a cleanup campaign, telling about clinic times, asking for health information.

- **make health posters** announcing visits from health visitors.

- **make record cards** to distribute to families for immunization programmes.

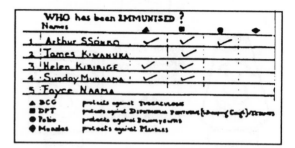

- **prepare school newspapers** with items about health activities, recipes, drawings and writings from all class groups. It can be on display at school, at the health centre.

- **story books** to read to other children.

- **make health posters** to use in health campaigns. They can draw the pictures or cut them out of magazines and newspapers.

4.6. Experiments and demonstrations

To help children understand health ideas and to discover principles for themselves is an important part of learning. Sometimes in explaining health ideas, health workers and teachers will need to give a demonstration. Whenever possible let the children experiment for themselves.

- Let them **make** things, **do** things, **grow** things, **weigh** things, **measure** things for themselves.

- Let them **observe** it, **talk** about it to each other, **record** what is done and observed, **discuss** the results and tell others about it. Children can incorporate these ideas in plays and puppet shows. They can repeat the experiment at clinics, at home, at school assemblies.

For example:

(i) learn how to mix the sugar and salt drink and when to give it to a child with diarrhoea.

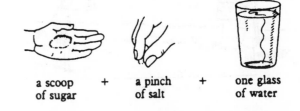

a scoop of sugar + a pinch of salt + one glass of water

DON'T USE TOO MUCH SALT

one glass each stool — two glasses each stool

CHILD   ADULT

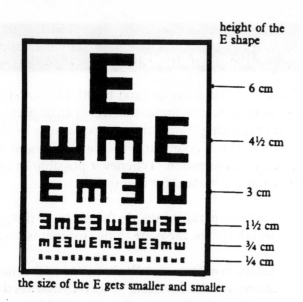

height of the E shape

— 6 cm

— 4½ cm

— 3 cm

— 1½ cm

— ¾ cm

— ¼ cm

the size of the E gets smaller and smaller

stains on inside. Dirty lungs! Discuss. What happens to our lungs with smoking?

(ii) make an eye test chart for the children at school. Tell the parents and health worker if some children have a problem.

(v) weigh babies. Measure young children regularly. Keep charts and records.

6 m or 20 feet

(iii) understanding principles of fluid loss and rehydration. (See page 21)

A gourd or plastic bottle with a hole top and bottom. Half filled with water and as water is lost fill from top to maintain water level. Discuss and draw analogy to body fluid loss with diarrhoea.

(iv) learning about dirty lungs from smoking.

Plastic bottle with eyes, nose and with a hole for mouth. Place cigarette in mouth, light and squeeze bottle so that it "puffs" cigarette. Watch for brown

4.7. Working in groups - in and out of school

Working in pairs or in groups on health projects encourages children to talk to each other about what they are doing. This kind of activity helps children learn to express opinions, to share their understanding, to discuss alternatives, to examine

CHILDREN CAN:

- Collect information

about? { current practice
programmes in the community
remedies
concerns
resources
facts and figures

how? { observe, take notes
ask questions
collect samples
draw maps
read books, papers

who from? { other children
families
neighbours
health workers
teachers

- Organize the information, interpret it, draw conclusions

- Present the information

to whom? { other children
teachers
families
health workers

how? { letters, posters, visits,
plays, puppets, songs,
showing, making, telling

when? { at assemblies
at meetings
on market day
health team visit

- Decide on what to do about it

for self: what shall I do?

for others: how can I help another?

for the environment: how can we make the place healthier?

- Take action

- Check up on result of action

choices and make decisions. In preparing the project results, they also learn how to organize and present information. All of these are important skills in health education.

Some activities the children can do in groups in the classroom are to:

- prepare a play
- make a poster
- make a map or a model
- help each other in language, maths, social studies lessons
- do an experiment
- find information from books, magazines and newspapers
- practise first aid.

Working with groups needs careful planning. A checklist might look like this:

Leaders and teachers need to:

- **Identify** the task, the problem, the topic
- **Involve** others who can contribute, need to be informed
- **Discuss and plan** with health workers and community leaders, what the children will do, when and how.

4.8. Working in the community

Children are members of several groups. They have relatives and neighbours at home and in the community, friends in and out of school. Health education is about the wellbeing of the children as members of these communities. They are learning to be responsible for their own health and the health of others. However their wellbeing is dependent on the care and protection of others. This can be by **direct action** like giving first aid, **indirect action** like telling the health worker about children who have not been immunized and

contributing to the care of the environment like planting fruit trees.

Children can do these things in the community:

ASK others for information

SHOW others how to do something

TELL others about what they know

DO SOMETHING for others to help them

WORK with others for better health for all

AT HOME
AT SCHOOL/CLASS/CLUB
IN THE NEIGHBOURHOOD

For example:

- **conduct surveys** to find out about:

  accidents at school, at home, in the neighbourhood

Bad accidents in our families			
	BABIES	OLDER CHILDREN	GROWN-UPS
BURNS	///	/	
CUTS AND FALLS	/	///	/
ROAD ACCIDENTS		//	///
SWALLOWING BAD THINGS	///	/	

food and nutrition at school, at home, in the neighbourhood

food eaten at home	
from the garden	
from the market	
from the store	
from the river	

- get information about

  immunization programmes at school, at the clinic and tell parents and others the time and place to attend.

  games children play at school, at home and then teach other children.

- conduct campaigns.

4.9. Campaigns

As part of school or club and community activities, teachers and headteachers might decide to have a health campaign. This might be for a day, a week or a month. It might be organized once a term, once a year or to coincide with a health event in the community like World Food Day or a visit from the immunization team. It might focus on improving a particular aspect of the neighbourhood or the school like making the school a healthy place, putting in a well, building a toilet, planting fruit trees. It might be conducted by class groups or by Red Crescent and health society groups. It can link to the local radio and contribute items to the local newspaper as part of a publicity campaign. Here is an example of a campaign for clean and safe drinking water:

CAMPAIGN FOR CLEAN AND SAFE DRINKING WATER

- use the checklist for water supply.

- find unhealthy places with flies, snails, mosquitoes.

- clean up by organising groups and allocating places.

- make posters telling people about the safe drinking water campaign.

- organize a play or puppet show about the effects of drinking dirty water.

- make water filters and give them to the families.

Checklist for WATER SUPPLY   Group_____Class_____

1. Complete the checklist
   Put a cross (x) where something is bad
   Put a tick (✓) where something is good

2. Put a circle around each "x" after you have fixed it.

3. List the jobs you need your leader or teacher to help you with.

What to check	Findings	Action to be taken
SOURCE - LOCATION - SURROUNDINGS		
- upland stream or river or spring - away from pit latrines		
- rain in clean tank		
- clear from plants and trees		
- no rubbish in the area		
- safe path to water		
- safe place to stand		
STRUCTURE		
- fenced from animals		
- clean unbroken pipes, not rusting		
- taps not leaking		
- covered if tank or well		

4.10 Games – with materials

Children enjoy games. If the games have health ideas incorporated in them it helps them practise what they know. It is a way to spread ideas to others at school or at home.

Teachers or older children can make health games, for example: snakes and ladders, dominoes, card games.

Children can make the games. They can decide on the rules of the games themselves.

• card games

• snakes and ladders

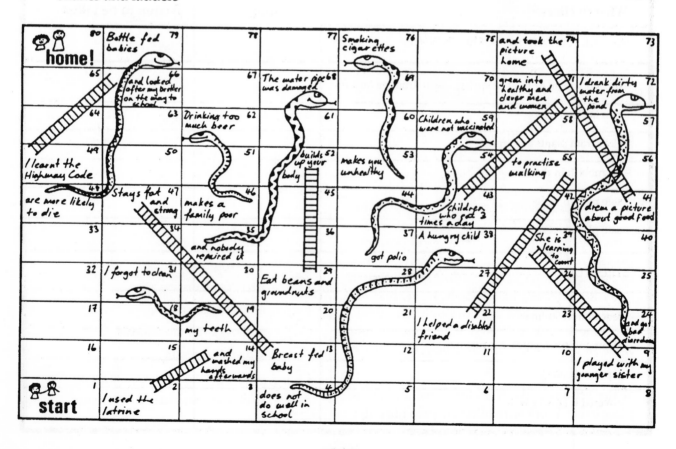

5. MATERIALS TO COLLECT AND USE

Using materials in health education can help teachers to do these things:

- make it easier for the leader or teacher to explain something about health

- make it more interesting for the children

- be more active in the learning process of health education

- help children to find out or do something for themselves in order to be healthy.

Some teachers may have a lot of ideas and resources for making materials to use in health activities. Other teachers may have to rely mainly on the environment, and what they have in the classrooms, at the school or in the neighbourhood. Here are some ideas showing how to make use of the environment and to make some of the materials used in activities in the earlier part of the book.

The best resource for health education is to be able to make use of people, places, things and events in the neighbourhood.

5.1. Using the environment

As well as collecting things and ideas for health activities, make use of the situation in the classroom, at school, in the neighbourhood.

- **in the classroom** encourage personal hygiene habits and make the classroom a clean and attractive place to be. Encourage children to present their workbooks and project work in a careful and attractive way. Use the chalkboard for health slogans and messages. Have children share their stories and work through 'newstime' and 'show and tell' sessions. Let children work in pairs or groups and help each other learn.

- **at the school** make it a clean and attractive place to be. Work with others to provide toilet and drinking water facilities, have safe places to play, shelter for wet and hot seasons. Hold assemblies for different classes to share their work, to hold puppet shows, put on plays. Organize pairing between children for safety on the way to school, for problem sharing, for helping with learning, for health checks.

- **in the neighbourhood** make visits to the clinic, the dentist, the hospital, the market, the gardens. Invite visitors to talk about their work at home, in the fields, at the health centres. Create safe places for children to play. Help maintain community toilets and drinking wells. Use the neighbourhood - its places, people, activities, as the major source of learning in health as suggested throughout this book.

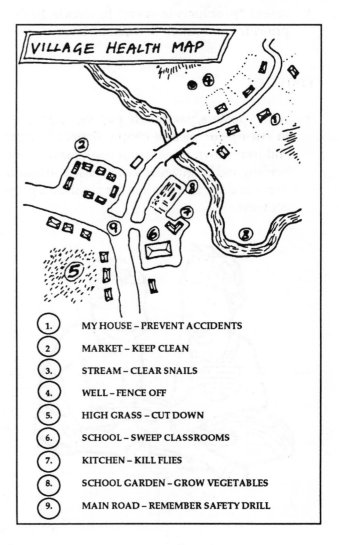

VILLAGE HEALTH MAP

1.	MY HOUSE – PREVENT ACCIDENTS
2	MARKET – KEEP CLEAN
3.	STREAM – CLEAR SNAILS
4.	WELL – FENCE OFF
5.	HIGH GRASS – CUT DOWN
6.	SCHOOL – SWEEP CLASSROOMS
7.	KITCHEN – KILL FLIES
8.	SCHOOL GARDEN – GROW VEGETABLES
9.	MAIN ROAD – REMEMBER SAFETY DRILL

5.2 Collecting things and materials

Teachers can involve children and others in the neighbourhood in collecting objects and ideas for use in health activities.

IDEAS

• collect **stories** to tell, to tape, to act, to write down about beliefs and experiences of health

• collect **information** about facts, figures, recipes, treatments, instructions to help understand or take action for health

• collect **'problems-to-solve'** to decide health priorities and action that can be taken.

OBJECTS

• collect **posters, pamphlets, papers, magazines** to cut up for picture charts, flannel boards, children's own posters and book making, for reading and language activities based on health items and for information for children's project work

• collect **containers** for experiments, growing things, storing clean drinking water

• collect **mirrors** for children to see themselves - a clean face, a happy, sad, angry face; to draw an eye, to be well-groomed

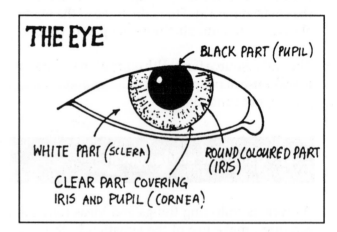

THE EYE

BLACK PART (PUPIL)

WHITE PART (SCLERA)

ROUND COLOURED PART (IRIS)

CLEAR PART COVERING IRIS AND PUPIL (CORNEA)

• collect a **first aid box** and learn how to use it.

MATERIALS

There is a need to collect materials to make puppets, toys, games, posters and for drama.

Collect:

• Clay, grass, straw and fibre.

• Tins, boxes and wire.

- Paper, cardboard and charcoal.

- 'Left over' materials. Often shops and small businesses have material which they cannot use and teachers and children can use, such as:

  - Pieces of cloth and paper.
  - Dyes and paint.
  - Wood or cardboard.

5.3 Health tools

Many household materials need to be collected, made and used to help us become healthier.

Keeping clean:

Collect and make: brooms, latrine covers, food covers, fly swats, rubbish containers.

Clean safe water:

Collect and make: filter, ladle, water pot, water covers

Detecting and managing disease:

Collect and make:

things to measure with (arm strips, scales, measuring tapes);

ways of telling time (clocks, hour glasses);

materials for treating cuts (soap, clean cloth for bandages);

things for rehydration drink (measures, glasses, sugar, salt).

CHILD-TO-CHILD

DOING IT BETTER

A SIMPLE GUIDE TO EVALUATING CHILD-TO-CHILD ACTIVITIES

INTRODUCTION

This section has been written to help people who are doing good and useful things do them even better. It is for everyone who is involved in Child-to-Child activities and not just for people who are called "Evaluators". Indeed one of the most important points that this booklet makes is that EVERYONE EVALUATES . . . and that includes the children themselves.

In everything we do, we continuously check to see if everything is progressing as it should and to make sure that this is the case we look at how we are doing it and the effects of our actions. Is "something" better than it was? The "something" will depend on what we are doing. In health education, our ultimate aim is to improve health, so we are looking for improvements in health . Are the children and their families healthier? Are there less cases of malnutrition, diarrhoea, measles?

The **knowledge** the children have acquired and their **understanding** of that knowledge is important. Do they know more about the local immunisation programme? Do they understand how immunisation works? However, Child-to-Child is not just concerned with **knowledge, but knowledge leading to action** and this also involves skills as well as changes in attitudes and behaviour. (This is what distinguishes the Child-to-Child approach to health education from many academic subjects studied at school.) Because skills, attitudes and behaviour are so important, we need to evaluate them too, even though this may be more difficult. Can the children prepare the oral rehydration drink? Are they cleaning their teeth more often? Are they spending more time playing with younger brothers and sisters?

The aim of this section is to show teachers and children that they too should and can evaluate their activities and how and when to evaluate Child-to-Child activities in order to make them better. However, the general principles can be applied whenever we want to evaluate our activities.

The preparation of this module began in a workshop in London, attended by Grazyna Bonati, Elisabeth Dumurgier, Hugh Hawes, David Morley, Barnabas Otaala, Gunadi Tanuputra and Sonal Zaveri. The text was finalised by Hugh Hawes and Richard Lansdown, with the help of Grazyna Bonati and Elisabeth Dumurgier.

PART I

EVALUATION AND THE CHILD-TO-CHILD APPROACH

1. CHILD-TO-CHILD

Child-to-Child is an approach which helps children to help others. In many countries all over the world they already do this. Child-to-Child encourages them with knowledge and ideas of how to make what they do more useful and more fun. Child-to-Child activities in health education are being used in different ways all over the world. In this section, we emphasise the two main ways in which the approach is used, i.e.:

● In schools and within the communities around the schools;

● In youth groups where children join together to spread health ideas to communities.

Child-to-Child approaches can also be used in other subject areas such as agriculture and environmental studies, but here we concentrate on health.

1.1. Three important goals of the Child-to-Child approach

1. It helps to link health and education together within communities and so improves the life of both children and adults.
2. It involves children as well as adults in actively improving health in communities.
3. It encourages children to take action both individually and as a group so they can benefit both themselves and others, without giving themselves extra burdens.

1.2. An active methodology - fun for children

Child-to-Child emphasises:

● meaningful, active learning, using a variety of approaches and methods;

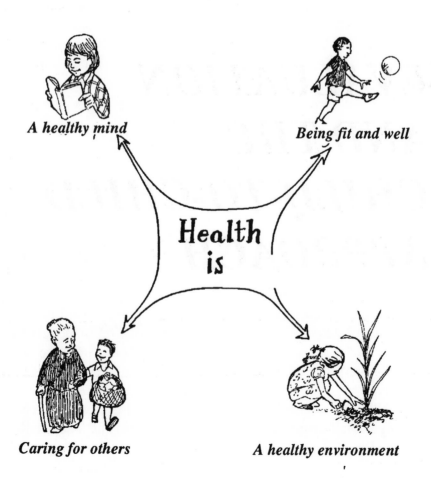

A healthy mind

Being fit and well

Health is

Caring for others

A healthy environment

- activities which are interesting and fun for children to do.

1.3. How the Child-to-Child approach helps children

1.3.1. Knowledge and skills

- It develops knowledge and understanding of important health issues in communities.

- It promotes a wider understanding of health as something more than absence of disease and thus an awareness of:
  — links between a healthy person and a healthy environment;
  — links between physical health and health of the 'whole person' (mind, body, spirit).

- It develops active skills to help children prevent disease and help those who are sick.

- It develops thinking skills of:
  — identifying problems and solving them;
  — communicating ideas to others;
  — examining actions and results: 'What have we done?' 'Was it useful?' 'How could we do it better?

This knowledge and these skills increase children's capacity to improve their own lives.

1.3.2. Attitudes

Child-to-Child also aims to develop desirable attitudes in children both through what children learn and how they learn it. It develops:

- their self-confidence, because they are planning and taking action;
- their sense of responsibility, because they are being trusted to do things which are important both for themselves and for others;

- their sense of cooperation, because they are working together.

1.3.3. Changes in behaviour and practice in children

Child-to-Child also aims to achieve changes in behaviour and practice in both younger and older children, e.g.:

- improved health habits resulting in better personal and community hygiene (e.g. children wash their hands more often and fill in mosquito breeding places);
- more care and attention to the health of others (e.g. children care for safety of younger children);
- better use of available resources to improve health care (e.g. children provide oral rehydration using rice water).

1.3.4. Effects on families, schools and communities

In addition to helping children, the Child-to-Child approach also helps families, communities and schools through:

- helping to make closer links between education and health workers, at community level (and at higher levels too);
- helping to bring changes in health knowledge and practice, through the knowledge that children can spread and the example they can provide (with the help of their teachers, youth leaders and health workers);
- helping to provide a model of an active methodology in health linked to doing and helping in the community so that these approaches may be used in other subject areas;
- increasing the respect that a community gives to its children (as it sees how they can take responsibility to improve health).

2. EVALUATION

2.1. What is evaluation?

To evaluate means to assess the value of something. In the context of the Child-to-Child approach, it has two broad aims:

1. To establish whether we are achieving our goals and if so whether the programme is being carried out in the most effective way.

2. To discover not only whether the programme is working as planned, but also why it is or is not. When we know this we can improve it and also extend our knowledge to similar programmes.

An everyday example of evaluation comes when we undertake a journey. First we decide where we want to go, that is our main aim. Then we decide when we want to go, and next we think about the best way to travel. Once the journey is over we can consider:

● Did we arrive exactly where we wanted to go, at the correct time?

● If we did not, what went wrong?

● If we did arrive correctly, could we have made the journey:
   a) more comfortably, given the money we had?
   b) more quickly?
   c) more cheaply?

● Are we now in a good position to advise someone else who is going to undertake a similar journey?

Sometimes we need not wait until we have finished the journey before asking ourselves these questions. As soon as we have started or are half-way through we can ask ourselves, "Is this bus the fastest (or cheapest) one? Should I get off and catch a better one?" or even before we start, we can ask ourselves, "Is this the right bus?" "Is there a better one?" "Will we be going in the right direction?"

2.2. When to evaluate

There are three main stages when evaluation is especially important:

● At the **planning** stage of the programme;

● At the **doing** stage;

● At the **conclusion** of the programme (the "**outcomes**" stage).

Every Child-to-Child programme and activity needs to be evaluated otherwise we shall not be able to learn from experience. We learn from our failures just as much as we learn from our successes.

Evaluation helps us gain confidence because we know more about a programme and about what works and what does not. It also gives us the ability to make better and more useful decisions.

We need to evaluate many separate aspects of an activity before we can evaluate the activity as a whole. Thus evaluation occurs at every stage of what we do. It is never too late to evaluate. Often there is no evaluation at the planning stage, but we can still gain very useful information later. Any activity, however large or small, which helps us know more and make better decisions is a useful evaluation activity.

TABLE 1

WHEN AND WHAT TO EVALUATE

ACTIVITIES	WHAT TO EVALUATE
1. At the planning stage	
Establishing Needs	● Which Child-to-Child activities are most important to the children, their families and their community?
Planning Objectives	● Are the objectives set realistic and relevant? Can they be achieved in small steps?
	● Are there long-term goals?
Drawing Up a Plan of Action	● Is it sensible and workable?
Considering Resources	● Are they the best available? Are they sufficient?
2. At the doing stage	
The Programme	● Is it well-managed?
The Materials	● Are they being used effectively?
	● Are they adapted to local needs?
Training	● Is the right training provided for the right people?
3. The outcomes stage	● Changes in **knowledge**
	● Changes in **attitude**
	● Changes in **practice** for both children and communities.

2.3.   What can be evaluated?

When we evaluate, we investigate:
  a) changes in what people know;
  b) changes in the skills people have;
  c) how they use these new skills and this new knowledge;
  d) how their attitudes have changed;
  e) what effects these changes have on people's lives.

In Child-to-Child activities, we may wish to find out the effects on children, teachers and youth leaders, health workers, families and communities.

In our list of the changes we expect the Child-to-Child approach to achieve, there are many things which are difficult to measure. Changes in attitude in the children ("They take more responsibility." "They cooperate more.") and changes in the community ("better health practices") are two examples. We may be able to describe both but we cannot always measure them easily. This does not mean that we should give up; often things which are difficult to measure are very important. What is more, we may not always be able to say with certainty, "This action caused that effect", but there are times when we have to say, "It is very probable, therefore let us say that it is so".

TABLE 2

EVALUATION - EXAMPLES OF GOOD AND LESS GOOD EFFECTS

	EXAMPLES OF GOOD EFFECTS	EXAMPLES OF LESS GOOD EFFECTS
Children	Took more action to improve health	Learned new facts but did not apply them
Teachers	Liked Child-to-Child and changed their methods	Found Child-to-Child approaches took a long time and interfered with covering the syllabus
Health workers	Cooperated with teachers	Resented children because 'they were not trained'
Families	Learned better child care because older children provided a good example (e.g. toys for children)	Resented children telling them what to do
Communities	Supported children's immunisation campaign	Showed no interest. Failed to attend school health fair.

We nearly always need to evaluate the cost of an activity (in terms of time, work for people, and materials as well as money) to find out whether it was worth doing. When we measure whether an activity was worth doing, we need to think of the long-term as well as the short-term effects although it is very much harder to measure them.

Unexpected results

Child-to-Child activities often have unexpected results. For instance, in Botswana older children were encouraged to act as "little teachers" to help pre-school children before they entered school. Evaluation suggested that the older children later performed better in class.

2.4. Who evaluates?

Everyone who takes part in an activity should be involved in its evaluation. This includes: *insiders*, the participants in an activity and the planners and organisers, and also *outsiders*, who can take a more dispassionate view. (Outsiders do not always have to be specialists in evaluation.)

Outsiders in a Child-to-Child activity can include:

- **Doctors** and other **health workers** (who can check whether the health messages are correct);

- **Administrators** and **planners** (who can assess whether the activities are "cost/effort effective");

- **Community leaders** and **community members** (who can assess the effect on children and the community).

2.5. Who we evaluate for

We evaluate for different people and for different purposes. For ourselves: children, teachers, programme organisers, and for others: funders, decision-makers, the community. All these people may need to know different things. So we should always think of what they need to know when we decide what and how to evaluate and how to present the results.

In Child-to-Child activities we also have different people who will want to know different things.

Doctors and Other Health Workers

Administrators and Planners

Community Leaders and Members

Outsiders as evaluators

TABLE 3

WHO NEEDS TO KNOW WHAT?

WHO	WHAT THEY NEED TO KNOW
The children and teachers	How they can improve their activities next time they do them.
The parents and community leaders	What the children have achieved and how they can help them.
The heads or youth group organisers	How they can plan their activities more effectively.
The health workers	Whether the children are spreading correct messages and whether they continue to remember them correctly.
People from different areas	What is happening and how they can learn from the experience in this area.
People at central level	What kind of resources were being used, what results have been achieved and whether the resources were being used effectively.
Funding agencies	How and how well their money was used.

2.6.   What evaluation need not be

- It is not necessarily something complicated which can be done only by experts and outsiders.
- It is not mainly aimed at judging the success or failure of an activity; rather at finding ways of improving it.
- It is not a way of finding fault either with the programme or its participants. Rather, it seeks to find things to praise or encourage.
- It need not involve complicated measurements and statistics.
- It is not something done only after an activity is finished. It needs to start right at the beginning to help us choose the "right road" and keep travelling it.
- It is not a waste of time and resources. It helps us to use what we have better.

PEOPLE OFTEN THINK OF EVALUATION BEING DONE BY PEOPLE LIKE THIS.

BUT IT IS USUALLY BETTER DONE BY PEOPLE LIKE OURSELVES.

3. HOW DO WE EVALUATE?

There are many ways in which we collect, analyse and assess information.

All the methods we describe in this section are likely to be used at some time or another at every level. Often different methods are likely to be used at the same time to give a clearer and fuller picture.

This section can only give a short introduction to various techniques; for further ideas and guidance on these we recommend the book, 'Partners in Evaluation', which is easy to use and easily available. At the end of this section we include a short guide which tells readers what they can find in this book and where. For those who will be involved in more complicated evaluations of programmes and their outcomes, we have also listed some other books which describe the techniques in much more detail.

3.1.   Observation

3.1.1.   What can we observe?

Observation is the basis for all other techniques, but good observation requires both skill and the right attitudes towards it. We must be able to observe clearly and carefully and to see and record what is really there and what is really happening rather than what we wish to see and what we want to happen. This is not easy.

Examples of what we can observe:

● Things we can count
   e.g. If we are evaluating an activity on "Clean Safe Water":
   — how many water containers are there at home?
   — how many are covered?
   — how many have ladles?

● What people are doing
   e.g. If we are evaluating the amount of child stimulation in a community:
   — how many people talk and play with babies?
   — who plays most of the time?
   — what are people doing when they are not playing with the baby?

3.1.2.   Recording

Once we have decided what to observe we have to decide how to record it. We need to be able to record in such a way that others will understand what we have put down. It is better to record as soon as we have observed rather than waiting until the end of the day since waiting can lead to our forgetting some important aspects.

● Observing events many times makes you surer of the results.

> **Example:**
>
> Five older children were told to observe how younger children behaved when crossing the road. They all observed that the younger children often crossed too near a certain corner where the motorists could not see them.

● It may be possible to allow space on the records to note the unexpected as well.

Example:

Children were observing foodsellers at school to see what they sold and whether they kept flies away. At the same time they noticed that their friends did not pay any attention to whether the stalls were clean or not. They bought from certain foodsellers because they were more friendly.

● Records of observation are not only written records. Maps, pictures and diagrams also help.

Example:

A project worker was asked to observe how a Child-to-Child school was operating. She took photographs of the school compound and of the children doing different health activities.

3.1.3. Making sure that we observe accurately

It is quite possible for three people who have witnessed an event to give accounts of what happened that differ a great deal. They may disagree on the height of one of the people observed, or the sequence of events. If observers are trained the chances of big differences in reporting are lessened but it will still be necessary to check on the level of accuracy of those taking part in an evaluation exercise.

One way to do this when children or teachers are concerned is to turn it into a game: have four or five observe something, then record it, then compare their records to see how similar they are.

3.2. Asking questions

Through asking questions we can find out more about what people know, do and think and even why they think and act in the way they do. But this information can only be gathered if questions are asked for the right reasons and in the right way. Many questions are asked and answered to give people the information they want to hear rather than the true information necessary in evaluation. Deciding what are the right questions to ask is vital to good evaluation. If we do not ask the right questions we will not get the information we need, however well we ask them and record the answers.

3.2.1. What questions to ask ... and how to ask them

- Think carefully about the information you need and the other information you may get from asking your proposed questions. Then plan your questions. Usually a line of questioning which leads to further information is more useful than a completely 'closed' set of questions which only seeks to get some answers and rejects others.

Example:

"Do you boil water?" will only get one (probably false) answer.

"How do you use water at home?" will get much more useful information including (if you are skilful) an answer to the first question.

- Use a step-by-step approach to build up questions in sequence. Ask simple and general questions first, and bring in more difficult and specific questions later.

- Link questions with what people tell you. Either let them talk freely and then bring in questions, or ask further questions based on their answers until you get all the useful information you can. Usually it is not wise to proceed like a machine through a set of prepared questions.

- Avoid questions which suggest the answer you would like to receive, e.g. "Do you clean your teeth every day?"

- Be very careful to recognise sensitive and embarrassing questions, e.g. "How much do you earn?"

3.2.2. Written questions

Sometimes we will wish to use a written questionnaire. Experience shows, however, that:

- such questionnaires are only useful for some (and not all) information gathering.
- it is usually not worthwhile to send them out without explanation to large numbers of people. (Very few will reply and many will not understand the questionnaire or its purposes.)

If a written questionnaire is given, it should:

1) be as short as possible, with very simple questions;

2) be directed to one or two specific purposes;
3) require short, simple replies;
4) only be used with people who can read and understand the questions and answer them in writing;
5) if possible, be given at a time when people have an opportunity to complete it, e.g. at an in-service course.

All answers should be treated with respect - in some cases, people may not like their names to be disclosed.

Note:
Oral and written questions may often be combined. A short written questionnaire can form the basis for wider and more open questions.

Example:

A group of children, well-prepared by their teachers, have been conducting a nutrition survey. They have five simple questions about food grown and eaten in the family, but they have also been encouraged to ask more, and wider, questions based on these and to record the answers.

3.3. Meetings and discussions

It is often very helpful for groups to discuss what is happening and what has been achieved, just as it often helps if groups decide which information to collect and take part in collecting it.

Group discussions:

● enable us to share experience, to learn from each other and obtain feedback.
● assist us to obtain information because group discussions encourage people to contribute.
● allow everyone involved in an activity to participate in the evaluation.

The group must feel relaxed and friendly, so small, informal groups are better than those that are large and formal. Seating arrangements should help create a friendly atmosphere.

The discussion should be organised and managed but free discussion should be allowed. Thus the organiser can have a programme checklist and encourage the group to cover it all but allow other ideas to come up.

The ideas and opinions of all participants should be respected.

It is useful to summarise the discussion from time to time.

Recording a group meeting can be difficult and it is important that this be done correctly. Two heads are often better than one. Training people in simple ways of recording is very useful and can help them to gather good evaluation information.

3.4. Using written material

We need to examine written records:

● to know what has happened in the past;
● to be aware of what exists and is happening now;
● to compare contexts, activities and results both from place to place and from time to time.

What written records can we examine?

- Written records from 'outside', e.g. health records.
- 'Inside' records, e.g. pupils' exercise books, planning documents, diaries, activity sheets.
- Our own records, either individual or group.
- Textbooks and curricula.
- Child-to-Child books and materials.
- Teachers' preparation.
- Attendance records in schools.
- Displays and posters.
- Reports made by inspectors or health workers on the effect of Child-to-Child approaches.

3.5. Assessing changes in knowledge and skills

3.5.1. What we need to find out

It is important not only to find out whether **knowledge** and **skills** have been gained, but also whether they have been **retained** and whether there has been any **change in behaviour** as a result of the new knowledge.

We need to find out:

- what people know and do already;
- how well do they understand the new material;
- how long they keep their new knowledge and skills;
- whether they are applying their knowledge and skills;
- whether they are spreading their knowledge and skills.

3.5.2. How to assess knowledge and skills

a) **Simple tests**

Often it is important to find out whether a whole group of children or adults can do

something. We therefore need to ask very clear and simple questions.

Examples:

"What are the most important signs of pneumonia in babies?" (quick breathing - even when lying down quietly, etc).

"How can you rehydrate children with diarrhoea?" (get or make oral rehydration solution, rice water makes excellent oral rehydration solution).

We may also need to do practical tests:

- making a sling in first aid;

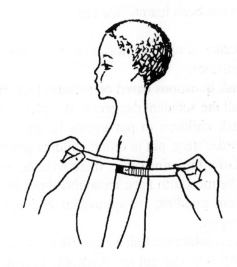

- using an arm circumference strip correctly.

In these tests we should not be satisfied unless nearly all those tested get the right answer. We should aim for at least 4 out of 5 correct answers for a knowledge test and, if possible, fully correct skill tests. If not, the individuals who do not understand must be re-taught.

b) More difficult questions

Simple questions are not always enough. We need to ask more difficult questions to see whether children understand the reasons for what they are doing.

> **Examples:**
>
> ● why does dehydration kill?
> ● why should food be covered?
> ● how can we help babies learn to talk?

Here, too, we need a measure of success. We should be unhappy if less than 2 out of 3 children gave correct answers to these questions.

c) Other ways of assessing knowledge and skills.

There are many different ways of finding out what has been learnt. We can:

● make simple games such as crossword puzzles;
● ask questions based on pictures (e.g. find all the accident dangers in this picture);
● ask children to put events in the 'right order' (e.g. put in order: children got malaria; the rains came; there were holes in the mosquito nets; mosquitos bred in the rain puddles; mosquitos bit children at night);
● get children to finish a story (e.g. we found Ali who did not go to school because he could not walk well, so we ....);
● observe skills in action (e.g. watching road safety drill).

Note: These are just some of the ways of testing. Many other ways can be thought of. Children, teachers and youth leaders should be encouraged to think of new and interesting ways. Thinking about how to test also helps to build understanding of the ideas and activities of Child-to-Child.

3.6. Assessing changes in attitudes and behaviour

If people gain new knowledge and skills they need to put them into practice before real changes can be made. Before acting they need to want to act. That is why changing attitudes is so important.

3.6.1. How to measure changes in attitudes and behaviour

Asking questions is one way to find out about attitudes and behaviour, but it is often difficult to get true information in this way. Careful observation of behaviour, including very careful listening, is a better guide.

Sometimes written records tell us what people have done. Sometimes group discussion or group simulation (where people act out what they would do in a certain situation) helps to show changes. Often we may need many different kinds of evidence to help us decide how far attitudes and behaviour have changed.

I'm up to date. I don't breast feed like the village women. I give my baby wondermilk in a bottle.

How would you answer her?

4. RECORDING AND PRESENTING RESULTS

When we evaluate we must present our findings to somebody so that they can then learn from them and "do it better". Sometimes people think that the only way of doing this is to write a long report full of quite difficult language and figures. This is not so.

4.1. Rules for preparing and presenting reports

1. **A report must be accurate.**

   If there are mistakes in the facts, if the figures are wrong, if the mathematics or statistics are incorrectly used, or if there are serious omissions or misunderstandings, no-one will take the report seriously. Be sure to check for accuracy.

2. **A report must be directed at the people who will use it.** (Always keep them in mind when writing the report.)

   Sometimes different people with different levels of knowledge about evaluation will use the same report. In this case it is best to produce a report in the simplest possible way and add on additional material such as statistical information for those who can understand it.

3. **A report should be designed to promote discussion leading to improvement.**

   A report which is dull, or which just delivers judgements and raises no questions, will not promote discussion.

   A report which is negative in tone and full of badly phrased criticism will discourage people who have worked hard on their programmes. Always be positive and praise where possible.

4. **A report must be prepared quickly.** If it is late it may be of little value (no matter how well it is presented).

4.2. Some techniques for presenting reports

4.2.1. Written descriptions

Sometimes observers will want to describe programmes they have seen, schools they have visited, classrooms or youth group activities they have seen.

Even a brief description can be informative and worthwhile.

Sometimes comparative tables of different cases observed can be valuable.

TABLE 4 : USE OF CHILD-TO-CHILD ACTIVITIES			
	Use of materials	Methods used	Link with activity at home
CLASS 1		*Brief description*	
CLASS 2		*of each case*	
CLASS 3			

4.2.2. Photographs, pictures and maps

Often these can be very valuable to show what has, or has not, been accomplished. Remember - always photograph positive as well as negative points.

Pictures drawn by children and their teachers are often good evidence of what has been achieved and what has been understood.

4.2.3. Videos

Videos can show activity well, but we need to take great care that they present a balanced picture and do not leave us with too one-sided a view of what has happened.

Both videos and pictures need to reinforce written and oral reports. They cannot replace them.

4.2.4. Presenting numbers

When we present numbers and comparisons between them (as is often the case in evaluation), we need to consider effective ways of showing what we want to show.

We may sometimes wish to use **tables**, but we may also want to use:

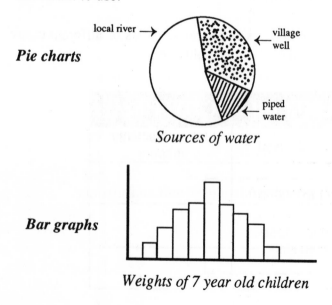

Pie charts

Sources of water

Bar graphs

Weights of 7 year old children

Line graphs

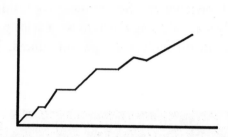

Use of Child-to-Child materials over 2 years

Pie charts and bar graphs are useful when we are comparing. Line graphs are useful when we want to show how activities are growing, or getting less, over time.

4.2.5. Verbal presentations

Remember not all evaluation reports have to be written.

The advantage of a verbal presentation, to a seminar of project workers, for instance, is that it is possible to discuss what has been observed and amend the report as a result of feedback obtained.

4.3. Key points about reports

Remember again the "four C's" about report writing.

They must be: CORRECT
CLEAR
CONSTRUCTIVE
CURRENT (i.e. produced on time).

PART II

EVALUATING CHILD-TO-CHILD ACTIVITIES

In this part we give examples from four levels of evaluation. We look at:

● Evaluating a **Child-to-Child activity** — taking as an example one done by teachers and the children themselves;

● Evaluating a **small-scale Child-to-Child project** — usually done by the project organisers with help from the participants;

● Evaluating **Child-to-Child approaches introduced nationally from curriculum centres**.

● Evaluating Child-to-Child **materials**.

5. EVALUATING A CHILD-TO-CHILD ACTIVITY

We give below an example of an activity involving children in a village who decide, in the first instance, to concentrate on just one Child-to-Child theme ... SAFETY.

5.1. The planning stage

5.1.1. Deciding to begin

> In village X, 2-year-old Ali was burnt badly when the cooking pot toppled over. The teacher, health worker, youth leader and some parents thought it would be a good idea to introduce the activity on home accidents both in youth groups and in the school. It would be better to begin with accidents at home and then later to take up those on the road. There were a lot of things that children could do for themselves as well as for others (e.g. brothers, sisters, etc), when they had learnt about this topic.

Evaluation questions:

- Who decided on the activity?
- Was there an agreement?
- Why did they decide on a particular activity?
- Was it the most relevant?
- Was it one where the Child-to-Child approach could be used?

5.1.2. Finding out the current needs

> The teacher discussed with the children why this topic was taken up; what they needed to find out and where they would get the information. She had already written down **burns** and the children made the list longer. They added **cuts, wounds**, etc. They decided

> to ask their parents and older members of the family for other examples of common accidents, in the evening when people were more relaxed. Some of the children finished very quickly and came back to show the teacher but the information was not sufficient. After explaining its importance, she sent them back to complete the task.
>
> Two children went to the Health Centre and asked the nurse there about it. The local medicine man was out of the village and so no one collected information from him, although the teacher did feel that this should have been done. When the children returned, they discussed what they had collected and found out.

Evaluation questions:

- Was the information collected appropriate, relevant, accurate, complete?
- Were the children able to collect it?
- Who prepared the "finding out" proforma?
- Did children know/understand how to fill it in correctly and to ask questions based on it?
- Were there any information gaps?

5.1.3. Writing out objectives

(a) Knowledge objectives

> The school teacher invited the children to list "what every family should know about causes of accidents". The children listed these topics: **burns, wounds, falls, dangerous things to eat and drink, insects and animals and electricity** and then agreed on what everyone needed to know to prevent these accidents.

Evaluation question:

● Are the knowledge objectives simply and clearly stated?
● Is the knowledge to be gained relevant and related to needs assessment?
● Is all the really important knowledge included?

(b) Skills and attitudes objectives

The teacher also decided that there were important **skill** objectives and explained these simply to the children. For example, to develop **skills** in **finding out more** about the problem, **thinking about some solutions**, to encourage children to **work cooperatively**, and to **encourage communication with others** especially the family.

The youth leader was keen to include **attitude objectives**, for example, to encourage children and families **to be aware of and willing to use this new knowledge and skills and to increase their self-confidence in doing so.**

Evaluation questions:

● Are the skills in question well-defined and related to Child-to-Child?
● Would the children/others get an opportunity to develop them?
● Are children (and teachers) being encouraged to work for attitude changes?

(c) Expected changes in practice

Everyone also agreed on the need for the activity to lead to **changes in practice at home**. The children and their teachers listed the following expected outcomes.

All homes will keep their stove on a higher level, above the ground, as well as matches, knives and other unsafe things. They should put all rubbish in the trash can, especially small bits which could be eaten by a crawling baby ... etc, etc.

Evaluation questions:

● Are the expected changes clearly listed?
● Are they reasonable?
● Can they be easily observed and recorded?

5.1.4. Preparing a simple plan

The teacher and youth leader involved some of the children in making a very simple plan of what they hoped to do.
(i) The plan was made but it was not full enough or clear enough. Several people who could help, e.g. the local nurse, were not listed. No mention was made of local remedies.
(ii) The time schedule was too long. It should be shortened to 3 months because after that the rains would start and attendance drop.

Evaluation questions:

- Is the plan clear, related to finding out and objectives?
- Does it have room for some flexibility?
- Is it understood by all those involved in planning and doing the activity?

5.2. The doing stage

5.2.1. Discussion based on knowledge collected

> There was some discussion on why babies/young children have lots more accidents than adults do. This led children to change their activities based on a better understanding of the fact that little children do not think and act like big ones.

Evaluation questions:

- Is the knowledge being taught simple to understand, relevant, correct, brief?
- Does it build on needs assessed earlier?
- Are all the children participating in finding out more?
- Could the teacher guide the questioning to a final solution or alternative solutions?

5.2.2. Undertaking activities and planning new ones

> After discussions by the children, teacher and youth leader, it was agreed to:
> - maintain a monthly record of accidents;
> - talk to younger siblings and show them how to play safely;
> - visit the Health Centre and see how simple accidents can be treated;
> - learn how to prepare a First Aid Box to be kept at home;
> - draw posters and explain them.

Evaluation questions:

- Did the children understand what they had to do and why?
- Could they maintain it regularly and complete it? Did they do so?
- Did the agreement come genuinely from the children or was it mainly the teacher's ideas?
- Were the agreed tasks simple for children? Could they do them? How were they organised and performed? Could it have been better?

5.2.3. From children to community

> Children presented posters and drama to a parents' meeting at the local festival to show them what they were doing.

Evaluation questions:

- Was this meeting the best way of communicating with the community?
- Did a good number of people attend — who came and who did not come?
- How well did the parents participate?
- What knowledge was conveyed to them?
- What message did the drama want to convey?
- How was the drama organised?
- What feedback was there from the audience?
- What was the possible impact?

5.3.1. Changes in knowledge

The teacher had already tested the children before the programme started. She compared the two sets of answers. She could see that there was a difference and that all the children knew more than when the programme began. She did not just ask verbal questions. To find out how accidents occur, she put up a picture (one drawn by one of the children) of an unsafe home and said, "Baby Seema is one-year-old and walks/crawls into this home. What could happen?" This made all the children think and respond, even those who could not write very easily.

Evaluation questions:

- Has there been a gain in knowledge?
- Was there a pretest?
- Could the results of earlier enquiries be used as a pretest? If so, how did the two results compare?

5.3.2. Changes in skills

As a result of the lessons on First Aid many children gained *practical skills* and the confidence that went with them. Teachers reported that they frequently observed children testing each other.

The Deputy Headmaster, who had been encouraging the teachers and watching the children right from the start of the activity, also found changes in the way that *learning skills* were developing. One of these was the way that the children were participating in activities both in and out of class.

In the beginning, the teacher had to guide and coax them along. Most did not even ask questions but towards the end of the programme, even the shy ones were ready to talk to the class about what they had seen. Some parents were also asked (when they came to pick up the children after school) and they felt that the children were asking more questions at home, e.g. "Why is the stove on the floor? Can't we build a small platform?"

Evaluation questions:

- Have children gained really effective practical skills, e.g. in first aid (and the confidence that goes with them)?
- Have children been encouraged to develop skills of learning, of finding out and working together - or are activities still very teacher-directed?
- How far has this development of skills changed over the lifetime of the programme?

5.3.3. Changes in attitudes and behaviour

Both the teacher and the youth leader agreed that the only way to assess children's changes in attitudes was to observe their behaviour at school and at home.

The **youth leader** observed that the children were more aware of accident hazards in their homes. In fact, many children said that their friends and neighbours were not even aware of how careful one must be, especially with small children.

Since it was a large class of 50, the **teacher** selected about 25 children and went to their homes to find out how their behaviour had changed. She was helped by the health worker. All the homes had a First Aid Box which the children had prepared. About five were incomplete, i.e. had been used and not refilled. The mothers had found it very handy especially when they got accidently burnt/scalded while cooking. They reported that the children insisted that they move the stove away into a corner and asked their fathers to make a small platform. Another example was given by Ram's grandmother.

A few days before, a bottle had been broken and Ram just got up and very matter-of-factly swept up the broken pieces of glass, mopped up the floor and threw the glass on the dump outside. "That was a relief," said his mother, "because I was standing in the water line and would have had to rush home."

Evaluation questions:

● Do children talk more about the problems in homes and communities?

● In school and when children go home, do they really **do** some of the things that they have been learning about with other children and with their younger brothers and sisters? Do they talk about it back in the classroom? When problems occur (in this case an accident to one of their friends), what are the responses of particular children? Are they different?

● Are there examples of changes in the home? (In this case, is there a First Aid Box? When and how is it used?)

5.3.4. Changes in health in the family and the community
(in this case the number of accidents)

After the school had finished the activity, the health worker waited for three months and then compared her records with those of the same period last year. "I can't say for certain that it is the result of your Child-to-Child project," she told the children, "but what I can say is that fewer babies have been brought into the Health Centre with burns than during the same time last year."

Evaluation question:

● Are there any changes in health in the neighbourhood which have been observed over the time the activity has taken place? How far can these probably be linked to the action taken by Child-to-Child?

TABLE 5			

EVALUATING A CHILD-TO-CHILD ACTIVITY
CHECKLIST FOR ACTION

TASK	EVALUATION		
	Who evaluates what?	What did they find out?	What action did they take?
I. THE PLANNING STAGE			
• Deciding to begin			
• Finding out the current needs			
• Writing out objectives:			
(i) knowledge			
(ii) skills and attitudes			
(iii) expected changes in practice			
II. THE DOING STAGE			
• Discussion based on knowledge collected			
• Undertaking activities. Planning new ones.			
• From children to community			
III. THE OUTCOME STAGE			
• Changes in knowledge			
• Changes in skills			
• Changes in attitudes and behaviour			
• Changes in health:			
(i) in the family			
(ii) in the community			
• Probable changes in health of:			
(i) children			
(ii) families			

6. EVALUATING A SMALL-SCALE CHILD-TO-CHILD PROJECT

By a 'small-scale project' we mean one which is local but which aims to introduce the Child-to-Child approach within a number of schools and out-of-school activities.

6.1. The planning stage

6.1.1. Deciding to start a project, selecting a community and assessing needs

A national-level health education programme was anxious to try out a Child-to-Child approach in a small area. They planned to involve local schools and youth groups. Before starting they called two meetings: one with local leaders, teachers and health workers to discuss health education, the possibility of the project and the approach; the second (after it had been found out that the community was more than happy to try out the ideas) to discuss needs and priorities.

Evaluation questions:

● Have the right people been consulted?
● Were they given enough opportunity to give their views?
● Do all those who have to take action know and understand the project and its purpose?
● Have both Education and Health Workers been involved from the beginning?
● How carefully were needs identified?
● Were priorities effectively chosen?

6.1.2. Looking at where we are now

Before starting to design materials and plan activities, the organisers discussed with teachers and health workers what were the traditional health beliefs and practices in the

area. They also agreed to give a very simple test of knowledge and skills to children. Teachers also took the test and were surprised that **they** also lacked important health knowledge.

Evaluation questions:

● Have present practices and beliefs been surveyed?
● Has there been a pretest of health knowledge and skills in the selected priority areas?
● Was it clear and easy to use?
● Have the results been noted?

6.1.3. Setting objectives and making a plan for the project

At a first seminar with teachers and youth leaders the project organisers discussed and agreed objectives and a plan of action with them. Everyone was very enthusiastic and confident. As a result the plan was quite ambitious.

Evaluation questions:

- Has an effective plan of action been made?
- Are the objectives realistic?
- Are they clearly defined, measurable (in some way)?
- Are they relevant to needs?
- Have those who will be carrying out the plan had a great enough part in making it? Do they feel they 'own' it in some way?
- Is the plan arranged in small steps so that progress can be seen?

6.1.4. Checking the plan against the resources available

> The project organisers asked a wise and experienced planner from another district to visit the project area. He looked carefully at their plans and spoke to the teachers and the inspector. "You have to look at three kinds of resources," he said, "manpower, money and time. You have a shortage of all three, and though your plans are good, perhaps you are expecting a little too much. Why don't you try to do a little less, so that you can be sure of doing it well?"

Evaluation questions:

- Are there enough teachers, health workers and youth leaders to make the plan work well?
- Are there sufficient funds and materials available? ... and time?
- Has implementation of the plan been well discussed with all those who will take part? Are they happy with the parts they are expected to play?

6.1.5. Assessing and collecting materials needed

> At a planning meeting it was decided to concentrate on just five priorities. With these in mind, the group began to look through materials which were already available ... both school material and adult education material produced by the Ministry of Health. Some of this was found to be quite useful.
>
> The relevant Child-to-Child activity sheets were very carefully analysed and a plan made on how to adapt them, make supplementary material from them, and use them in training. One sheet was found totally unsuitable and a new activity was selected and planned.

Evaluation questions:

- Is the material relevant to:
  - those who will use it (children, teachers, youth leaders)?
  - the objectives set?

- Is the material usable?
  - Can the language be well understood?
  - Are the activities suggested possible?

- Is the material medically accurate?

6.1.6. Selection of schools and youth leaders

After a lot of discussion and some disagreement, there was agreement on which schools and youth leaders would be included in the project. One or two of those which were close and easy to monitor were not, however, included since the heads and organisers did not seem really keen to participate.

Evaluation questions:

● Were there sensible rules (criteria) for selecting participants?

● Are those who have been selected ready, willing and interested in taking part?

● Have we selected key decision-makers and not just individuals? e.g. At school are **heads** willing to participate and cooperate and not merely one or two teachers?

6.1.7. Training before beginning the project

The training group for youth leaders appointed one of the project planning group as an evaluator. She:

● Insisted that the course produced objectives and then criticised them.
● Conducted a pretest with participants.
● Attended sessions of the course and discussed them with staff and participants.
● Conducted a test and gave a questionnaire to the participants at the end of the course and held a discussion with them.
● Held a feedback session with the organisers.

Evaluation questions:

● Are the right people being given training?
● Have we decided clear and realistic objectives for our training?
● Have we attempted to evaluate changes in knowledge, skills, attitudes and behaviour of the participants both before and after the course?
● Have we attempted to assess their understanding of the Child-to-Child ideas and methodology?

6.2. The doing stage

6.2.1. Organisation of the programme

The programme planning committee then reviewed how the activities during the next year would be organised, and assigned responsibilities (including responsibilities for monitoring). The project got under way.

Evaluation questions:

● Is there a working group responsible for the management of the programme?
● Is everyone well-informed of the programme planning, methodology and results expected?

6.2.2. Operation of the programme at school level*

Following preliminary training, schools organised a teaching programme based round the five priority areas identified. They also tried to reinforce these messages in all subjects across the curriculum. School health

* [Note: a similar set of activities and questions would be relevant for out-of-school groups.]

action committees (including some children) were formed to try to ensure that the school itself was healthy and to plan health action in the community based on the school.

All these activities had to be monitored and schools were encouraged to draw up their own lists of self-evaluation questions. When the project monitoring team came round the school they discussed these with the health action committees and suggested improvements.

Evaluation questions:

● Is there a well-defined schedule for Child-to-Child activities in the school programme (time given, people involved, arrangement of activities)?
● Is the purpose of Child-to-Child understood in the school as a whole (head, teachers, children)?
● To what extent is the Child-to-Child approach being used?
  — how many classes?
  — how often?
  — other applications, e.g. maths, etc?
● What Child-to-Child materials are available and being produced? How good are they? Have they been evaluated?
● How is Child-to-Child being used in the classroom?
● Are children involved at each stage?
  — Understanding the problem;
  — Investigating, reporting and discussing;
  — Planning and deciding action;
  — Taking action;
  — Discussing and reporting results;
  — Evaluation.
● Is Child-to-Child part of school life?
● Are there health clubs, health committees? health scouts?
● Are the children involved? Are all of the children involved or just some?
● How far are the children involved in decision-making and evaluating?
● Have the school and teachers prepared their own work plan?
● Who helps the teachers in carrying out the activities?

6.2.3. Coordination and communication

It was agreed that coordination between all those working with the programme and communication of the ideas was vital to the project's success. The project workers selected one small area (two schools and one youth group) and studied how far the ideas and activities were shared. As a result a feedback meeting was called and the problems and possible solutions discussed with all heads and youth leaders involved in the project.

Evaluation questions:

- What links were made within schools through:
  — Teachers and teacher/parent meetings;
  — Different subjects in the curriculum;
  — Classroom and out-of-class activities?
- What links are being made between schools and youth groups involved in the programme?
- What links are being made between school and home?
- What links are being made with other professionals such as health workers and with other programmes in the community?
- How far are the media (newspapers, radio, etc) being used to spread interest among the wider national community?

6.2.4. Training

The first training which teachers and youth leaders received was not enough. Many new challenges and problems came up, so it was necessary to have short training meetings frequently during the project. Most of these were organised at school level. All those who took part were encouraged to evaluate each round of training, and in the end a very simple 'guide to training' was produced by the project organisers which proved very useful to schools.

Evaluation questions:

- How often and what kind of training do the teachers receive during the programme, e.g. individual help from supervisors or training groups in school?
- Did the training reflect the Child-to-Child methodology?
- What are the results of training, e.g. better skills/teaching/materials produced? Better understanding, more confidence?
- What problems were raised by training?

6.3. Evaluation of outcomes

6.3.1. Evaluating changes in knowledge in children and families

Children, helped by their teachers and club organisers, were invited to design their own knowledge tests both for other children and for the community members to whom they had taken the messages. They found this very difficult but learnt a great deal by doing it. They were helped by project organisers.

In some cases, these questions were the same as those which they had asked right at the beginning of the project. From asking these questions they discovered that most children and some parents had gained a good deal of knowledge, but additional questions showed that some of the messages had not really been properly understood. (Many parents and some children thought that the oral rehydration drink was a 'medicine' to be taken in small quantities.)

Evaluation questions:

● Has there been a gain in knowledge?
● Is the new knowledge correct, useful, relevant?
● Is there a better **understanding** of health problems and possible ways of overcoming them?
● Is the knowledge retained over a long period? (Ask the same questions six months later.)

6.3.2. Changes in skills*

In the project schools, children were 'paired' with older children responsible for the hygiene and safety of the younger ones. Older children also had responsibilities for the health committees.

"MY SCHOOL BROTHER NEVER CHECKED MY FINGERNAILS TODAY"

A survey made over a number of schools reported a considerable improvement in hygiene ... both older and younger children

had gained skills (e.g. older children had taught younger ones how to clean their teeth more thoroughly and, in so doing, learnt a lot themselves).

Some comments also reflected that older children were getting more skilful in helping the younger ones help themselves (instead of just telling them what to do).

Evaluation questions:

● What health skills do children or their families now have that they did not have before?
● Do they practice these skills?
● Have older children taught new skills to younger ones?
● What has been the effect on the older children ... have they become more confident?
● Have teachers, health workers or youth leaders gained any new teaching, management or communication skills as a result of working with a Child-to-Child project? If so, which ones?

6.3.3. Changes in attitudes in children, teachers, health workers and youth leaders, administrators and managers, community members*

Health workers, youth leaders and project organisers had a long discussion on how to evaluate attitudes. They all agreed that tests were not likely to be useful to them. Finally they made a list of some of the ways of behaving (**indicators**) which they should look for in children, e.g.:
● attends health club regularly;
● notices and reports poor hygiene or safety hazards;
● makes a toy for baby, etc, etc.

*Note: Here we are talking about two rather different things: health skills in children, teachers and community members, as well as problem-solving and communication skills.

*Note: Changes in attitudes are usually demonstrated by changes in behaviour. This can be observed over time and recorded, but it cannot easily be tested.

Making the list taught them a lot about what to look for and encourage.

They enjoyed this activity and found it useful and so decided to do something much more difficult: to make a similar list of **indicators** for parents and even for themselves, e.g.:
● praises children on health activity;
● gives children more responsibility;
● encourages child to join health club;
● asks 'did you learn anything new about health this week?'

Evaluation questions:

● Do children demonstrate more interest and concern over the health of:
— themselves?
— others?
● Do they give their time and energy to activities related to health?
● Do they give up other things for such activities?
● Do teachers display more interest and confidence in working with health topics in school?
● Do they take more time and show more interest in working with parents and health workers outside school time?
● Do parents show more interest in the health messages the school teaches? Do they show more concern about health problems?

6.3.4. Note

There are two more things which we would look for at the outcome stage.

The **first** is **changes in health of children or families**.

Whether we can measure this depends on what activities are being attempted. In some cases a simple medical message (e.g. detecting and treat-

ing scabies) can be passed on by children and the results measured (i.e. less cases of scabies were seen and reported).

In some cases, we may be able to say *probably* a Child-to-Child programme has effected a change in health. (For example, health workers say that more cases of pneumonia in babies were brought to the clinic and cured.)

Nevertheless, we must not believe that medical outcomes are easy to measure and we must not neglect Child-to-Child activities like hygiene or playing with children or helping the handicapped because their direct effects cannot be measured.

The **second** is **unexpected results**.

We must always look for these in a small-scale programme. We may discover changes in children:
● in the other subjects they learn;
● in what they do at home.

Many may discover new interest and new cooperation in the community ... or we may find that the programme causes bad feeling and competition.

Unexpected results can often be very important and lead to changes in projects and their evaluation.

TABLE 6

EVALUATING A SMALL-SCALE CHILD-TO-CHILD PROJECT
CHECKLIST FOR ACTION

TASK	EVALUATION		
	Who evaluates what?	What did they find out?	What action did they take?
I. THE PLANNING STAGE			
• Deciding to start a project, selecting a community and assessing needs			
• Looking at where we are now			
• Setting objectives and making a plan for the project			
• Checking the plan against resources available			
• Assessing and collecting materials needed			
• Selection of schools and youth leaders			
• Training before beginning the project			
II. THE DOING STAGE			
• Organisation of the programme			
• Operation of the programme at school level			
• Coordination and communication			
• Training			
III. EVALUATION OF OUTCOMES			
• Changes in knowledge:			
(i) in children			
(ii) in families			
(iii) in communities			
• Changes in skills:			
(i) in children			
(ii) in actions			
(iii) in problem solving			
(iv) in communication			
(v) in teachers			
(vi) in families and communities			
• Changes in attitudes (observed through practice):			
(i) in children			
(ii) in teachers			
(iii) in health workers and youth leaders			
(iv) in administrators and managers			
(v) in the community			
• Changes in health:			
(i) in children			
(ii) in families			
• Unexpected results			

7. EVALUATING CHILD-TO-CHILD APPROACHES IN A NATIONAL PROGRAMME

Very often countries are now introducing Health Education in a much more serious and positive way within their school curricula. Sometimes they are doing this through the medium of one subject. Sometimes they wish Health to be introduced across the curriculum and into many subjects. Often they wish to introduce a Child-to-Child approach into Health Education.

They need to evaluate:

● Whether the approach is needed and worth-while.
● How it is being introduced.
● Whether it has value, both in spreading health to children and communities and as a way of educating children and helping them to 'learn how to learn'.

In other cases, countries may introduce large-scale Child-to-Child approaches *outside* the formal school system, possibly using youth groups. Here also a national evaluation is needed. However, in this section, we concentrate on national programmes based on the formal school.

WHEN AND WHAT TO EVALUATE

As in the small-scale programmes, there will need to be evaluation of the **Planning, Doing** and **Outcome** stages. But it is never too late to evaluate. (Even if the programme has already started, we can still evaluate both **Doing** and **Outcomes**.)

7.1. The planning stage

7.1.1. Adopting the Child-to-Child approach

Evaluation questions:

● Are the *reasons* for introducing a Child-to-Child approach clear?

● Does the curriculum centre understand that introducing a Child-to-Child approach implies:

— closer links with school and community;
— more active approaches in schools, etc?

Evaluation in action:

A Curriculum Centre set up a group to study the introduction of a proposed new Health Education syllabus using Child-to-Child. They agreed that the approach implied many new methods and some changes in school organisation. It was therefore decided to start the approach in a small number of schools around a teachers' training college before spreading it more widely.

7.1.2. Objectives

Evaluation questions:

● Do the *objectives* for the curriculum effectively include those of the Child-to-Child approach (especially those emphasising new attitudes and practices within the curriculum)? If not, can they be revised?

Evaluation in action:

The Curriculum Centre, together with an outside consultant who had worked with Child-to-Child programmes, looked at health needs and formulated new objectives. In each case attitudes and practices were emphasised. The new objectives stressed what children could do for others as well as what they could do for themselves.

7.1.3. Materials

Evaluation questions:

- Have the Child-to-Child materials nationally available for the teachers and children been surveyed?
- Have decisions been made regarding their use:

  — Can any materials be used without adaptation?
  — How far do others need to be translated and modified to suit local needs?
  — Who is available to do this?
  — What are the cost implications?

> **Evaluation in action:**
>
> Child-to-Child readers were received by the Curriculum Centre and examined by a panel of teachers and health workers against a list of questions. They were then tried out with a number of children of different ages and in different places. As a result some were considered suitable, but others were not. Therefore new titles will be prepared at a writing workshop.

- Have new Health Education materials incorporating the Child-to-Child approach been planned and by whom?

- How far is this material cost-effective ... (can it be used for more than one purpose, e.g. for teaching reading and health at the same time)?

7.1.4. Training

Evaluation questions:

- Are there enough Teacher Educators, Health Educators and Curriculum Workers who understand and support Child-to-Child approaches - or will some further training be needed?
- If *training* is planned, is it affordable and can it be made as cost-effective as possible?

> **Evaluation in action:**
>
> At a national course on Health Education, an evaluation (by questionnaire) supported by experience from the course, showed that very few participants understood how to use active methods with children and in communities. As a result, it was decided to identify core teachers in each district who could be trained and encouraged to spread these approaches.

7.1.5. Who evaluates at the planning stage?

The following might undertake such an evaluation:

A Special Working Group (convened by the Curriculum Centre)
Such a group might be convened only at the planning stage to look at plans, resources and objectives and could also gather evidence from surveys in different parts of the country. It would include a wide range of expertise including specialists in health, people knowledgeable about Child-to-Child approaches and 'users'.

Experts in Particular Fields for Different Tasks
The current Child-to-Child materials could be assessed for medical relevance (by doctors), for readability (by language specialists), for teachability (by teacher educators), for local acceptability (by health workers and teachers).

An Evaluator or Evaluation Group (for Health Education), Appointed by the Curriculum Centre
Such a group needs to be appointed right at the beginning of a project to plan its evaluation all the way through. The group would not be full time and could include expertise from outside the Centre. It should meet regularly. One of its main tasks would be to encourage the 'users' of the approach to evaluate themselves.

7.2. The doing stage

Evaluation questions:

Once the Child-to-Child approach is being introduced into the curriculum, we need to look at:

(1) Whether any *plan* that has been made is being followed. If not, what are the reasons for changes in action or for lack of action?

(2) How it is being introduced in different contexts:

- Are some programmes and schools more active than others? If so, why?

- Are some teachers or schools failing to introduce the approach or misunderstanding it? If so, why?

Evaluation in action:

A group from the Curriculum Centre was appointed to visit a number of schools, colleges and 'Health Scout' programmes in different areas. In one district, far more activity was noted than another. Questioning revealed that:

- the organising committee was more active;
- transport was available to visit schools and clubs;
- a local in-service centre was particularly involved and interested.

Visits were arranged so that others could come to the area to see the good work that was going on.

(3) Is the *approach spreading* outside the original planned action? As it spreads, is it changing (or weakening)? Why? Are *new ideas* about Child-to-Child beginning to emerge? Do they incorporate both in-school and out-of-school activities? How and why?

Evaluation in action:

A seminar was called to discuss Child-to-Child approaches. During this seminar it was discovered that several schools had started Health Clubs and that they were very popular and successful. They will now be encouraged.

(4) Is *training and material production* taking place and with what frequency and quality? Are training materials being used? If so, of what quality?

TABLE 7

CRITERIA FOR GOOD TRAINING MATERIALS

WHAT TO LOOK FOR	WHAT TO FIND OUT
1. Relevant to local needs.	Make a list of the priorities. Check to see that the materials cover these.
2. Medically correct.	Doctors must read them.
3. Suggest many useful, varied and practical ideas and methods.	Teacher trainers should read them.
4. Encourage Child-to-Child approaches.	List Child-to-Child approaches. Check materials to see if they are used.
5. Flexible: can be used in different situations.	Discuss materials with groups of teachers. "What can you use?"
6. Readable.	Test with teachers and health workers who will use them.
7. Interesting.	Discuss with groups. "How could you use them?"

(5) Which Child-to-Child messages and materials are *being most and least used?* What are the reasons?

(6) Which *groups and agencies* (including international agencies) seem most interested and supportive of Child-to-Child and which least interested?

7.2.1. Who evaluates at the doing stage?

1. *An evaluation team from the Centre*
Already mentioned at the planning stage. There needs to be some group, not full time, which looks not only at how the implementation is working, but also at how it fulfils the plans and objectives made earlier. Remember! One of the main purposes of this group is to encourage others to evaluate.

2. *Evaluation groups at local level*
At local level, there should also be individuals (or, better still, a group) who evaluate 'how the programme is doing'. These can include local organisers and supervisors of the programme, but also other people who already have the task of helping local people to improve, such as the school inspectors, or district health workers. From their reports, it will be possible to make a national picture of successes and difficulties.

3. *Everyone working for Child-to-Child (including children)*

If everyone thinks of themselves as an evaluator and is prepared to make simple reports, to discuss what they have done with others and to answer simple questions, then the task of a national team is made much easier. For local workers to do this, two things are necessary:

● They must feel that their information is welcome and will not be 'used against them';
● They must know *what* needs to be evaluated and *why*. (So sharing this information is very important.)

7.3. The outcomes stage

At this stage, evaluation becomes more technical and professional. Its purpose may be:

● to decide how widely to spread the Child-to-Child approach through formal and non-formal education;
● to assess how easily it can be absorbed;
● to examine whether, and in what way, the approach should be encouraged to spread from Health to other areas.

At this stage, the question will have to be considered of whether Child-to-Child is cost-effective (providing a worthwhile educational return for the time and effort it requires to introduce it).

This will *prove very difficult to answer* because the chief gains from Child-to-Child activities are likely to be changes in attitudes and behaviour of children and communities. These, too, need to be measured over a long time (and possibly over generations as these children become parents themselves). Such attitudes are very difficult to measure. Yet any programme that ignores them

and merely measures the impact of Child-to-Child in terms of short-term gains in knowledge and short-term effects on health status is not measuring the full, true impact of the approach.

What to evaluate:
At this stage we want to evaluate the following outcomes:

7.3.1. Changes in children

Evaluation questions:

● What are the knowledge and skills gained, possibly measured against a set of minimum health knowledge and skill objectives? A wide variety of situations need to be examined. We need to repeat the measures after, perhaps, a year to find out how far they are remembered.
● What are the changes in attitudes in children (again over a longer period)?

Evaluation in action:

Following an agreement on a set of Minimum National knowledge and skill competencies, partly based on the UNICEF document 'Facts for Life', a very simple test was devised which could be administered either by teachers or by secondary school children in Youth Groups. Children were tested. Some of these were in schools and youth groups already using the Child-to-Child approach; some in schools or groups about to start.

In both groups, it will be necessary to test the children again in a year's time. In the latter group a 'before' and 'after' comparison will be possible. From the results it will be possible to identify variations in interest and effectiveness between schools.

7.3.2. Changes in approaches in school and out-of-school programmes and in curriculum centres

Evaluation questions:

- How far has the approach actually been taken up and does it continue to operate? This provides an easy and useful measure. People do not regularly take up an idea and *go on doing it* if it does not appear to work or if it does not seem to be worthwhile.
- How far has the approach led to changes in methodology and classroom practice?
- How far can we detect changes in the way in which schools, colleges or curriculum centres plan and implement programmes (e.g. more or less integration; more or less flexibility; greater or less relations with the community)?

Evaluation in action:

As part of a Master's study in Education, three students were encouraged to write dissertations about classroom and out-of-school approaches in schools using the Child-to-Child approach. They were attached to schools and stayed in them for a fortnight observing and recording activities.

7.3.3. Changes in relations between institutions and sectors

Evaluation questions:

Has the introduction of the Child-to-Child approach led to closer cooperation between:

- schools, preschools, youth groups and communities?
- education and health programmes at any or every level?

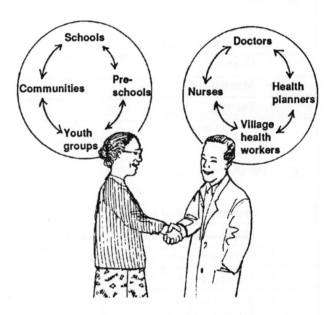

Evaluation in action:

A three-person team was identified from outside the programme. At an initial session, objectives and major evaluation questions were identified. Thereafter the team was given a free hand to observe activities and ask questions as it wished. As a result, a report 'The Impact of Child-to-Child Approaches' is being prepared quickly and will be discussed with the national organisers. The same group will revisit the activities in a year's time.

TABLE 8

EVALUATING CHILD-TO-CHILD APPROACHES IN A NATIONAL PROGRAMME CHECKLIST FOR ACTION

TASK	EVALUATION		
	Who evaluates what?	What did they find out?	What action did they take?
I. THE PLANNING STAGE			
• Adopting the Child-to-Child approach			
• Objectives			
• Materials			
• Training			
• Making the plan			
II. THE DOING STAGE			
• Implementation of the plan			
• Modification to suit different contexts			
• Spread and change of the approach			
• Training and materials production			
• Reasons for using or not using different methods			
• Take up by which agencies and why			
III. THE OUTCOMES STAGE			
• Changes in children			
• Changes in approaches:			
(i) in school			
(ii) in out-of-school programmes			
(iii) in curriculum centres			
• Changes in relations between institutions and sectors			
• Changes in practice and attitudes across communities			
• Probable health gains			

7.3.4. Changes in practice and attitudes across communities

Evaluation questions:

- How far are there any observable changes caused by the children's interaction with their communities and, if so, what are these?
- How far have Child-to-Child programmes made a probable health impact on communities? (Very difficult to measure with certainty.)

Evaluation in action:

Three case studies are commissioned from an evaluation group to look at the impact of Child-to-Child on carefully selected communities. They will record how far messages have been transmitted by children to communities and how far these have been received and understood by those for whom they were intended. They will also be asked to observe and record changes in practice and health status within the community resulting from the use of the new approach by the children.

7.3.5. Who evaluates at the outcomes stage?

When national level evaluations are mounted, there needs to be expertise in evaluation. However, such expertise is within the range of any competent planner or curriculum worker. No long and complicated training in Evaluation Techniques is necessary. All that is necessary is to ask the right questions and interpret results objectively and sensibly. Technical help can always be enlisted for statistical analysis (though, in fact, little will be necessary).

Remember also that if smaller scale evaluations have been done, one of the main roles of a central evaluator is to collect and analyse these.

At this stage, however, an 'Outside View' is probably essential to complement observations and judgements made by planners and implementors within the programme. Discussions with such 'outsiders' to determine what questions are worth asking are essential. It is vital that those who evaluate at this stage understand the nature and purpose of the Child-to-Child approach.

8. EVALUATING CHILD-TO-CHILD MATERIALS

8.1. What materials?

Sometimes Child-to-Child activities are introduced as an addition or as part of another programme, through use of Child-to-Child materials.

A common example of this is when story books with a Child-to-Child message are introduced into the language programme; another instance is when sheets or books on toy-making are used in a youth group programme.

Sometimes the books are imported or adapted. Sometimes they may be made locally but usually they need to be evaluated.

8.2. Key evaluation questions

Here are some key questions:

(1) *Is it correct?*
Check the text **and** the illustrations.

(2) *Is the language and are the pictures easy to understand?*
One easy way of checking the language is to copy out a passage and leave a blank on every eighth word. If a reader can fill in the blanks sensibly (never mind about the exact wording or the spelling) the text can be understood. If he cannot or writes nonsense in the blanks, it cannot be.

(3) *Is the main message getting across?*
Ask key questions.

(4) *Are the pictures suitable?*
Ask the children to describe them to you.

(5) *Is it interesting?*
Ask the children to retell the story or describe the content and tell you whether it is 'like something you know' (in other words, whether it matches with children's experience). You will soon be able to decide from the way they respond whether they were interested. (DON'T ask them "did you like it?" They will probably say 'yes' because that is the answer you want.)

(6) *Does it lead on to other interesting activities?*
Good Child-to-Child materials suggest new things that children can do in their schools and communities.

(7) *Is it acceptable to the culture?*
Get someone like a religious leader to read through any parts which you may have doubts about.

(8) *Is it worth the money?*
Check the cost against other books which children might buy.

(9) *How could it be made better?*

APPENDIX

1. **Marie-Thérèse Feuerstein.** *Partners in Evaluation*, **(1986) London: Macmillan.**

This book provides an excellent practical guide for field evaluators. It was written in the belief that participants in programmes can and should help in their evaluation.

All the chapters are relevant, but Chapters 3 and 4 on methods of collecting information and Chapter 5 on reporting the results of evaluation are invaluable as the extract from the Contents in Table 9 shows.

2. **Other Useful Books and Resources**

McCormick, R and James, M. *Curriculum Evaluation in Schools*. (1983) Croom Helm.

Peil, M. Social Science Research Methods. In: *An African Handbook*. (1982) Hodder and Stoughton.

*Rossi, P H and Freedman, H E. *Evaluation: A Systematic Approach*. (1982) Beverley Hills: Sage Publications.

Werner, D and Bowers, W. *Helping Health Workers Learn*. (1983) Palo Alto: Hesperian Foundation.

WHO Health Programme Evaluation. *Health For All Series*. (1981) Geneva: WHO.

Young, B and Durston, S. *Primary Health Education*. (1987) London: Longman.

*Herman, J L (Series Editor), *Program Evaluation Kit* (2nd edition). (1988) London: Sage Publications:

Volume 1:   *Evaluator's Handbook.*

Volume 2:   *How to Focus an Evaluation.*

---

*   provides a comprehensive guide to evaluation technique and is also quite lengthy and expensive.

Table 9
Techniques Analysed in Chapters 3 to 5 of 'Partners in Evaluation'

Chapter 3
Making and keeping records
Using reports
Case studies
Meetings and workshops
Mapping
Observations - Using pictures, photographs and tape recordings
Writing profiles
Using written materials

Chapter 4
Sampling and surveys
Interviewing
Analysing and summarising

Chapter 5
Reporting
Written and verbal reports
Numbers
Tables and graphs
Overlays and charts
Pictures and photographs
Tape recordings

Volume 3:	*How to Design a Program Evaluation.*
Volume 4:	*How to Use Qualitative Methods in Evaluation.*
Volume 5:	*How to Assess Program Implementation.*
Volume 6:	*How to Measure Attitudes.*
Volume 7:	*How to Measure Performance and Use Tests*
Volume 8:	*How to Analyze Data*
Volume 9:	*How to Communicate Evaluation Findings*

Child-to-Child

How to Run
A Workshop
and similar occasions

by
William Dodd and Christine Scotchmer

INTRODUCTION
This section has been prepared in order to share the experience of those, from many countries, who have organised and run Child-to-Child workshops. It is designed to help people involved in organising workshops or similar occasions, whether at national or local level, where Child-to-Child approaches and activities are to be discussed and developed.

ABOUT WORKSHOPS
There are many words used to describe people coming together for study or training, for example **conference, congress, symposium, seminar, course**. They all have slightly different meanings and the special meaning of the word **WORKSHOP** is that people come to **work together** and to **work things out together. However this booklet may also be helpful in the organisation of symposia, seminars and courses.**

Child-to-Child workshops have different purposes, including:

• Spreading awareness of Child-to-Child.

• Sharing existing experience of Child-to-Child and similar approaches, nationally and/or internationally.

• Preparing a programme of action.

• Learning how to use materials.

• Learning how to use a particular methodology.

• Writing new materials or adapting and translating existing ones.

The workshop may be:

• Part of a series.

• Part of a broad programme of action.

• Part of another training course, e.g. a national teacher training course on new methodology; a training course for primary health care workers or scout leaders, etc.

• Part of what people are already doing.

SETTING UP THE WORKSHOP

It is useful to form a **planning group**, made up of people who will themselves be attending the workshop, rather than leaving all the advance planning to **one** person. The group should:

- Plan well ahead. Arrangements often take much longer than expected, i.e. months rather than weeks.

- Liaise with the appropriate people, e.g. Ministries of Health and Education, voluntary bodies, funding agencies, teacher training colleges, key speakers, etc.

- Secure funding well in advance.

- Obtain local and national political support.

- Study previous experience, e.g. obtain reports of previous Child-to-Child workshops.

- Appoint a **coordinator** who will oversee the planning activities.

ORGANISING THE WORKSHOP

Consider:

- **When** the workshop will take place. The dates should not clash with other important events for participants (e.g. local or national events, school terms, university terms, etc.)

- **How long** it will be.

- **Where** the workshop will take place.

  — Consider, for example, whether a college or hotel would be the best setting. This will depend on the purpose of the workshop. College accommodation may be less costly and may facilitate greater participation of college tutors, and teachers and students from associated schools. Participants may, however, be distracted by other duties. Holding the workshop in a hotel often leads to more consistent attendance.

  — Everyone, staff and other participants, should have appropriately good accommodation.

  — Meeting rooms must be sufficient in number and suitable for group work and practical sessions; one big room alone is often not adequate.

- **Whom** you are going to invite, e.g. a mixture of education and health workers; community leaders; parents and children. Sometimes it is useful to invite a large number of people for initial, awareness sessions, and a smaller number to participate in other parts of the programme.

- **Sending out necessary materials** in advance, e.g. books, articles, or any background documents you want participants to read and think about beforehand.

- **Requesting participants to prepare reports** and other information, or statistics, about their local area or projects with which they are involved. Give precise instructions, well in advance, regarding the information required and how it should be organised. Only request such reports and information if you are sure they will be used during the workshop.

- **Financial arrangements**, including travel and subsistence allowances for participants.

CHECKLIST FOR FINANCIAL ARRANGEMENTS

Have you taken into account:

✓ The boarding and feeding costs per participant, multiplied by the number of participants, multiplied by the number of nights;

✓ The travel costs of participants to and from the workshop;

✓ The cost of books, materials and stationery;

✓ The travel and residential costs of the staff (including support staff such as secretaries);

✓ Daily subsistence allowances (where appropriate)?

- **Support services**, e.g. food, transport, equipment and stationery, clerical support, electricity supply.

- **Liaising with ministries or agencies** who can provide support services.

- **Arrangements for registration**, including provision of name badges.

- **Publicity**, which includes alerting local/national press, radio and TV. (It is often worthwhile writing out a description of the workshop and its purpose which newspapers may well use.)

- **Joining instructions**.

- **Delegation** of the above tasks.

CHECKLIST FOR JOINING INSTRUCTIONS

Have you included:

✓ The place where the workshop will be held;

✓ The dates of opening and closure, as well as the date and time of assembly/registration;

✓ The travel arrangements, with special reference to 'travel warrants' where these are issued, and what trains or buses will be met by official transport;

✓ Details of daily subsistence allowances (where appropriate);

✓ The nature of the boarding accommodation, specifying whether those attending should bring such items as towels, soap, blankets, and eating utensils, and what arrangements there are for laundry;

✓ The postal address of the workshop;

✓ The arrangements for any salary or other payments which may be due to participants during or after the workshop;

✓ The syllabuses, textbooks, and notebooks, or information about their own activities, which those attending should bring with them?

EVALUATION RIGHT FROM THE START

✎ Check that you have set reasonable and attainable objectives for your workshop.

✎ Check that your arrangements are satisfactory and that everything will be ready on time.

✎ Get a second opinion to make sure.

PLANNING THE ACTIVITIES

OBJECTIVES OF THE WORKSHOP

Child-to-Child workshops have different purposes. The nature and range of each meeting will affect both its objectives and the shape of its programme or timetable.

**OBJECTIVES OF
A SCHOOL HEALTH
ACTION PLAN
WORKSHOP**

➤ To consider and agree the nature and purpose of health education in our country.

➤ To discuss and agree the part children can play in that endeavour.

➤ To consider our country's national priorities for health education, their application to communities and their implications for children learning in primary schools.

➤ To select key priorities as examples and then consider these in relation to methodology and activities in selected schools.

➤ To consider and evaluate current materials.

➤ To produce an outline for a national school health action plan.

➤ To consider and agree guidelines for the production of local school health action plans.

➤ To consider and agree criteria for the monitoring and evaluation of the project.

➤ To decide how the project is to be managed.

➤ To decide and agree a plan of action for the coming year.

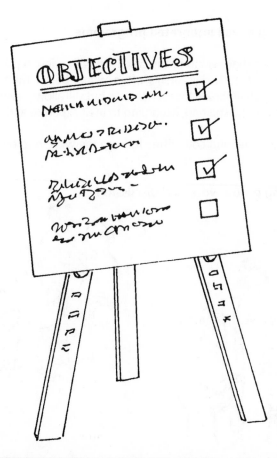

It is useful to display the objectives on a wall poster, or on a blackboard, throughout the workshop. This helps to keep the workshop on course and acts as a checklist, with each objective being ticked as it is achieved.

**THE PROGRAMME
OR TIMETABLE**

Think about:

☞ **Opening and closing ceremonies.**

- What will you do if the invited dignitary does not turn up? Can you be flexible and re-arrange sessions? (This applies to unexpected events throughout the programme.)

- Make the most of these ceremonies by organising photo sessions for publicity. Have a group of children ready to sing songs with health messages.

☞ **Making the most of more formal speeches and speakers.**

- Ask for papers in advance, for distribution to participants, and suggest that speakers **summarise the main points rather than read their entire papers** at the workshop.

- Brief chairpersons fully.

- Choose respondents to begin the questioning when the speaker has finished.

☞ **Including question and answer sessions.** These are very useful for getting across basic facts.

☞ **Maintaining a well integrated programme.**

- Appoint a chairperson of the day, who will review proceedings at the end of each day. (This often works better than having a different chairperson for each session but still allows several people to share in the chairing, according to their expertise and interests.)

- Choose a steering committee to keep the workshop on course.

☞ **Organising group work and discussions.**

Bear in mind:

- Composition of groups, e.g. whether of similar professionals or a mixture.

- Size of groups.

- Providing clear, brief, written instructions to groups and checking that these are fully understood before work starts. See sample instructions below.

PROJECT ON CHILD GROWTH AND DEVELOPMENT

INSTRUCTIONS TO GROUP A

You are **teachers** in a **primary school**. Plan a project in which the school children will learn how to help children who do not go to school.

Use the Child-to-Child Activity Sheet 1.4 as resource material.

A. **Check the information.** Is it appropriate? How can you link these ideas with topics in the school curriculum?

B. **Decide on the aims for your project.**

C. **Now plan the children's activities for each stage of the project:**

1. **Understanding the issue.**
   Think of ways in which the children can start to think about the problems of children who don't come to school.

2. **Finding out more about the issue in their community.**
   What information can the children find out? What questions can they ask?

3. **Discussing possible solutions.**
   What solutions exist? What kind of discussion will help the children assess possible solutions and decide on which solution to adopt?

4. **Taking action to help other children.**
   Through what activities can children, as individuals and as a group, help children who do not go to school?

5. **Evaluation.**
   How can the children and teachers evaluate the impact of the project?

Prepare ONE activity as a role-play to show to the other participants in the workshop.

- Selection of group rapporteurs, i.e. those who report on behalf of the group. It is not a good idea to choose either the weakest or most dominant member of the group for this task. Consider who holds the pen - do they also hold the power?

- Reminding rapporteurs to focus on the main results of the group work when they report to plenary sessions. Asking groups to produce a poster which highlights, for example, three proposals for action will help to focus the discussion and be simple enough for the rapporteur to mention in one or two minutes.

- Suggesting introductory activities. Particularly when group members do not know each other, initial introductory activities can help to create an atmosphere where people can work together creatively.

- Restraining over-dominant members of groups and encouraging shy participants to contribute.

- Allowing enough time for the exploration and development of ideas. **Insufficient time for group work is a frequent complaint during workshop evaluations.**

- Involving older children in the group work. It may be appropriate to include secondary school students, perhaps in their own group so that they are not intimidated. Some workshops have successfully appointed students as chairpersons of group reporting sessions.

☞ **Arranging practical sessions, e.g. drama, puppets, writing, translating.**

- These are often better in the afternoon, as a change from the more 'academic' activities.

- Again, allowing sufficient time for the activity is as vital as the provision of the right type and quantity of materials, and discussion afterwards of what has been done.

- If possible, it can be useful to take photographs of practical sessions or to record them on video or audio tapes: the material thus produced can be used for publicity during the workshop and later in action programmes.

OUTSIDE VISITS AND ACTIVITIES

Outside visits or activities add interest to a programme. They can either involve **participants going out** to visit a particular place or to take part in an activity, or **outside contributors (e.g. a drama group or horti-culturalist) coming in** to share experience and knowledge and demonstrate activites.

Points to remember:

✎ Survey beforehand any place you plan to visit. Make sure you know how to get there and how long it will take. Allow plenty of time for travel and the activity involved, and make arrangements for refreshments if necessary.

✎ To avoid surprises on the day, liaise with the outside contributors to make sure you know what they will be doing.

MONITORING AND EVALUATING ACTIVITIES

There are various ways of monitoring and evaluating activities during the workshop:

- Knowledge of factual topics can be pre-tested and post-tested, to assess gains in knowledge.

- A member of each group can be appointed to report daily to the steering committee about progress of the workshop, including any practical complaints.

- Participants can be asked to score activities, orally or in writing, using a simple system such as categorising them as **'Very Good'**, **'Good'** or **'Fair'**. (Nobody ever grades an activity as 'Poor' even though they think it is.)

  When a number of participants have given lower ratings, discuss their reasons for doing so.

- Informal discussion with participants can identify good points and problems.

THE SOCIAL PROGRAMME

This is important. People who are working hard must have time off. The social programme might include informal and more formal events. You are advised to think about:

- Allowing free time for people to do whatever they want.

- Having tea and coffee breaks.

- Allowing enough time for main meals.

- Including cultural events and visits to places of interest not related to the workshop.

- Arranging for a list of addresses to be available so that participants can keep in touch with one another after the workshop.

- Organising a video or slide show by any visitors, showing life in their country or region.

- Having a musical evening.

- Arranging a group photograph.

- Having a 'goodbye' meal on the last evening.

INVOLVING CHILDREN IN ACTIVITIES

Children should be appropriately involved in workshops:

- In group work (please see above).

- In demonstration 'lessons' or activities.

- In displays of work (e.g. drawings, toys, puppets).

- In playlets or choirs.

OUTCOMES OF THE WORKSHOP

There are likely to be several outcomes, including:

☞ Agreement on a plan of action following the workshop.

☞ The report of the workshop. The first thing to consider will be what type of report is required. The nature of the report will depend on the type of workshop and to whom the report is addressed, e.g. donors, ministers, trainers, etc.

   • Sometimes it is better to have two reports: a quickly produced, brief account of the workshop, followed by a longer, useable document at a later (but not too much later) date which might include, e.g. activity sheets or stories produced; training material concerning methods such as using pictures, puppets or songs.

   • The report should include objectives and practical recommendations for action which clearly state who will do what and by when.

   • The report should have a readable format and layout and may benefit from a little humour, with examples of things that people said and amusing events. Consider illustrations.

☞ A certificate of attendance for participants. This will be more useful if it states what the workshop covered.

MONITORING AND FOLLOW-UP

Workshops easily become isolated events having no connection with activities in the 'real world'. It is therefore important to consider:

✎ The objectives of the workshop and which of them have been achieved ... in the short term? in the longer term?

✎ Whether the achievements have in fact been different from those expected.

✎ Appointing participants to monitor action in the long term in relation to the objectives.

In the monitoring and follow-up it is useful to consider the **implications for future workshops and similar occasions.**

CHILD-TO-CHILD

PUBLICATIONS

WHERE TO GET CHILD-TO-CHILD PUBLICATIONS

(By Alphabetical Order of Country)

1. FRANCE

1.1. **L'Enfant pour l'Enfant, Institut Santé et Développement, 15 rue de l'Ecole de Médecine, 75270 Paris — cedex 06, France.**

French:

- Activity Sheets.
- Readers.
- Newsletter.

1.2. **Unesco, 7 place de Fontenoy, 75700 Paris, France.**

English and French:

- Child-to-Child, Another Path to Learning: Hugh Hawes, (UIE Monographs 13), 1988. ISBN 92820 1049X.

- L'Enfant pour l'Enfant: Une Autre Voie pour la Santé et l'Education: Hugh Hawes, traduit et adapté par Elisabeth Dumurgier, Colette Hawes et Lucien Michon, (Monographies de l'IUE 13), 1990. ISBN 92820 20495.

N.B. This book is available through sales agents for Unesco publications or bookshops worldwide. In case of difficulty, contact the Unesco Press, Commercial Services, Unesco.

- Child-to-Child in Africa: Towards an Open Learning Strategy: A K B Tay, (Digest 29), 1989.

- L'Enfant pour l'Enfant en Afrique: Vers une Pédagogie Ouverte: A K B Tay, (Digest 29), 1989.

Contact: Unit for Inter-Agency Cooperation in Basic Education, Unesco.

- Children, Health and Science: Child-to-Child Activities and Science and Technology Teaching, 1991 (Unesco Science and Technology Education Document Series No 41) — For primary science teachers. Shows the links between health and science education and how Child-to-Child provides good examples for both. **(Arabic, French and Spanish versions forthcoming.)**

Contact: Section of Science and Technology Education, Division for the Development of Education, Unesco.

2. INDIA

2.1. **Aga Khan Foundation, Sarojini House, 2nd Floor, 6 Bhagwan Dass Road, New Delhi 110 001, India. (English and Hindi)**

LANGUAGE KEY:		
Amharic	—	Section 6
Arabic	—	Sections 1 and 6
Chinese	—	Section 6
English	—	Sections 1, 2, 3, 6 and 7
French	—	Sections 1 and 6
Gujerati	—	Section 2
Hindi	—	Section 2
Nepali	—	Section 4
Portuguese	—	Section 6
Spanish	—	Sections 1 and 6
Swahili	—	Sections 3 and 6
Tamil	—	Section 2

2.2. Centre for Health Education, Training and Nutrition Awareness, Drive-in Cinema Building, 3rd Floor, Thaltej Road, Ahmedabad 380 054, Gujarat, India. (English and Gujerati)

2.3. Educational Multi Media Association, 32 College Road, Nungambakkam, Madras 600 006, India. (English and Tamil)

2.4. National Council of Educational Research and Training, Department of Preschool and Elementary Education, Sri Aurobindo Marg, New Delhi 110 016, India. (English)

2.5. Voluntary Health Association of India, Tong Swasthya Bhavan, 40 Institutional Area, Near Qutab Hotel, New Delhi 110 016, India. (English and Hindi)

3. KENYA

3.1. AMREF, Wilson Airport, PO Box 30125, Nairobi, Kenya.

English:

● Child-to-Child Activity Sheets — Complete pack.

Swahili:

● Adaptation of CHILD-to-child: Audrey Aarons and Hugh Hawes, first published in 1979 in the International Year of the Child.

4. NEPAL

4.1. Centre for Health Learning Materials, TU Institute of Medicine, PO Box 2533, Kathmandu, Nepal.

Nepali:

● Adaptations of Child-to-Child English Readers Numbers 2, 3, 4, 5 and 6.

5. PAKISTAN

5.1. Hamdard Foundation, Pakistan, Hamdard Centre, Nazimabad, Karachi 18, Pakistan.

Urdu:

● Adaptation of Child-to-Child English Reader Number 7 currently available. More to follow.

6. UNITED KINGDOM

6.1. Child-to-Child Trust, Institute of Education, 20 Bedford Way, London WC1H 0AL, UK. (Free of charge unless stated otherwise.)

Amharic:

● Child-to-Child Activity Sheets (24 titles) — Reference set held. **N.B.** Charge normally made for photocopying and postage.

Arabic:

● Child-to-Child Activity Sheets — A few titles only, produced in 1979. New translations underway and expected to be available from TALC (see below) from mid-1992.

Chinese:

● Child-to-Child Activity Sheets (12 titles) — Reference set held. **N.B.** Charge normally made for photocopying and postage.

English:

● Half-size sample pack of Child-to-Child Activity Sheets. **N.B.** Full-size complete pack sold by TALC — see below.

● Child-to-Child Newsletter — Annual issue.

● Child-to-Child Annual Report.

- Child-to-Child Introductory Leaflet.

- Do You Know a Handicapped Child? — A few copies remain of this booklet produced in 1984.

Portuguese:

- Child-to-Child Activity Sheets (11 titles) — Reference set held. **N.B.** Charge normally made for photocopying and postage.

Swahili:

- Child-to-Child Activity Sheets (19 titles) — Reference set held. **N.B.** Charge normally made for photocopying and postage.

6.2. Macmillan Education Ltd, Houndmills, Basingstoke, Hants RG21 2XS, UK.

English:

- CHILD-to-child: Audrey Aarons and Hugh Hawes, first published in 1979 in the International Year of the Child.

6.3. TALC (Teaching-aids At Low Cost), PO Box 49, St Albans, Herts AL1 4AX, UK.

Arabic:

- Child-to-Child Activity Sheets — Complete pack as English titles to be published mid-1992.

- Adaptations of Child-to-Child English Readers Numbers 1, 4, 5, 6, 8 and 10. More to follow.

- Adaptation of CHILD-to-child: Audrey Aarons and Hugh Hawes, first published in 1979 in the International Year of the Child.

English:

- Child-to-Child Activity Sheets — Complete pack now contains over 30 titles on the following themes:

  Child Growth and Development

  Nutrition

  Personal and Community Hygiene

  Safety

  Recognising and Helping the Disabled

  Prevention and Cure of Disease

- Child-to-Child and the Growth and Development of Young Children — A report and resource book from the International Seminar held at Nyeri, Kenya in 1989.

- Child-to-Child Readers:

  Level I
  Dirty Water (1)
  Good Food (2)
  Accidents (3)
  Not Just a Cold (7)

  Level II
  A Simple Cure (4)
  Teaching Thomas (5)
  Down with Fever (6)
  Diseases Defeated (8)
  Flies (9)
  I Can Do It Too (10)

  Level III
  Deadly Habits (11)

- Child-to-Child: A Resource Book, edited by Grazyna Bonati. Contains the following sections*, the current set of activity sheets and examples of Child-to-Child in action.

- Approaches to Learning and Teaching*: Audrey Aarons — A guide to taking action for health education with the Child-to-Child approach; for leaders, trainers, teachers and writers.

- Children, Health and Science: Child-to-Child Activities and Science and Technology Teaching, 1991 (Unesco Science and Technology Education Document Series No 41) — For primary science teachers. Shows the links between health and science education and how Child-to-Child provides good examples for both. (**English Edition**.)

- Doing It Better*: Hugh Hawes et al. — A simple guide to evaluation of Child-to-Child programmes and projects.

- How to Run a Workshop*: William Dodd and Christine Scotchmer — A short guide based on experiences from many countries.

  * These titles are also available separately.

- Health into Mathematics: William Gibbs and Peter Mutunga — For teachers and student teachers. The first in a series, Health Across the Curriculum, incorporating the Child-to-Child approach. Illustrates how health education can be taught through maths and how maths can be taught using health examples.

- Primary Health Education: Beverley Young and Susan Durston — How to teach health education in the classroom. Ideal for primary and student teachers. Incorporates the Child-to-Child approach.

- Toys for Fun: edited by June Carlile — A book of toys for pre-school children in Arabic, English, French, Portuguese, Spanish and Swahili (all in one volume). Many illustrations.

- We Are On the Radio!: edited by Clare Hanbury and Sarah McCrum — This pack, available from mid-1992, contains a booklet and two companion tapes designed to help adult organisers involve children in broadcasting to other children about health.

French:

- Adaptations of Child-to-Child English Readers Numbers 3 and 4 plus new titles published by L'Enfant pour l'Enfant, Paris.

Portuguese:

- Criança para Criança — Portuguese version, produced in 1981, of original CHILD-to-child book.

Spanish:

- Child-to-Child Activity Sheets — Complete pack as English titles, recently translated in Ecuador.

- Adaptations of Child-to-Child English Readers Numbers 1, 2, 3, 4, 5 and 6.

7. ZIMBABWE

7.1. **Longman Zimbabwe (Pvt) Ltd, PO Box ST125, Southerton, Harare, Zimbabwe.**

English:

- Child-to-Child Readers Numbers 1, 2, 3, 4, 5 and 6.